Return to Beauty

Restoring the Ecology of Imagination

BENJAMIN SELLS

SPRING PUBLICATIONS

THOMPSON, CONN.

Published by Spring Publications
Thompson, Conn.
www.springpublications.com

First edition 2022 (1.3)

Cover art © 2022 by Margot McLean

Library of Congress Control Number: 2022910703

ISBN: 978-0-88214-970-7

for Jill

CONTENTS

PROLOGUE   7

INTRODUCTION   11

ONE
Bird Watching   19

TWO
The Blindness We Make for Ourselves   33

THREE
What the Blackbird Knows   53

FOUR
A Taste for the Beautiful   77

FIVE
An Ecology of Imagination   105

SIX
Animal Mundi   123

SEVEN
An Eye Grafted on the Heart   136

EIGHT
Terrible Beauty   161

NINE
Homo Aestheticus   181

TEN
Return to Beauty   201

CODA   215

ACKNOWLEDGMENTS   216

BIBLIOGRAPHY   217

PROLOGUE

Thirteen Ways of Looking at a Blackbird
by Wallace Stevens

I

Among twenty snowy mountains,
The only moving thing
Was the eye of the blackbird.

II

I was of three minds,
Like a tree
In which there are three blackbirds.

III

The blackbird whirled in the autumn winds.
It was a small part of the pantomime.

IV

A man and a woman
Are one.
A man and a woman and a blackbird
Are one.

V

I do not know which to prefer,
The beauty of inflections
Or the beauty of innuendoes,
The blackbird whistling
Or just after.

VI

Icicles filled the long window
With barbaric glass.
The shadow of the blackbird
Crossed it, to and fro.
The mood
Traced in the shadow
An indecipherable cause.

VII

O thin men of Haddam,
Why do you imagine golden birds?
Do you not see how the blackbird
Walks around the feet
Of the women about you?

VIII

I know noble accents
And lucid, inescapable rhythms;
But I know, too,
That the blackbird is involved
In what I know.

IX

When the blackbird flew out of sight,
It marked the edge
Of one of many circles.

X

At the sight of blackbirds
Flying in a green light,
Even the bawds of euphony
Would cry out sharply.

XI

He rode over Connecticut
In a glass coach.
Once, a fear pierced him,
In that he mistook
The shadow of his equipage
For blackbirds.

XII

The river is moving.
The blackbird must be flying.

XIII

It was evening all afternoon.
It was snowing
And it was going to snow.
The blackbird sat
In the cedar-limbs.

From *The Collected Poems of Wallace Stevens,* edited by John N. Serio and Chris Beyers (New York: Vintage Books, 2015)

We are by nature aesthetic animals. We exist to appreciate beauty, to create beauty, and to be beautiful. That is all the world asks of us. Nothing more is required.

It is odd that we wonder about what our place is in the natural world. Somehow, we have come to feel separated and estranged from the other animals and the greater world that lies beyond ourselves. We have even come to think of nature as something apart from us, and that it exists only where we are absent.

The source of our discontent, and its remedy, lies in beauty. As aesthetic animals our fundamental bond with nature is through beauty. We live among other aesthetic animals, and it is through our mutual recognition of and respect for one another's beauty that we find our roles in the natural order of things. Even the many things of the world that we think of as inanimate are nonetheless first encountered within an aesthetic array of display and presentation where each thing appears as itself and not otherwise. We encounter and engage the world through aesthetic images that are sensate, sensual, and sensible, and so our primary obligation is to appreciate how these images present themselves in form and action. Because we exist within the context of beauty, we are perceived, imagined, and known by others long before we ever have our first thoughts about knowing ourselves. In the first instance, then, the world is not something to be understood and explained, but to be appreciated and loved.

If we exist to appreciate beauty, and if we are bound together with the natural world through beauty, then what happens if our bond with beauty is broken? What happens to us and the world of which we are a part if we lose the connecting power of beauty? If beauty constitutes the world and establishes our place within it, then what is left in its absence? Can we sustain life without beauty?

These are the questions that we will address in the pages to come. I maintain that we have lost our connection with nature by repressing beauty, defending against it, even abusing it. The repression of beauty has left us estranged from our animal place in the world, leaving us adrift, excluded from nature, and set apart from our fellow animals. Even worse, the repression of beauty has resulted in transgressions against our fellow animals and our shared environment. These consequences are inseparable from the effects that the repression of beauty has on us. The repression of beauty affects both individuals and society, taking various forms of dis-ease, among them anxiety, depression, intolerance, and toxic partisanship. Meanwhile the greater world suffers elemental decay and ecocide through anthropogenic climate change, scarcity of water, pollution, deforestation, and a dramatic loss of biodiversity—all brought about by the actions of one species alone. And all because we have forsaken beauty.

If the connection between beauty and the symptoms that plague us seems farfetched, then that is simply an indication of how far we have strayed from our aesthetic responsibilities. When we appreciate something for its beauty, we grow closer to it, want to care for it, and keep it alive and well. Often beauty leads to love, and with love comes a deep sense of attachment and belonging. It is difficult to imagine the woes listed above in a world where human actions are motivated by appreciation and love. Caring for the world because it is beautiful is different than wanting to preserve the world so it can provide us what we want and need. Aesthetic appreciation leads to loving care that is freely given, a far cry from burdensome feelings of duty and obligation.

That we have arrived at this place where beauty beckons but goes unanswered has historical and cultural antecedents but cannot be reduced to history alone. For millennia, our Western tradition has declared humans to be not only separate from but superior to the other animals and the greater world that we all inhabit. We have been told that we are more akin to god and the angels than to the other animals, that we have dominion over them and their home, and that they are there to serve our wants and needs. We have been told that the other animals lack consciousness, perhaps even the ability to feel and suffer. We have declared ourselves the pinnacle of evolution, alone on the top rung of nature's ladder. And we have defined evolution in such a manner that beauty is only a handmaiden to survival and reproduction.

Although these beliefs are widely held, they are devastatingly wrong. We will work our way through the purported separation of humans from nature, the denial of consciousness to non-human animals, and the single-minded resistance against beauty as playing an essential role in evolution. Each of these, in its own way, has contributed to the repression of beauty, and each represents a psychic dislocation that cannot be fully explained by historical or cultural analysis. Fortunately, all of these ideologies—and that is what they are—have weakened in recent years. The bulwarks they have erected against beauty have begun to crumble from within, and new ideas, and old ideas wrongly discarded, are straining to return. Despite the shadows that these defending walls cast, beauty once again glimmers through the cracks.

Although the first part of this book will also deal with scientific ideas and theories, this book is not about science properly speaking. I espouse no scientific theories and make no scientific claims. Nor will I posit choices between warring dualities such as soul/body, subject/object, or religion/science. We really have had quite enough of such pointless dualisms. Instead, I will suggest that such dualisms are false prophets offering promises that they cannot keep. By returning to beauty, we will find a way beyond their horned dilemmas.

That is not to say that we will not inquire into how such dualisms have gained such power over us. There is much to be gained from seeing from whence they came and how they operate. But our effort will be to see through them to discover their deeper significance. They are blinders that limit the range of our vision, designed to keep us running according to the will of the jockey on our back. We will stop running, buck the jockey, and seek to make our own way.

After a brief introduction to different ways of looking at the images that beauty provides us, we will begin with the purported separation of humans from nature. For millennia, humans have labored under the illusion that we are separate from the many other things of the world. Almost incredibly, we have created an idea of Nature (and that capital "N" will become important) that allows Nature to exist only where humans are not. This separation is primarily due to a monotheistic cast of mind that has likened humans unto God and the angels and that has declared us separate from and above the other animals, plants, indeed the earth itself. Adam might have been made from the dust of the earth, but he never regained his earthly footing. Here, too, we will encounter the destructive idea that humans have dominion over the rest of God's Creation.

Next, we review beliefs and theories that deny consciousness to non-human animals, declaring them incapable of joy, desire, grief, or any depth of emotion or imagination. We will see that these beliefs and theories, for which both philosophy and science have advocated, cannot be separated from monotheism's continuing influence. Both philosophy and science have a long tradition of declaring non-human animals mere robotic automata, and there are still philosophers and scientists who remain under the sway of such claims. In accord with one view of Christianity's claims, Western philosophy and science have proclaimed humans exceptional because of our God-given rationality that supposedly sets us apart from the mindless, instinct-driven lives of pure action purportedly lived by non-human animals. We will see the sad consequences of these ideas and find ways to restore a proper accord with our fellow animals.

Meanwhile psychology, or what's left of it, has followed René Descartes down the rabbit hole of subjectivity. Based on Descartes' wearisome and wrong separation of mind and body, much of psychology's tradition has declared an "ego" or "self" that is locked within the individual brain of its possessor. This secret self is said to be available only through personal introspection and is held to be the only true arbiter of our being. This "self," and here again psychology follows philosophy and science as if imprinted upon them, is also said to be the projecting source of any consciousness that we think we experience in other animals or the many things of the world. It is the human self, says psychology, that projects soul onto the world. Here psychology joins philosophy and science in rejecting the idea of a truly ensouled world as mere mythmaking, where "myth" means false, fiction, and whimsy.

If there has been a serious challenge to Christian monotheism in our Western tradition, it has been evolution. But although today many would still set evolution over against Christianity, we will see that evolution, too, remains subject to monotheism's fundamentalist tendencies, mimicking monotheism's preference for overarching, unified theories. The ubiquitous insistence that natural selection is the *only* modality for evolution is thoroughly imbued with the monotheistic cast of mind. Indeed, both the ubiquity and the insistence of this single-minded approach to evolution are tell-tales of the invisible, guiding hand of monotheism. When evolutionary theory declares that all manifestations of beauty must somehow benefit survival and reproductive success, it ceases to be a theory and becomes an ideology. We will seek a different route that acknowledges beauty's essential role in evolution and the inherent creativity of life.

Embedded within each of these traditions is the repression of beauty, and it is one task of this book to show how this is so and how this repression is of ultimate concern. What is clear at the outset, however, is that the results of such traditions have been devastating. They have led to moral atrocities against our planet and its many inhabitants, a stultifying obstinance in our refusal to learn about, and from, our fellow sentient beings, and psychological breakdown among humans, both individually and socially. We will see that these catastrophes are inextricably bound together. When we declare that the world and its inhabitants are essentially different from and apart from us, then they become things to be used, and abused, at our whim. When we pre-determine and denigrate the capabilities of non-human animals, we blind ourselves to their potentials and nobility. When we insist that every human is an island, we are left trapped behind borders that cannot be crossed and walls that cannot be felled. And when we try to yolk beauty to utility, as if that is the only way it can be of any worth whatsoever, we create a world declared to be essentially selfish, a world ruled by struggle, sword, shield, and strife.

The good news is that in the last several decades some of these old ideas have begun to collapse under the weight of their own hubris. The environmental impact of human abuse and neglect has led us to a precipice that endangers the entire planet. The realities of anthropogenic climate change have left little doubt to those with open minds of the essential interdependence between humans and nature. The natural sciences, especially evolutionary biology and the study of animal behavior, are embracing new ideas that recognize more fully the capabilities, intelligence, and imagination of non-human animals. We are increasingly recognizing that our misinformed claims about non-human animals' perceived shortcomings are more often than not really comments about the limitations of our own methods of inquiry.

At the same time, around the edges of conventional evolutionary thought, attempts are being made to restore Charles Darwin's actual theory that there is more to evolution than natural selection and adaptations for survival and reproductive success. These attempts suggest that perhaps there is also an aesthetic impulse that infuses and motivates sentient life as much as does a selfish struggle to survive and reproduce. Perhaps we have moved too quickly beyond the actual appearances and manifestations of life in its dazzling diversity to instead search for hidden explanations that fit our predetermined theories. We will see that beauty lies at the heart of evolution.

The idea of an isolated self is also being challenged as some psychologists insist that "psyche" or "soul" cannot be equated with "self" and that soul cannot be limited to being a personal, individual possession. Some psychologists are even espousing an "ecopsychology" that says it makes no sense to limit soul only to humans, and that we must also attend to soul in the context of the greater world that lies beyond the human. Such views challenge old dualities and propose new ways of overcoming the purported separation of human and nature and the isolation of soul into a private "self." The burgeoning fields of environmental and conservation psychology are also emphasizing that our views of nature and of our relationship with nature need to be expanded and deepened to include psychological ideas and methodologies.

Taken together, these new ideas are pushing back against the repression of beauty and are attempting to encourage beauty's return. We are witnessing a rebirth of the sensate and the sensual, a rising up of the irrepressible aesthetic power of the many things of the world. As they reassert themselves, we can feel how weak and insufficient our current attempts to understand ourselves are when we leave out the many other things of the world that are so assertively real, here, and now. Even as we marvel at our technical advances, we cannot help but recognize amidst our preening a deep longing that is neither touched nor satisfied by our tools and toys. This longing finds its answer in the redemption of old words that have for too long been excluded by the sterile demands of the laboratory—imagination, myth, love, soul—but in all of these, beauty comes first.

Our millennia-long efforts to repress beauty's foundational, essential necessity are failing, and with the return to beauty comes the offer of salvation of a different sort, not one of transcendence beyond the world but of a grounded participation with and respect for our fellow inhabitants of the world. The many things of the world have always been animated and ensouled, whether or not we choose to admit them as such. Our Fall did not come from being cast out into the world, but from our refusal to actually land there. Instead of embracing, and being held by, the many things of the world we have insisted upon remaining aloft on clouds of belief and denial. Belief that we are not of this world but are closer to God than to the animals; denial that we are in fact but one among many, not exceptional but simply different, as Darwin said, in degree, not kind. This is the nature of our psychic dislocation, but with the return to beauty we are offered a way to cease our perpetual orbit.

The second part of this book explores how we can restore our connection to nature and our place in the natural order of things through beauty. I will emphasize that our deepest relationship to nature is through our imagination and the power of myth. We are *Homo aestheticus* before we are *Homo sapiens,* and the latter depends on the former. Beauty, love, soul, imagination, and myth are our foundations, and it upon those foundations that our powers of reason and rationality rest. We will see that we embody the same animal certainty and sureness of action that we see in the other animals, and that by restoring our animal faith in the inherent sensibility of the world we can regain our place in the ecology of imagination that we inhabit as aesthetic animals.

The project of this book, then, is to briefly review some of the most glaring examples of how we have repressed beauty and then to imagine ways that we might return to beauty. To do this we will depend on the very things that we have sought so hard to exclude – the many things of the world, and most especially the other animals with whom we share so much. If we are to craft new ideas, or reclaim old ones mistakenly discarded, in such a manner that they will really matter, it will ultimately be up to the other animals to validate our efforts. We have had enough anthropocentric attempts at redemption. The plain fact is that we do not deserve it, at least not until we prove ourselves worthy in their eyes. The actualities of the world are such that the tables have turned. It is the other animals, the plants, the earth, air, fire, and water that will now be the judge of our actions. They never forsook beauty, and so have no need to seek its return. The task is ours alone, and success is far from certain; but what is certain is that we will never succeed without their help.

ONE

Bird Watching

There are between 48 and 60 million bird watchers in the United States, maybe more with the dramatic increase in interest that occurred during the Covid-19 pandemic. Within that large number of people drawn to our feathered friends, subtle distinctions are sometimes drawn between bird watchers and birders. Bird watchers are taken to be the more amateur of the group and can include pretty much everyone who feeds birds or watches them around the house. Birders are more accomplished at identification and often travel beyond the home in search of birds. Birders are also more likely to be "listers" who keep a list of the birds they see. Most have a "life list" that lists all the birds they have ever seen and identified. When a birder sees a bird they have never seen before it becomes a "lifer." Some birders become more competitive. In the movie *The Big Year,* Steve Martin plays a successful businessman whose true passion is birds and who strives to collect the most species among all American birders for a given year—a "big year." When a colleague criticizes him for wasting valuable business time on mere "bird watching," Martin sternly corrects him that "it's called birding."

I am a bird watcher and apprentice birder. My wife Jill, who is a scientist and accomplished birder, introduced me to bird watching several years ago and two of our close friends are both ardent birders and prominent ornithologists. It is a great treat for me to go birding with them because of their knowledge and experience—their ability to identify hundreds of species of birds and to make fine discernments between birds that look so similar amazes me. They can identify more birds by their songs and vocalizations alone than I can by sight. But what I lack in expertise, I equal in delight. We all thrill at the flash of a bird on the wing or freeze in place when a shape high in a tree attracts and holds our eyes' attention.

Hiking through the woods held little appeal to me before I became a bird watcher. It was a monotonous exercise to me, and I found little of interest. For me hiking was just a walk in the woods, and the woods was an undifferentiated place—one tree looked like another to me. In retrospect I now see that it wasn't the woods that was boring and uninteresting but me. Instead of paying attention to the things around me I was usually thinking about something else, ruminating over how bored I was, or wondering how much farther we had to go before we could call it a day. I wasn't seeing anything because I wasn't looking for anything.

When I was a boy my family had a subscription to *Reader's Digest* and at the bottom of the page of some of the articles there was sometimes a joke or anecdote. I only remember one, but it is one that has stuck with me indelibly for decades. Two men are walking down a city street when one man says "Oh, listen to that robin!" The other man, amazed, says "How in the world did you hear that with all the city noise?" The first man takes a quarter out of his pocket and tosses it on the sidewalk, causing people all around to stop and look for the coin. "We hear what we listen for," says the first man. He was a birder.

As I became more involved with bird watching the woods came alive. Although nominally there to be looking for birds, I began to see other things, too. In fact, one of the first things that a new bird watcher learns is the necessity of looking at the natural habitat first. To find birds that are in trees or bushes, you are watching for a shape or form that is different, perhaps a silhouette that is unlike its surroundings, or a flicker of movement against a still backdrop. The more attuned and accustomed you become to a bird's habitat the more easily you will be able to see a bird when it appears.

Birds are not static pictures on a page. They display not only in their plumage but in their behavior. Some birds feed by "hawking," which means catching insects in the air. Some birds prefer to hawk by "sallying" out from a perch, catching an insect, then returning to the perch to eat it. This is called "flycatching," and there are several species of birds that are called flycatchers. Other birds, like swallows or swifts, catch and eat insects while in flight. In contrast to hawking, other birds feed by "gleaning" which means plucking insects from foliage or the ground, from crevices such as rock faces and under the eaves of houses, or even off other animals. And then there are birds that forage for seeds and fruit. For many birds, all of the above behaviors are possible even if they favor some more than others. The more one watches birds the more fascinating these various feeding behaviors become.

And they fly. Of the many things that birds do that enthrall us, none is more enchanting than their gift of flight. When we watch them fly, we feel drawn aloft by their graceful wings. Birds have many styles of flight —woodpeckers dip and climb, hawks soar, hummingbirds streak and hover. Ornithologists have words for these different patterns of flight, too, (undulating, static soaring, flap and glide, etc.) and over time a bird watcher can even learn to identify birds by their particular style of flight, by how they move through the air.

Birds are also social creatures. They interact with one another, shooing each other away from a favored spot or calling to one another among the trees. They display personalities both individually and as species. And, lest we forget, in the stories and fables of indigenous peoples just about everywhere, birds are often seen as spirit animals, winged divinities. Bird watching opens one's eyes to worlds previously unseen.

That certainly has been my experience. The woods are no longer monotonous. What before seemed like a silent slate is now filled with motion, color, and sound. As so nicely put by fellow bird watcher Jonathan Rosen, once I started looking I began to see the diversity and beauty that "had been hidden from me by my own blindness."[1] Whereas before I had shielded myself from what the woods had to offer, now I see that there are wondrous things everywhere. All of this given to me by the birds who so selflessly help me to share their world.

Once you start looking you cannot stop seeing. Now I can be doing anything, driving, sitting writing at my desk, in the middle of a conversation, and if I catch a flash out of the corner of my eye I am immediately drawn to look. I'm even getting a little more adept at hearing a *seep* from on high and seeking to find the little body that goes with the voice. As I venture out more and more, I have also realized that bird watching is not a passive or solitary endeavor. Although bird watching often requires

---

1. Jonathan Rosen, *The Life of the Skies: Birding at the End of Nature* (New York: Farrar, Straus, and Giroux, 2008), 38.

stealth, quiet, and patience, it is an active encounter between the watcher and the watched that can only proceed when both are present. And many a bird watcher has had the extraordinary experience of having the tables turned, when a bird suddenly turns its eyes upon the birder. Having a raptor's piercing eyes size you up is an experience not forgotten.

Prior to the early 1900s, "birding" meant hunting for birds and only later gained the added meaning of observing birds for naturalistic and aesthetic pleasure. Obviously, humans have long delighted in the beauty of birds, but bird watching as a pastime became more formalized in the late nineteenth century. The phrase "bird watching" first appeared in 1901 as the title of a book by the British ornithologist Edmund Selous.[2] It was during this time that bird watching also became closely affiliated with bird identification. With advances in optics, people no longer had to kill birds to identify them. (John Audubon painted over 1000 birds and shot almost every single one.) One of the earliest field guides designed to help bird watchers identify what they were seeing rather than shooting, was *Birds through an Opera Glass* by the American ornithologist Florence Augusta Merriam Bailey published in 1889.[3]

Bird watching as we know it today came into its own in 1934 with Roger Tory Peterson's influential *Field Guide to the Birds*.[4] The book used drawings instead of photographs to give an idealized version of a given bird along with diagnostic "field marks" to be used for identification. Peterson even included little arrows pointing to the relevant field marks. As Peterson himself put it:

> The "Peterson System," as it came to be known, was essentially a shortcut: by means of schematic drawings and little arrows it taught birdwatchers to look for those few diagnostic marks or patterns that would allow them to name almost every bird they saw. The very

---

2. Edmund Selous, *Bird Watching* (London, J. M. Dent & Co., 1901).

3. Florence A. Merriam, *Birds through an Opera Glass* (Boston and New York: Houghton, Mifflin and Company, 1889).

4. Roger Tory Peterson, *A Field Guide to the Birds Giving Field Marks of All Species Found in Eastern North America* (Boston and New York: Houghton, Mifflin and Company, 1934).

simplicity of this method, it has been suggested, was a major reason for the spectacular growth of birding.[5]

Peterson recognized the inherent limitations of this approach. "With every new edition...I have struggled with the dilemma: how schematic should the drawings be? And how much detail should I include?"[6] Even birds within a given species are not static in their appearance but vary widely both as they mature and according to their mating and non-mating plumage. Warblers might offer brilliant colors during the spring migration only to return in the fall migration as "LBJs" (little brown jobs). A field guide that attempted to address all the variations found among actual birds would have to be towed behind a bird watcher in a wagon.

Today's bird watcher is blessed with an abundance of field guides from the general to the specific. In our own home library, we have guides for birds of North America, birds of Illinois, and birds of the Forest Preserve District of Cook County, the county where we live. There are also numerous mobile apps available for the bird watcher. These have the enormous benefit of being able to include actual recordings of bird vocalizations that a bird watcher can take into the field in his or her back pocket. One amazing volume claims to include all birds of the world— 11,524 species in a book weighing almost nine pounds!

After World War II, the availability of good quality binoculars from military surplus was a boon to bird watching. Improved optics, ease of travel, and new and better field guides made bird watching more and more available to larger numbers of people. With this increase, a new attitude of competition began to grow among bird watchers. More and more bird watchers started keeping lists, not only as a diary of their observations but to compare and compete with the lists of other bird watchers. Before long, it became a race among some birders to see who could have the longest list. As Scott Weidensaul puts it in his history of American birding, a polarity overtook modern bird watching:

5. Roger Tory Peterson, "Editor's Note," in Kenn Kaufman, *A Field Guide to Advanced Birding: Birding Challenges and How to Approach Them* (Boston: Houghton Mifflin Company, 1990), v.

6. Ibid.

At one extreme you have birds as a source of inspiration and awe, as objects of curiosity, whether intensely scientific or at the layman's more general level. At the other extreme, you have birds as tick marks on a list, as inventory, treasures in a scavenger hunt that may encompass one's backyard or the planet, a single day or a lifetime.[7]

There is an odd contradiction here. In its earlier scientific days, the study of birds focused on taxonomy and careful field studies. Great precision was given to identifying and classifying birds, but the focus remained on the birds. When bird watching became a popular competition the focus shifted away from the birds to the bird watcher and his or her list. Weidensaul describes "a growing unease...between the burgeoning enthusiasm for birding and a pervasive apathy about the birds themselves."[8] There is a lesson here—the more we see a thing in terms of what it means to us, the less we seem to care about the thing itself. The more we turn our attention away from the birds to instead focus on competition and listing, the less we care about protecting and preserving birds. Lack of attention begets neglect. It is tragically ironic that at the same time bird watching has exploded in popularity since the 1970s, three billion birds have vanished from North America.

This does not mean that there is a necessary antagonism between appreciating birds in their own right and identifying them to compile a list. But the distinction deserves a closer look and came into focus during a local birding project that a group of bird watchers conducted in my hometown. I live in Riverside, Illinois, which sets beside the Des Plaines River and is within the Mississippi flyway for migratory birds. Every spring and fall more than 325 species of birds bring bits of South America and Northern Canada through Illinois as they migrate north and south in spring and fall via the Mississippi flyway. In April, among the first migrants to arrive in Riverside are the Eastern Phoebe, various sparrows, and the Golden-crowned and Ruby-crowned Kinglets. Then comes May and many species of warblers take center stage alongside other migrants such as the Great-crested Flycatcher, Scarlet Tanager, Indigo Bunting,

7. Scott Weidensaul, *Of a Feather: A Brief History of American Birding* (New York: Harcourt, 2007), 281.

8. Ibid., 271.

Baltimore Oriole, and Rose-breasted Grosbeak to name but a few. It is a joyous, almost intoxicating time and one that is anxiously awaited by bird watchers. There are even websites that follow the migration with radar and weather forecasts to aid in predicting the arrival dates for various species. Spring migration is a big deal.

To draw more attention to Riverside's natural setting and the richness of its environment, a group of bird watchers decided to try to have Riverside designated an Important Bird Area by the Audubon Society. The Important Bird Area (IBA) program was started by BirdLife International in Europe in 1985. It is an international effort to identify, conserve, and monitor a network of sites that provide essential habitat for bird populations. The Audubon Society partnered with BirdLife in 1995, and in the ensuing years has designated 2,758 IBAs in the United States. We wanted Riverside to join that number.

The process for becoming an IBA is daunting. There are various criteria under which a location can be designated an IBA. Riverside's significance was as a stopover for migratory birds. Audubon provided us a list of migratory bird species that we might be able to see in the area of our proposed IBA and established a baseline of how many of those species we would have to document. Audubon also told us how many individual birds for each species we would need to see in a single day to reach a required "significant number." So, for example, to meet a significant number set by Audubon we needed to document five Pine Warblers in one day. Overall, Riverside needed to document significant numbers for at least nineteen different species of migratory birds to support its application to become an IBA.

With bird list in hand, our volunteer bird watchers hit the woods to start identifying and counting species and individual birds. This was a different kind of bird watching than what I had experienced previously. Before, I was looking at individual birds as they appeared to my newly opened eyes. My gaze lingered, drawn to the appearance of a singular creature and its behavior. My intent was seeing and appreciating, and the beauty of a given bird would often stop me in my tracks. Significantly, the pleasure I experienced was simply in seeing and appreciating the bird and there was no other purpose involved. On more than one occasion the sudden appearance of a bird would take my breath away. Anyone who has been startled by an animal in the wild knows the experience.

But now I had a list to fill out, numbers to meet, and sheets of photographs of birds with their Latin and common names. The warblers, especially, were at once marvelous and maddening. So many of them were like feathered jewels with their bright colors and refinements, but at the same time some of the different species looked so similar to my untrained eye that I struggled to tell them apart. Luckily some of the species distinguished themselves by their mannerisms—the Palm Warbler, for example, can be readily identified by the way it twerks its tail up and down. The biggest challenge for a newbie like me was learning how to identify the various birds that had similar field marks, a challenge made all the more difficult because many of the species didn't seem capable of staying in one spot for more than a fleeting second.

When learning to identify birds, beginners are taught to pay attention to four key indicators: size and shape, color patterns, habitat, and behavior. Size and shape are best learned by association with known birds, e.g., bigger than a sparrow but smaller than a robin. Color patterns can refer to many different aspects of the bird, from a dominant color to wing bands to eye-rings to a flash of white on the rump seen as the bird flies away (Northern Flicker!). Paying attention to habitat helps to more fully integrate the bird watcher into the bird's world—our twerky Palm Warbler (about sparrow-sized) likes to forage on the ground while Golden-crowned Kinglets (smaller than a sparrow) prefer to glean, hover, and hawk in trees and shrubs. I came to expect finding Yellow Warblers on fallen trees and bushes down by the river. Behavior is also stylized and can be distinctly characteristic among species. Kinglets, both Golden-crowned and Ruby-crowned, give the appearance of nervous nellies as they constantly flit and hover to pluck insects from branches and twigs. The Great Crested Flycatcher prefers to sit stationary on a perch waiting for a prey to come within range before sallying forth. And, for the more advanced birder, calls and songs become audible identifiers in addition to visual cues. Sometimes it is even easier to distinguish between various species by their vocalizations than by their appearance. With the goal of becoming an IBA firmly in mind I would need all of these tricks of the trade if I was going to help collect the data we needed.

This was a different kind of looking. I was now interested not in the bird as a singular presence but as representative of a given species. In focusing on identifying different species and trying to reach the required significant number of sightings, I became less interested in the birds themselves. With the goal of achieving the IBA as our pressing concern, the birds became primarily a means to an end. The list and numbers came first.

I want to be careful here because learning to identify birds does not necessarily limit a bird watcher's appreciation for birds. Indeed, learning to identify birds can teach a bird watcher to see more precisely and with greater refinement—was that one wing bar or two, an eye-ring or an eyebrow? Learning to identify birds can also help us to appreciate nuance, subtlety, and difference. The problem arises when identification becomes the dominant reason for looking, an end unto itself. Yes, the Prothonotary Warbler was still incredibly beautiful, but I needed five of the damn things to meet my daily goal! I had to keep moving and counting, which meant I had a less time to linger and look.

The wonderful novelist Walker Percy, who was a physician before taking up writing full time, commented on the effect of looking at something through what we might call an identifying or representational lens:

> [T]he scientist, in practicing scientific method, cannot utter a single word about an individual thing or creature insofar as it is an individual but only insofar as it resembles other individuals. This limitation holds true whether the individual is a molecule of NaCl or an amoeba or a human being. There is nothing new or startling about this and nothing a scientist would disagree with. We all remember taking science courses where one was confronted with a *sample of* sodium or a *specimen of* a dogfish to dissect. Such studies reveal the properties shared by all sodium chloride and all dogfish. *We have no particular interest in this particular pinch of salt or this particular dogfish.* (Last emphasis added.)[9]

Percy goes on to extend this same situation to psychiatry, paraphrasing Harry Stack Sullivan as saying that as a psychiatrist Sullivan was only

9. Walker Percy, *Diagnosing the Modern Malaise* (New Orleans: Faust Publishing, 1985), 10.

interested in a person's symptoms insofar as they resembled other individuals and other symptoms.

Percy contrasts this limitation of scientific method with his efforts as a novelist, saying the novel can be "a serious instrument for the exploration of reality, a cognitive instrument."[10] He argues that art in general, and literature in particular, can be instruments "for exploring the great gap in our knowing, knowing ourselves and how it stands between ourselves and others."[11] We will return to this idea of art as a naturalistic endeavor capable of providing knowledge about a particular thing later, but for now we can post Percy as a marker on our journey of looking.

Another way of describing these two ways of looking—the particular and the general—comes from the archetypal psychologist James Hillman who distinguished between images and symbols. Images are independent displays complete unto themselves with an inherent individuality, integrity, and intelligibility. Symbols are representations that point beyond an image to a meaning or an interpretation. So, for example, if a person dreams of a black snake, then you can look at that snake as an image by being interested in the snake as it appears and behaves in the context of the dream or you can look at the snake as a symbol representing something other than the snake. Describing the latter move, which is so typical of psychological analysis and interpretation, Hillman concludes that:

> the moment you've defined the snake, interpreted it, you've lost the snake, you've stopped it, and the person leaves the [therapeutic] hour with a concept about my repressed sexuality or my cold black passions or my mother or whatever it is, and you've lost the snake. The task of analysis is to keep the snake there, the black snake...see, *the black snake's no longer necessary the moment it's been interpreted,* and you don't need your dreams anymore because they've been interpreted. [Emphasis added.][12]

I take Hillman's imagistic approach as a psychologist to mirror that of Percy as a novelist. Both are committed to attending to a particular thing

10. Ibid., 12.

11. Ibid., 15.

12. James Hillman, *Inter Views: Conversations with Laura Pozzo on Psychotherapy, Biography, Love, Soul, Dreams, Work, Imagination, and the State of the Culture* (Woodstock, Conn.: Spring Publications, 1991), 54.

(*this* dogfish, *this* black snake) through an appreciation of the thing's precise qualities and presentation, including the context in which it appears. Both Hillman and Percy insist on the inherent integrity of the individual thing as an individual and not as a sample, specimen, or symbol of something else. And, notably, both Hillman and Percy rely on aesthetic means as the proper method for approaching things as individuals.

The distinction between these two ways of looking is clearly seen in Peterson's decision to use illustrations instead of photographs for his field guides. He chose to use drawings in his books precisely because they are generalized representations of birds. The drawings emphasize idealized field marks that a bird watcher can use to identify different species of birds, that is, the field marks are approximations of what one might see in the wild. Real birds are much more diverse and varied in their ornamentation than their field guide representatives, but the illustrations provide a baseline for identification. A photograph of a bird is always a photograph of a particular bird, so it is more difficult to use photographs as a reference when learning how to identify birds. Drawings are more useful because they represent the shared general characteristics of a given species.

If you watch the same group of birds, or for that matter the same group of anything, over time you will begin to discern differences between the individuals. Even the mass-produced objects of the assembly line, produced to the specifications of sameness, can be distinguished by those who know how to look. So, when we look at Audubon's painting of Pileated Woodpeckers and see them as displaying what we might call individual "personalities" we are seeing what objective observers of wildlife see all the time—that no two birds are alike despite being the same species or coming from the same nest. It is certainly possible, and indeed common, for humans to project human traits onto the other things of the world. But it is also possible that we recognize characteristics in non-human animals for which we simply have no other descriptive language than our own. In that instance, anthropomorphism is not a projection but rather reflects the limitations of our own language and concepts. When we look at Audubon's painting of mockingbirds defending their nest against a snake and see anger, rage, and desperation it is difficult to say whether we are projecting or recognizing kindred spirits.

There is enormous satisfaction in correctly identifying a Pine Warbler. They look very much like other warblers and they are not common visitors to Riverside during migration—we only needed to see five of them in a day to reach our Audubon goal while we needed to see one hundred Yellow-rumped Warblers to reach the magic number. So, during our bird count a Pine Warbler was an elusive find and when we did see one it was a special occasion. As I write this in January, I have just returned from visiting my mother-in-law in South Carolina. She is an avid and skilled birder, and her feeders attract a wide range of birds that we don't commonly see in Illinois. Sitting and watching one afternoon I was mesmerized by the Tufted Titmice (yes, that is the plural for Tufted Titmouse) and Eastern Bluebirds. A Brown-headed Nuthatch (a lifer!) stopped by, and then, all of a sudden, a Pine Warbler appeared. It struck me anew with its graceful form and subtle colors. Freed from the pressures of the count I was able to both appreciate it and identify it without losing it. It was at once new and familiar. At first, I thought it might be a Yellow Warbler and so I had to look more closely. I finally had to consult a field guide to settle the matter, but the identification did not diminish the pleasure I had of seeing the same bird several times during my visit. I knew it was the same bird precisely because of the enhanced focus that the identification had required. I *identified* it as *a* Pine Warbler, yes, but I also *recognized* it as that *particular* Pine Warbler.

After seeing the Pine Warbler for the first time I looked forward to seeing it again. This points to another aspect of bird watching—when we head out to look, we do so in anticipation of what we might see. Our attention heightens, and we become alert to the things around us. We also prepare for the occasion. Ritual practice has long identified that the soul must be prepared to receive the divine, and so the bird watcher dons special clothes, hangs her binocular amulet around her neck, agrees to be bound by rules of etiquette, and adopts the proper receptive reverence for the occasion. Think of how similar this is with the rituals that we associate with what we have come to call the higher arts, how the lights dim, the audience ceases its chatter and becomes alertly silent in anticipation of the music or the play to come, and then the stage lights come up and the performance begins. Or think of the muted respect of the museumgoer as she walks quietly among the paintings and sculpture, pausing to sit on a bench provided just for looking. Or the silence of a sacred place where human voices are muted so that other voices might be heard.

Despite, or perhaps because of, this preparation and anticipation, the bird itself is always a surprise that can never be taken for granted. You never know what you are going to see or even if you will see—many bird watching trips yield no sightings. And yet you prepare yourself and head out to look, encouraged in part by remembrances of things past and in part by the very promise of nature's fecundity and diversity.

By the end of our bird count several of us had what bird watchers call warbler neck from constantly craning with our binoculars to catch every flitting movement high in the trees. We were rewarded in our efforts when Riverside was awarded IBA status, but to a person we all expressed our relief that our data collecting days were over and that we could once again focus on bird *watching* instead of bird *counting*.

I have touched on only two generalized ways of looking and have distinguished between the eye of the novelist who seeks to bring to life a particular character and that of the scientist who seeks to classify and categorize. So, too, for a depth psychologist an image remains forever mysterious and cannot be removed from its particular appearance while a symbol points elsewhere and then become irrelevant. Once I know that a dove in a religious painting means peace or the Holy Spirit then the dove is replaced by its symbolic meaning and I no longer need that particular dove. Actual birds resist such symbolism by the sheer power of their individual presence and beauty. When we go bird watching we are not looking for meaning and when birds appear, they do not signify meaning. We go looking for birds because they are beautiful, and their beauty needs no further explication. Or, better, their beauty is their meaning.

The beauty of a bird, or of anything, really, is complete in its presentation. More, the beauty of each thing can educate our styles of looking. How we look at one thing might not be appropriate for looking at some other thing. Some birds hold our steady gaze while others require quick eyes to follow their lead. There are as many ways of looking as there are things to be seen, indeed there are many ways of looking at any given thing—Wallace Stevens had thirteen ways of looking at a blackbird.

What bird watching teaches us is that these manners of looking depend on the birds we watch. If we try to impose a certain manner of looking then we no longer see what is before us but rather a reflection of our own making. This is akin to what happens when we take something as a symbol, replacing the precise image that presents itself to us with a predetermined, abstracted meaning created by us. Appreciation keeps us connected with the imaginative power of things, and our sensing of images is guided by images themselves as innately sensate, sensual, and sensible. An image, then, is both what is sensed and how it is sensed; not only what we see but how we see.[13]

Beauty calls upon us to constantly refresh and refine how we look at things. Sometimes that means we need to stop looking so hard and instead simply wait for something to catch our attention. Beauty draws the senses to it. We cannot look away when beauty confronts us, our interest is held by the power of the image because the image is inherently interesting. This power exists in all things, and no matter how seemingly insignificant something might appear to us, there is someone somewhere that will find it fascinating beyond measure. Ask them why they find it so fascinating, and they likely will tell you that there was something about it that called to them, something that they cannot set aside, that holds them there fixated, attached, devoted, something like love. This is beauty's gift, and that is why the bird watcher sets out, to see what there is to be found. The old trope that beauty is in the eye of the beholder has always missed the mark. It is beauty that calls the eye to behold.

---

13. Throughout this book I rely on James Hillman's usage of "image." He presented his meaning of the word in three essays first published in *Spring: A Journal of Archetype and Culture*: "Inquiry into Image" (1977), "Further Notes on Images" (1978), and "Image Sense" (1979), and reprinted in *Uniform Edition of the Writings of James Hillman*, vol. 4: *From Types to Images*, edited by Klaus Ottmann (Thompson, Conn.: Spring Publications, 2019). For an extended discussion of "image," see Chapter Seven.

TWO

The Blindness We Make for Ourselves

M any of the ideas that we hold as commonplace we have not really thought about all that much. We are born into a world that is already underway with a long history of ideas and mental habits that we learn much the same way as we learn our native tongue, which is to say organically and largely unconsciously. Many of our ideas feel innate to us, as if given with the world itself. Without realizing it we accept and enact thoughts and mental patterns that are hundreds, sometimes thousands of years old, carried to us by the winds of tradition. Ironically, the ideas that we think least about are often the ones that are most foundational for how we understand the world and our place in it. These foundational ideas feel solid, permanent, and sure. We adhere to them without doubt, and where we are most sure is where we are most unconscious. Among these ideas is how we think about nature.

In 1966, Lynn White, Jr., an historian of medieval science and technology, gave a lecture at the American Association for the Advancement of Science conference that was published the next year as "The Historical Roots of our Ecologic Crisis." In it, White claimed that "the victory of Christianity over paganism was the greatest psychic revolution in the history of our culture."[1] He insisted that although modern people might not think that our current ideas follow those of early Christianity, "the substance [of our thoughts] often remains amazingly akin to that of the past."[2] He pointed to our belief in the possibility of perpetual progress as such an idea that was not found in Greco-Roman or Eastern thought but was directly traceable to the Judeo-Christian world view. "We con-

---

1. Lynn White, Jr., "The Historical Roots of our Ecologic Crisis," *Science* 155, no. 3767 (March 10, 1967): 1205.
2. Ibid.

tinue today to live," said White, "very largely in a context of Christian axioms."[3]

As White pointed out, Greco-Roman mythology does not have a creation story like those found in other mythologies, in part because the Greco-Roman view of time was cyclical and not linear. By contrast, Christianity adopted from Judaism the idea of linear and non-repetitive time along with a very distinct creation story. According to this story (Genesis 1:26), God first created light and darkness, followed by the heavenly bodies, the earth, and all of the plants and animals. Finally, God created Adam and, so Adam would not be lonely, God made Eve from Adam's rib or side. Unlike the rest of creation, only Adam was created in God's own image. (A later creation story told in Genesis 2 has Adam created before the animals and the animals then created to keep him company. In both renditions, the animals are made subservient to Adam.)

According to Genesis, God then gave Adam the task of naming all of the animals. This naming is significant because it emphasizes that Adam is distinctly different in kind from the animals. By naming the animals, Adam claims sovereignty over them. Moreover, in the ancient world, it was believed that a name expressed the essential nature of the thing named and controlled its destiny. Only Adam possessed the God-like ability to perceive the intrinsic character of each animal and so was able to give it an appropriate name suitable to its nature. Adam's ability to name the animals reinforced the idea that Adam was more akin to God and was unlike the animals.

The Judeo-Christian creation story told in Genesis is explicit when it comes to the relationship between humans and nature:

> Then God said, "Let Us make man in Our image, according to Our likeness; and let them rule over the fish of the sea and over the birds of the sky and over the cattle and over all the earth, and over every creeping thing that creeps on the earth." God created man in His own image, in the image of God He created him; male and female He created them. God blessed them; and God said to them, "Be fruitful and multiply, and fill the earth, and subdue it; and rule over the fish

---

3. Ibid.

of the sea and over the birds of the sky and over every living thing that moves on the earth."[4]

According to this story, not only are humans separate in kind from nature, they have dominion over nature. "Christianity," says White, "in absolute contrast to ancient paganism and Asia's religions (except, perhaps, Zoroastrianism) not only established a dualism of man and nature but also insisted that it is God's will that man exploit nature for his proper ends."[5]

Another aspect of Hebrew tradition dovetails with the elevation of humans over nature. In contrast to the mythologies of the Greeks and Romans, nature for the Hebrews was demythologized in the sense that the divine ceased to be an active participant in the natural world.[6] For the Greeks and Romans, the things of the world, including animals, were full of gods—an owl did not represent Athena but rather *was* Athena, and so the divine was present in each instance that an owl appeared. Monotheism replaced the many gods with one and removed that god from direct involvement with nature. This relationship is captured in the metaphor of God as the Supreme Watchmaker. According to this view, nature exists unto itself and operates without need of God's interference. The nature given by God to humans is devoid of divine or demonic powers, and so it can be treated without regard to ethical or moral concerns. "By destroying pagan animism, Christianity made it possible to exploit nature in a mood of indifference to the feelings of natural objects."[7]

The idea that nature operated according to divine law without need of God's oversight blended nicely with early scientific efforts to decipher the laws of nature. The early scientific view was that because nature operated according to God's design, the more we understood nature's laws the closer we became to God. The idea that there were objective, immu-

---

4. New American Standard Bible.

5. White, "Historical Roots," 1205.

6. James Austin Baker, "Biblical Views of Nature," in Charles Birch, William Eakin, and Jay B. McDaniel, eds., *Liberating Life: Contemporary Approaches to Ecological Theology* (Maryknoll, N.Y.: Orbis Books, 1990), 9–26. Available online at *https://www.religion-online.org/article/biblical-views-of-nature/*

7. White, "Historical Roots," 1205.

table natural laws that were an expression of God's will was the thrust behind the rise of science from the thirteenth century onward, where "every major scientist... explained his motivations in religious terms."[8] Rodney Stark compiled a list of 52 eminent scientists from 1543 to 1680— of these, 26 were Protestant and 26 Catholic; 15 of them were English, 9 French, 8 Italian, 7 German (the rest were Dutch, Danish, Flemish, Polish and Swedish respectively). One was a sceptic (Edmund Halley) and one (Paracelsus) was a pantheist. The other 50 were Christians, and Stark found that at least 30 of them could be characterized as "devout" because of "clear signs of especially deep religious concerns," and that the remainder were "conventionally religious."[9] It was not until Darwin in the mid-nineteenth century that a serious alternative to the Christian view of nature appeared. But in its formative centuries, "modern Western science was cast in a matrix of Christian theology."[10]

The Christian legacy of nature as separate from humans and operating according to natural law is clearly reflected in the philosophy of René Descartes (1596–1650). Descartes restated the human/nature dualism by asserting that there was a separation between mind and matter, mental and physical. According to Descartes, the mind is immaterial while matter exists separate from the mind and follows natural laws that can be scientifically and mathematically explained. Nature, for Descartes, was purely material, and he considered animals to be nothing more than living machines—they had no mind, no soul, no thoughts, no consciousness, no language, no emotions. According to Descartes, animals were simply one of the many ways that matter manifested itself in nature and all of nature was outside of and separate from the mind.

This latter point is crucial. For Descartes, the mind is what constitutes a person's essential, individual being. His famous *cogito ergo sum,* "I think, therefore I am," posits that I *am* my mind, and my mentality is exclusively and privately my own. You cannot know my mind as I know it; only I have access to my secret self. According to Descartes, each of us

---

8. Ibid., 1206.

9. Rodney Stark, *For the Glory of God: How Monotheism Led to Reformations, Science, Witch-Hunts and the End of Slavery* (Princeton: Princeton University Press, 2003), 162.

10. White, "Historical Roots," 1206.

looks out onto a natural world of mindless things that exist beyond our individual minds (*res extensa*), a mechanistic world devoid of soul, ticking away the time.

Descartes's mind/body dualism interiorized Christianity's human/nature dualism into the individual person. The body was base matter (nature) and therefore was subject to the natural laws established by God, while the mind (that which made us human) remained separate and immaterial. Humans thus became divided beings with no clear way of bridging the ineffable gap between mind and body, human and nature. Not only were humans separate from nature, they were estranged from themselves.

The Judeo-Christian and Cartesian views of the relationship between humans and nature came ashore with the European settlers of North America and guided how they interacted with the American landscape and the indigenous peoples they found there. The Pilgrim leader William Bradford described the Cape Cod shoreline that he saw from the deck of the *Mayflower* in 1620 as "a hideous and desolate wilderness, full of wild beasts and wild men."[11] As Leo Marx puts it, "the bias inherent in the Christian idea of nature as fallen—as Satan's domain—effectively erases the humanity of the indigenous Americans. To Bradford they are more like wild beasts than white men."[12]

By the time of Thomas Jefferson, such views had been somewhat tempered by the Enlightenment, but the underlying belief that the natural world was separate from humans still held. Jefferson moved the idea of natural law from science into politics, asserting in the *Declaration of Independence* that the right of the Americans to dissolve their political ties with England was based on their right "to assume among the powers of the earth, the separate and equal station to which the Laws of Nature and of Nature's God entitle them." Later, as President, Jefferson advocated an egalitarian view of land ownership imbued with what Jedediah Purdy, in his book *After Nature,* calls the "providential" view of nature. According to this view, nature's purpose is to provide for human

---

11. Quoted in Leo Marx, "The Idea of Nature in America." *Daedalus* 137, no. 2 (Spring 2008): 10.
12. Ibid.

needs, "but only if people do their part by filling it up with labor and developments."[13] This view, says Purdy, provided the justification for the expropriation of Native American lands because from a European perspective the Native Americans were not putting the land to its best and fullest use. Thus, the Biblical grant of human dominion over nature gained a new moral and political impetus that declared humans had a duty to alter nature to meet human needs.

Purdy posits three later developments of the American view of nature, the Romantic, the utilitarian, and the ecological. The Romantic vision saw nature as a place for inspiration and transcendence. This was the nature that appeared in the pristine and idealized landscapes of Frederic Church, Ashur Durand, and other painters from the Hudson River School, and in the writings of Henry David Thoreau and Ralph Waldo Emerson. It would later reappear in the creation of the national parks, all chosen, at least in part, because they represented the ideals of the Romantic vision of nature. But here, too, the separation of human and nature remained. "Philosophically considered," wrote Emerson, "the universe is composed of Nature and the Soul. Strictly speaking, therefore, all that is separate from us, all which Philosophy distinguishes as the NOT ME, that is, both nature and art, all other men, and my own body, must be ranked under this name, NATURE."[14] According to this view, humans can go to nature to commune with God, but they cannot be part of that nature. And the brighter the light, the darker the shadow. Purdy points out that there was no place in the Romantic landscape for indigenous people. John Muir supported removing the Miwok from Yosemite because he considered nature to be at its best when it was people-free.

With the winds of manifest destiny at its back, the frontier, that line that demarked the separation between European progress and unredeemed nature, pushed relentlessly westward. The "utilitarian" vision now took hold, a view of nature as a resource to be managed for max-

---

13. Jedediah Purdy, *After Nature: A Politics for the Anthropocene* (Cambridge, Mass.: Harvard University Press, 2015), 8.

14. *The Collected Works of Ralph Waldo Emerson,* vol. 1: *Nature, Addresses, and Lectures,* edited by Alfred R. Ferguson (Cambridge, Mass.: The Belknap Press of Harvard University, 1971), 8.

imum benefit. National forests were managed by the Bureau of Land Management and vast areas of the West were irrigated by the ironically named Bureau of Reclamation. Nature became something to be managed by experts.

Lastly, says Purdy, comes the "ecological" view where nature is seen as a network of complex and interpenetrating systems. This view began to coalesce in the 1960s and by the 1970s "nature" was increasingly replaced with "environment." In an attempt to avoid the ambiguities inherent in "nature," "environment" referred "to the entire biophysical surround—or environs—we inhabit; it implies no distinction between human and other forms of life; it encompasses all that is built and (so to speak) unbuilt, the artificial and the natural, within the terrain we inhabit."[15] Here at last was progress as humans finally began to see themselves as direct participants in the natural world. Unfortunately, this recognition was in part forced upon us as a result of human exploitation and recklessness with regard to nature and its resources. The first Earth Day was in 1970, the same year that Congress enacted the National Environmental Policy Act, the Clean Air Act, and the act establishing the Environmental Protection Agency.

Although the ecological perspective offered an alternative to earlier views that kept humans and nature apart, in the last part of the 20th century the very idea of nature was deemed suspect. In a 1984 essay, Fredric Jameson, a prominent theorist of postmodernism, wrote that "Postmodernism is what you have when the modernization process is complete and nature is gone for good."[16] From such a deconstructionist view, nature is a cultural construction having no actual referent in the real world, and is merely a concept that is seen as mere discourse. According to this view, not only are humans separate from nature, the idea that humans could have any direct, unmediated knowledge of the material world is naïve if not laughable.

---

15. Marx, "The Idea of Nature in America," 17.

16. Fredric Jameson, *Postmodernism, or the Cultural Logic of Late Capitalism* (Durham, N.C.: Duke University Press, 1991), ix. Quoted in Marx, "The Idea of Nature in America," 17.

In 1989, Carolyn Merchant declared nature "dead" because of the widespread acceptance of a mechanistic, male oriented, Newtonian-Cartesian worldview. "The removal of animistic, organic assumptions about the cosmos," wrote Merchant, "constituted the death of nature."[17] Despite this bleak conclusion, Merchant held out hope that the harsh realities of an ecological crisis might drive humans to restore a more organic view of nature. That same year, in *The End of Nature*, Bill McKibben concluded that nature came to an end when the earth's atmosphere was altered by greenhouse gases and other manufactured chemicals.[18] For McKibben, the all-pervasive, globe-encircling presence of humankind's detritus made the very idea of nature meaningless. This idea continues today in the increasing use of "Anthropocene" to refer to a new epoch in which humans have become the defining force shaping the planet. Purdy advances this idea in his aptly titled *After Nature*.

It is hard to know which is worse, the idea that humans are separate from nature or that our estrangement has become so severe that we have lost the idea of nature altogether. Under either scenario the practical consequences are likely the same. "Any way of looking at nature that encourages us to believe that we are separate from nature," wrote William Cronon in 1995, "is likely to reinforce environmentally irresponsible behavior."[19] With the catastrophic realities of anthropogenic climate change already upon us it is difficult to disagree.

This short review of the history of the idea that humans are separate from nature barely hints at the many strands and nuances of the idea. It is hardly news that the *idea* of nature is itself a human construct, despite Christian theological claims of a divine origin for the natural world. And it is certainly debatable whether the Christian view that humans are separate from nature can be held responsible for the many varieties

---

17. Carolyn Merchant, *The Death of Nature: Women, Ecology, and the Scientific Revolution* (San Francisco: Harper, 1989). Quoted in Marx, "The Idea of Nature in America," 18.

18. Bill McKibben, *The End of Nature* (New York: Random House, 1989).

19. "The Trouble with Wilderness; or, Getting Back to the Wrong Nature," in William Cronon, ed., *Uncommon Ground: Rethinking the Human Place in Nature* (New York: W. W. Norton, 1995), 87.

of environmental abuse perpetrated by humans. Dominion over nature does not necessarily lead to the exploitation of nature. But even if we take a more benevolent view that humans have stewardship over nature and should care for it responsibly as a matter of moral duty, we do not bridge the gap between humans and nature that Genesis proclaimed, Christian doctrine reinforced, and monotheistic-influenced philosophy and science perpetuated.

Today most people in America probably feel that they hold the modern ecological view described by Purdy. But the old ideas are still with us. Whenever we think of humans as superior to other animals, much less so-called inanimate nature, we perpetuate the Christian idea that humans are separate from nature. We do not have to be Christians or believe in the Christian faith to think and behave as Christians. Whenever we think of ourselves in terms of inner subjectivity or limit the idea of *psyche* or soul as being a human possession located within the human body, we are Cartesian dualists quite apart from whether we have ever heard of or read a word written by Descartes. The checkerboard farmland that we see when flying over the Midwest is a visual testament to the providential landscape that resulted from Jefferson's egalitarian vision of individual farms co-existing within a larger pattern of mutually dependent land uses. When we extoll the virtues of wilderness or denigrate the city as being unnatural, we transcend with the Romantics. And when we blissfully ignore climate change in the sanguine belief that technology will find a way to fix things, we place our faith, and our lives, in utilitarian hands.

In one study, people were asked if they felt like they were part of nature or separate from nature. A majority responded that humans were part of nature, but when that same group was asked to describe nature, they uniformly described nature as places where there were no humans.[20] A beach belonged to nature—so long as there were no human footprints in the sand.

---

20. Joanne Vining, Melinda S. Merrick, and Emily A. Price, "The Distinction between Humans and Nature: Human Perceptions of Connectedness to Nature and Elements of the Natural and Unnatural," *Human Ecology Review* 15, no. 1 (Summer 2008): 7.

This study perfectly portrays the psychological paradox of the modern ecological imagination. Despite centuries of being told and taught otherwise, the human animal knows that it is an animal. It knows that nature is its home and that it shares the planet with an incredible diversity of worldly things. It knows that the bird's nest, the beaver's lodge, and the suburban bungalow differ only in degree, not in kind. It knows that soul is not imprisoned within the brain but reverberates within a greater soul that lies beyond the body. It knows when it sees joy or pain in the eyes of a non-human animal. It knows the sadness of a forest stripped of life and left behind to suffer in silence. And it knows that attempts to dismiss such truths as mere anthropomorphisms are desperate, dogmatic attempts to buttress the old lies.

And yet we currently are at a loss for how to talk about these things we know. There is a disconnect between the immediate facts of our animal, embodied lives and the reigning cultural ideas and language that deny those facts. This is a blindness of our own making. Psychology, especially, is at a loss to even discuss the greater part of the soul that lies beyond the body. For the most part, the extent of psychology's reach beyond personal subjectivity is at best extended to family or interpersonal relationships, although a small group of psychologists begun to advocate for a psychological perspective that includes nature.[21] What is needed are psychological ideas that take into account the full range of psychic reality that includes the natural world of which we are a part. Recall that White's point was that the victory of Christian monotheism over paganism, and the resulting separation of humans from nature, was "the greatest *psychic* revolution in the history of our culture." (Emphasis mine.) Dualism, whether Christian or Cartesian, can no longer be allowed to repress nature's psychic presence, and mechanistic explanations can no longer pretend to satisfy psyche's need for ideas that match its actual, felt animal vitality.

Psychology's withdrawal from nature was part of the fallout from Descartes's dualism. "Practically all philosophy since [Descartes],"

---

21. See, e.g., Theodore Rosak, Mary E. Gomes, and Allen D. Kanner, eds., *Ecopsychology: Restoring the Earth, Healing the Mind* (San Francisco: Sierra Club Books, 1995).

wrote Owen Barfield in his wonderful *History in English Words*, "has worked outward from the thinking self rather than inwards from the cosmos to the soul."[22] Barfield called this cultural and psychological shift "internalization," by which he meant "the shifting of the centre of gravity of consciousness from the cosmos around him into the personal human being himself."[23] With this shift, "impulses which control human behavior and destiny, are felt to arise more and more from within the individual."[24] And with psyche now denied in nature, "the spiritual life and activity felt to be immanent in the world outside—in star and planet, in herb and animal, in the juices and 'humours' of the body...grow feebler."[25] The more we retreat into ourselves the less we hear the voices that surround us, and the more we turn our eyes inward the less we see the other eyes that cast their gaze upon us.

Sigmund Freud, who so desired psychology to be considered "scientific," encapsulated the Cartesian *cogito* into the concept of the ego. "There is nothing of which we are more certain that the feeling of our self, of our own ego. This ego appears as something autonomous and unitary, marked off distinctly from everything else."[26] And what was that "everything else"? Nature, which Freud understood as "impersonal forces and destinies,"[27] that were "majestic, cruel, and inexorable."[28] Nature is "eternally remote,"[29] and it is out to get us: "She destroys us—coldly, cruelly, relentlessly."[30] Our only recourse is to try to "humanize" nature, because then:

> We can apply the same methods against these violent supermen outside that we employ in our own society; we can try to adjure them,

---

22. Owen Barfield, *History in English Words* (Great Barrington, Mass.: Lindisfarne Press, 1988), 170.

23. Ibid., 171.

24. Ibid.

25. Ibid.

26. Sigmund Freud, *Civilization and its Discontents*, translated by James Strachey (New York: W. W. Norton, 1961), 14.

27. Sigmund Freud, *The Future of an Illusion*, translated by James Strachey (New York: W. W. Norton, 1961), 16.

28. Ibid.

29. Ibid.

30. Ibid., 15.

to appease them, to bribe them, and, by so influencing them, we may rob them of a part of their power. A replacement like this of natural science by psychology not only provides immediate relief, but also points the way to a further mastering of the situation.[31]

And yet in the face of psychic powers ("impersonal forces and destinies") that clearly need to be reckoned with (via "humanization"), Freud and so much of the psychology that has followed him have steadfastly refused to recognize the psychological reality of these powers or to seek ways to psychologically engage them on their own terms. Instead we have retreated to the sterile walls of the laboratory, or to Skinner's box, or to the darkened consulting room with drawn curtains where the ego is safe to pursue its interior dreams of interpretation.

The way forward is daunting but two of the writers we have heard from in this chapter offer similar clues for how to proceed. "Until [the human-nature dualism] is eradicated not only from our minds but also our emotions," wrote White, "we shall doubtless be unable to make fundamental changes in our attitudes and actions affecting ecology. *The religious problem is to find a viable equivalent to animism.*"[32] (Emphasis mine.) White goes on to pose the question "Do people have ethical obligations toward rocks?" and points out that "to an ancient Greek, to an American Indian, or perhaps certain kinds of Buddhists, the question would have meaning."[33] Indeed, not only would it have meaning, "for quite different reasons they would probably reply 'Yes.'"[34] But "to almost all Americans, still saturated with ideas historically dominant in Christianity (although perhaps not necessarily so), the question makes no sense at all."[35] White concludes that only if we are able to reach a point where we no longer consider such a question ridiculous will we have any hope of answering the ecological crises we face.

---

31. Ibid., 17.
32. Lynn White, Jr., "Continuing the Conversation," in Ian G. Barbour, ed., *Western Man and Environmental Ethics: Attitudes Toward Nature and Technology* (Reading, Mass.: Addison-Wesley Publishing Company, 1973), 62.
33. Ibid., 63.
34. Ibid.
35. Ibid.

Purdy starts from a different place. He wonders if perhaps part of the human-nature separation comes from taking "nature" abstractly, as a "coherent system of principles that somehow adds up to a whole and orders all the material activity of the universe, at all scales, living and nonliving."[36] This he calls "capital-N Nature." But then he ends up in a similar place as White:

> I think Nature, used this way, is a religious holdover. It's a mono-
> theistic idea, as if the universe had a single meaning because it's
> the work of a single mind...I wonder whether—to stay with the
> religious imagery for a moment—a polytheist or animist image
> wouldn't fit better today and going forward. It's just not true that
> Nature has a meaning, or that we have relations with it as a whole.
> But that doesn't mean we are disconnected from the living world.
> Quite the contrary. We have bonds and relations with particular
> places, species, seasons in a place. All of these are fragments of what
> I think we should keep calling the natural world.
>
> There's an ethnography of Alaska's Athabascan peoples, by
> Richard Nelson, called *Make Prayers to the Raven*. Its gist is that
> these "animist" folks don't revere an abstract Nature, nor do they
> see it as just a set of resources and logistical problems. They have
> relations to it, rather like the relations you might have with your
> partner's family, or the neighbors, or your co-workers: a bit opaque,
> touchy, a mix of affection, obligation, and prudence. And these rela-
> tions are specific—not with Nature, but with the salmon, or a river,
> or a tree. They are on many scales, again, much like our relations
> with individuals, institutions, countries, cultures, in our human-on-
> human lives.
>
> We can't decide to be Athabascan, of course, but this strikes me as
> a promising direction for a realistic, open-minded ethical practice.
> It takes very seriously that we live with the rest of the world, and it
> can be a big pain in the ass, or even hurt or kill us, but it is also the
> only possible site and source of all the joys we can have.[37]

---

36. Jedediah Purdy in Ross Anderson, "Nature Has Lost Its Meaning," *The Atlantic* (November 30, 2015), online at *https://www.theatlantic.com/science/archive/2015/11/nature-has-lost-its-meaning/417918/*

37. Ibid.

There is much wisdom here. And note especially that in both White and Purdy the ideas of animism and polytheism both take on an ethical dimension. It is as if once we consider the many things of the world as worthy in themselves, we have a "natural" tendency to want to relate with them in more suitable ways. Not our way, necessarily, but in ways that accept and honor their place, their needs, their integrity. Are we back to Hillman and the snake? If instead of *interpreting* nature, asking what it means, what if we were to attend to it, appreciate it, learn from it on its own terms? That, after all, is what we want to do. If nature really is separate from us, if we really are just lonely minds adrift among lifeless atoms in motion, then why are we so curious about the greater world, why do we care? Despite our nature-killing ideas, we cannot shake the feeling that we belong here.

Neither White nor Purdy are calling for an animistic or polytheistic religion based on literal belief in gods and spirits. White suggests "a viable equivalent to animism," and Purdy wonders if "a polytheist or animist *image* wouldn't fit better today and going forward" (emphasis added). We can open ourselves to the influences we feel coming from the natural world without need for belief; indeed, belief itself contributes to the blinders that belong to a monotheistic cast of mind. A polytheistic imagination simply accepts what is presented to it without need of belief; it doesn't ask what is "really" there, or what is "really" true because it does not belong to a style of thought that requires such questions. Cultures everywhere and for eons have perceived the world as animated, but the dominant psychological ideas of Western monotheistic culture, and especially American monotheistic culture, are incapable of talking about, much less relating, to such a world. Instead, we follow the monotheistic and Cartesian traditions that declare the world to be "inanimate" (literally, no *anima,* no soul). And so, rocks are inanimate and therefore insignificant, unless they are useful to us in some practical way, and any suggestion to the contrary is mere anthropomorphic projection.

But by denying soul to the greater world beyond the human, we are left isolated and alone, adrift in a vast sea of dead, mechanically reactive matter. Little wonder that the leading psychological complaints of the twenty-first century are anxiety and depression—objectless fear and sadness. There is a radical disconnect between our ideas and the realities that we nonetheless feel, and perhaps have felt since the dawn of our evolution. As aesthetic animals we feel and know the world as alive and ensouled even though our religious and intellectual traditions deny these feelings and knowledge. Can we even wonder if the scourge of suicide that plagues us, especially among our young people, is perhaps partly a desperate desire to reconnect with what we have come to call inanimate? Is it literal death that is desired or the death of a way of thinking that requires us to constantly deny the soul that we feel all around us, penetrating us, evoking undeniable feelings and thoughts of interdependence and relatedness? If I have to deny the life that I know is there, what is the point of living?

Purdy is also onto something important with his idea of "capital-N Nature." We have been talking about nature as if we know what that word means when in fact the word "nature," as Raymond Williams writes, "is perhaps the most complex word in [the English] language."[38] Williams goes on to say that "Any full history of the uses of nature would be a history of a large part of human thought."[39] The reason why becomes clearer the closer we look at the word.

"Nature" derives etymologically from the Latin *natura*, from a root in the past participle of *nasci*—to be born. The same root lies within *nation*, *native*, and *innate*.[40] The oldest meaning of nature referred to the essential quality or characteristic *of* something. It was used singularly in the sense of "the nature of" something in particular. Only later did it acquire the more abstract meanings of "the inherent force which directs either the world or human beings or both [or] the material world itself, taken as including or not including human beings."[41] This shift from calling attention to the qualities of particular things to asserting an abstract, overarching concept that includes all things was "structurally and historically

---

38. Raymond Williams, *Keywords: A Vocabulary of Culture and Society* (New York: Oxford University Press, 1985), 219.

39. Ibid. For a short history of some of the various meanings of "nature," see Arthur O. Lovejoy, *Essays in the History of Ideas* (New York: G.P. Putnam's Sons, 1960), 69–77.

40. Williams, *Keywords*, 219.

41. Ibid.

cognate with the emergence of *God* from *a god* or *the gods*."[42] Echoing this insight, Barfield notes that "At the beginning of the seventeenth century we find the word *Nature* employed in contexts where medieval writers would certainly have used the single word *God*."[43]

The monotheistic conflation of Nature and God goes hand in hand with Barfield's internalization of the cosmos into human subjectivity. When God and Nature become One, and when we declare that our being is defined by and limited to a wholly subjective self that is radically different and apart from nature then we are stranded on an island that no bridge can reach. We cannot discern the nature of particular things because they are essentially not like us—we feel no connection because there *is* no connection. We are alone in ourselves and all else is dead matter, soulless, inanimate. We lose our ability to discern and appreciate particular things when we reject the vibrancy of an animistic or polytheistic world view in favor of monotheism's unifying concepts. The ancient Greeks said that "all things are full of gods," and it is precisely when we deny the gods in things that we lose both. The many things of the world, and the many gods that animate them, are forsaken when we erect an idealized and transcendent Nature that remains forever out of our reach. Nature becomes an abstraction for something that exists forever elsewhere than where we are, a symbol for an inaccessible reality that evaporates with our presence.

The abstraction of Nature from its actual presence in and among the nature of things is the ideational dissonance that lies at the heart of the paradox that leads people to say that they are part of nature while simultaneously defining nature as places that are devoid of humans. The separation we feel from nature is because of how we think about nature; it is our *idea* of nature that gives rise to our abiding sense of dislocation, confusion, and loneliness. An idea of nature that places it always elsewhere means that for us it is nowhere. And with nowhere to call home we are left alone in our secret selves, unable to break free from the eddies and whirlpools of subjectivity and introspection.

---

42. Ibid., 220.
43. Barfield, *History in English Words,* 173.

When Nature becomes an abstraction that excludes our presence, both we and the many things of the world suffer. "Capital-N Nature" is a pathological idea that isolates humans from our proper place in the order of things, and in our isolation we begin to have delusions of superiority and grandeur, standing atop the ladder of creation with the many things of the world at our feet. From this transcendent and elevated position, we cannot help but see the other things of the world as being there for our use and disposal. How could they be otherwise? After all, it boils down to Us and Them, and there is nothing in between to bind us together. History has shown what this kind of thinking does to us and to the world.

Going back to "lowercase-n nature" would enable us to respectfully reengage with the many things of the world. From this humbler perspective, nature is not transcendent but rather exists everywhere and is immediately available by opening our imagination and senses to the natures of the specific things that are all around us. Cronon describes this shift in perspective as replacing "wilderness" ("capital-N Nature") with "wildness" ("lowercase-n nature"). Like the abstract idea of Nature, wilderness is a human cultural construct that contributes to our sense of separation:

> Indeed, one of the most striking proofs of the cultural invention of wilderness is its thoroughgoing erasure of the history from which it sprang. In virtually all of its manifestations, wilderness represents a flight from history. Seen as the original garden, it is a place outside of time, from which human beings had to be ejected before the fallen world of history could properly begin. Seen as the frontier, it is a savage world at the dawn of civilization, whose transformation represents the very beginning of the national historical epic. Seen as the bold landscape of frontier heroism, it is the place of youth and childhood, into which men escape by abandoning their pasts and entering a world of freedom where the constraints of civilization fade into memory. Seen as the sacred sublime, it is the home of a God who transcends history by standing as the One who remains untouched and unchanged by time's arrow. No matter what the angle from which we regard it, wilderness offers us the illusion that

we can escape the cares and troubles of the world in which our past has ensnared us.[44]

Cronon also zeros in on the consequences of a dualistic view that separates humans from nature:

[W]ilderness embodies a dualistic vision in which the human is entirely outside the natural. If we allow ourselves to believe that nature, to be true, must also be wild, then our very presence in nature represents its fall. The place where we are is the place where nature is not. If this is so—if by definition wilderness leaves no place for human beings, save perhaps as contemplative sojourners enjoying their leisurely reverie in God's natural cathedral—then also by definition it can offer no solution to the environmental and other problems that confront us. To the extent that we celebrate wilderness as the measure with which we judge civilization, we reproduce the dualism that sets humanity and nature at opposite poles. We thereby leave ourselves little hope of discovering what an ethical, sustainable, *honorable* human place in nature might actually look like.[45]

Cronon suggests that by focusing on "wildness" instead of "wilderness" we leave the spiritual haze of transcendence and are regrounded in the nature of things. "[W]ildness (as opposed to wilderness) can be found anywhere: in the seemingly tame fields and woodlots of Massachusetts, in the cracks of a Manhattan sidewalk, even in the cells of our own bodies."[46]

When we forgo abstractions that draw us away from the many things of the world we can begin to appreciate the natures of particular things as full of portents and potentialities, displaying qualities and characteristics that attract us to them, and embodying attributes that are waiting to be discovered and discerned. Peter Wohlleben tells the story of how he changed when he stopped looking at trees in term of their commercial value and began looking at them as individuals with intrinsic value. He says his love of nature was "reignited," and he suddenly became aware of "countless wonders."[47] Here is the return to beauty. Each thing an

---

44. Cronon, "The Trouble with Wilderness," 79–80.
45. Ibid., 80–81.
46. Ibid., 89.
47. Peter Wohlleben, *The Hidden Life of Trees: What They Feel, How They Communicate* (Vancouver: Greystone Books, 2015), xiv.

each, just as it is, but never alone. Each thing always present in a broader aesthetic array of other things, a thriving, animated context of relationships, microcosm and macrocosm always together, penetrating and implicating one another.

With the return to beauty comes the reanimation of our imagination. Our natural senses and skills are released from their internal prison within our alleged subjectivity so that they may fully engage the world in which we live. The tired debates over objectivity and subjectivity, outer and inner, nature and human are then seen for what they are—imaginal perspectives foisted upon the mind by the crushing weight of monotheism and Cartesian dualism. Although monotheism cannot help but posit choices between assumed opposites and then demand for us to choose between them, there is always a third way, the way of soul or *anima,* that refuses to choose, that refuses to be caught on the horns of a pre-ordained dilemma. Soul prefers the animal beneath the horns, imagining an animated and embodied world alive and rippling with diversity and delights. The visceral presence of things are at once readily at hand while remaining eternally mysterious. "You could not discover the limits of soul," wrote Heraclitus, "even if you traveled every road to do so; such is the depth of its meaning."[48] But this mystery is not separate from the many things of the world, it part of their nature.

When we return to beauty we also return to love and soul. This is the mythical trinity given to us in the old story by Apuleius, where Aphrodite, Eros, and Psyche (or more precisely in his Roman telling Venus, Cupid, and Psyche) all belong together, require one another, and implicate one another.[49] When guided by their examples, we approach the world as a place to be appreciated, loved, and deepened. Beauty, love, and soul give us a world that is sensate, sensual, and sensible, and together they evoke and sustain our insatiable curiosity for the many things of the world. And, as we discover and learn more about the natures of particular things, we cannot help but feel a growing kinship. No longer enclosed within

---

48. Philip Wheelwright, *Heraclitus* (Princeton, N.J.: Princeton University Press, 1959), 58.

49. Apuleius, *The Golden Ass,* translated by Jack Lindsay (Bloomington: Indiana University Press, 1960).

our own minds, our desires suddenly take wing, lifted by an empathy that connects us to a greater world of things that we discover are not so unlike ourselves after all. We come to see that surely Stevens is correct that "the blackbird is involved...In what I know."

THREE

What the Blackbird Knows

W ithin the broader context of monotheistic and Cartesian ideas that have misled us into believing that we are separate from nature is a corollary tradition that has, until recently, kept us from appreciating the creative, emotional, and intellectual powers of non-human animals. Through a sustained, almost incredible, intransigence, we have for millennia denied non-human animals the capacity for consciousness. The history of the debate over animal consciousness is a cautionary tale of how strict ideology and fundamentalism, both of which are varieties of rational experience, can repress natural affinities that exist among the many things of the world. This refusal to respect and appreciate the capabilities of non-human animals is a further repression of beauty because it continues the blindness of our own making, yet again creating a false divide, this time between human and non-human animals. As we have just seen with regard to our ideas about nature, this repression of beauty occasions personal and cultural aberrations, and ethical failings of the worst kind.

Aristotle wrote extensively about animals, including their psychological aspects. In his *De Anima, Historia Animalium,* and related writings he brought together his own extensive observations of animals and anecdotal animal lore from earlier times. Because of his emphasis on observation and reliance on inductive reasoning, Aristotle is considered by some to be "the father of comparative psychology, as well as the founder of the other biological sciences and of natural history in general."[1] Despite his admiration for their instinctive capabilities, Aristotle believed that non-human animals lacked a rational soul, which was possessed only by

---

1. C.J. Warden, "The Development of Modern Comparative Psychology," *The Quarterly Review of Biology* 3, no. 4 (December 1928): 486.

humans. In his taxonomy, Aristotle ranked non-human animals below humans and believed that non-human animals were subservient to humans. According to his taxonomic hierarchy, humans stood on the top rung of nature's ladder (*scala naturae*): "Plants exist for the sake of animals and the other animals for the good of man."[2]

After Aristotle, interest in animals waned among later Greek and Roman writers, who turned their attention away from nature to more metaphysical and ethical considerations. A few, like Pliny and Plutarch, compiled anecdotes about animals but in general natural history in the Aristotelian tradition faded away.

We have already seen how early Christianity emphasized the view that non-human animals are essentially different from and inferior to humans. Augustine believed that nothing could be perceived without reason, which is needed to judge and classify sensations, and that because non-human animals lacked reason they therefore "lack understanding or sensation or life altogether."[3] The lack of moral status for animals was also made clear by Augustine, who wrote that "Christ himself shows that to refrain from the killing of animals and the destroying of plants is the height of superstition, for, judging that *there are no common rights between us and beasts and the trees,* he sent the devils into a herd of swine and with a curse withered the tree on which he found no fruit."[4] (Emphasis added.)

2. Aristotle, *Politics* 1256*b*15, translated by H. Rackham, Loeb Classical Library 264 (Cambridge, Mass.: Harvard University Press, 1932), 37.

3. Augustine, *City of God,* vol. 4: Books 12–15, Loeb Classical Library 414, translated by Philip Levine (Cambridge: Harvard University Press, 1966), 16–17.

4. Saint Augustine, *The Catholic and Manichean Ways of Life,* translated by Donald A. Gallagher and Idella J. Gallagher (Washington, D.C.: The Catholic University of America Press, 2017), 102. Augustine refers here to two biblical stories. The first is an account of Jesus calling demons out from a man into a herd of swine that then are drowned in a lake. Mark 5:1–20; Matthew 8:28–34; Luke 8:26–36. The second is an account of Jesus cursing a fig tree that bears no fruit and is commonly taken to be a symbol directed at the Jews for not accepting Jesus as king. Mark 11:12–25; Matthew 21:18–22; Luke 13:6–9. This is in turn based on the symbolic representation in Jewish scripture of the people of Israel as figs on a tree. Hosea 9:10, Jeremiah 24. Both stories have also been taken to mean that Jesus was sent by God to redeem human souls and has little interest in their bodies or their "property," including animals.

Throughout the Middle Ages, interest in the mental capabilities of non-human animals was discussed primarily through theological considerations about the relationship of humans to non-human animals. The orthodox view was that non-human animals were driven by divinely implanted instinct while humans possessed a rational soul allowing for voluntary choice. Only humans, therefore, could rightly be considered moral or ethical beings.

A revival of natural history in the Aristotelian tradition began in the sixteenth century with Conrad Gessner's *Historia animalium* (1551–1587). Gessner purposefully chose the name of Aristotle's great work for his own and attempted to bring together all of the classical views on non-human animals, as well as views of his own time and his own observations. The five volumes of his profusely illustrated natural history spanned to 4,500 pages, and was the most complete encyclopedia of its kind. It included descriptions of animals and their habits as well as examples of how they appeared in literature, history, and art. It was widely read, despite the Catholic Church adding it to its list of banned books (Gessner was a Protestant).

It was Descartes, however, who most clearly encapsulated the orthodox theological view of non-human animals and infused it into the mechanistic language of the early scientific revolution. For Descartes, non-human animals were non-sentient mechanical automata driven only by reactions to stimuli. As he put it in a letter to Henry More, "I now came to realise that there are two different principles causing our motions: one is purely mechanical and corporeal...the other is the incorporeal mind, the soul which I have defined as a thinking substance."[5] Because non-human animals lacked the incorporeal mind, their motions were purely mechanical. Although there is disagreement over whether Descartes believed non-human animals were conscious or had feelings, the matter was clear to many of his followers. Malebranche, who was deeply steeped in the thought of both Augustine and Descartes, summed up the more extreme view:

---

5. Peter Harrison, "Descartes on Animals," *The Philosophical Quarterly* 42, no. 167 (April 1992): 223.

In dogs, cats, and other animals, there is neither intelligence nor a spiritual soul in the usual sense. They eat without pleasure; they cry without pain; they believe without knowing it; they desire nothing; they know nothing; and if they act in what seems to be an intelligent and purposive manner, it is only because God has made them fit to survive, and has constructed their bodies in such a way that they can organically avoid—without knowing that they do so—everything that might destroy them and that they seem to fear.[6]

Descartes's view of non-human animals took hold as an acceptable answer to both the emerging scientific sensibility and the orthodox theological tradition. It has proven remarkably resilient and still has adherents today. Nevertheless, it also sparked considerable disagreement, especially among people who had close contact with animals both wild and domestic. As the naturalist John Ray wrote in his *The Wisdom of God Manifested in the Works of Creation* (1691), if "beasts were automata or machines, they could have no sense, or perception of pleasure, or pain and consequently no cruelty could be exercised on them; which is contrary to the doleful significations they make when beaten, or tormented, and contrary to the common sense of mankind."[7] Thomas Hobbes adopted a thoroughly materialist view to counter Cartesian dualism, and although granting non-human animals a degree of consciousness, he maintained that they lacked the ability of self-consciousness, which belonged only to humans. Thus, non-human animals could understand and act upon words spoken by humans but did not understand the words as words—only humans could understand their own "thoughts and conceptions."[8]

This basic split between the Christian/Cartesian view that animals were machines of no moral or ethical status and the "common sense"

---

6. *Méditations métaphysiques et correspondance de N. Malebranche,* edited by F. Feuillet de Conches (Paris: H. Delloye, 1841), 75–76. Quoted and translated in Matt Cartmill, "Animal Consciousness: Some Philosophical, Methodological, and Evolutionary Problems," *American Zoologist* 40, no. 6 (December 2000): 838.

7. John Ray, *The Wisdom of God Manifested in the Works of Creation* (London: William Innys and Richard Manby, 1735), 55–56.

8. Thomas Hobbes, *Leviathan: Parts One and Two* (Indianapolis: The Bobbs-Merrill Company, 1958), 32.

view that animals were conscious, could feel pain, and therefore warranted at least some moral consideration pretty much sums up the debate over animal consciousness for the next two centuries. Indeed, many of these same issues still occupy the field of animal consciousness. Notably, during the period before Darwin, the discussion remained primarily within philosophy and theology while the scientific interest in animals focused on taxonomy and zoology, neither of which engaged in any significant way with the idea of animal consciousness.

The discussion changed with Darwin, who decisively moved (or at least tried to) the question of animal consciousness away from theology and philosophy to what we today would call comparative psychology:

> [T]he difference in mind between man and the higher animals, great as it is, certainly is one of degree and not of kind. We have seen that the senses and intuitions, the various emotions and faculties, such as love, memory, attention, curiosity, imitation, reason, &c., of which man boasts, may be found in an incipient, or even sometimes in a well-developed condition, in the lower animals. They are also capable of some inherited improvement, as we see in the domestic dog compared with the wolf or jackal. If it could be proved that certain high mental powers, such as the formation of general concepts, self-consciousness, &tc., were absolutely peculiar to man, which seems extremely doubtful, it is not improbable that these qualities are merely the incidental results of other highly-advanced intellectual faculties; and these again mainly the result of the continued use of a perfect language. At what age does the new-born infant possess the power of abstraction, or become self-conscious, and reflect on its own existence? We cannot answer; nor can we answer in regard to the ascending organic scale...That such evolution [the evolution of mental and moral faculties] is at least possible, ought not to be denied, for we daily see these faculties developing in every infant; and we may trace a perfect gradation from the mind of an utter idiot, lower than that of an animal low in the scale, to the mind of a Newton.[9]

---

9. Charles Darwin, *The Descent of Man and Selection in Relation to Sex,* 2nd ed. (London: John Murray, 1874), 126–27.

And more:

> Of all the faculties of the human mind, it will, I presume, be admitted
> that *Reason* stands at the summit. Only a few persons now dispute that
> animals possess some power of reasoning. Animals may constantly be
> seen to pause, deliberate, and resolve. It is a significant fact, that the
> more the habits of any particular animal are studied by a naturalist,
> the more he attributes to reason and the less to unlearnt instincts.[10]

Despite his prolific writing, Darwin did not really attend to philosophical questions of definitions, commenting toward the end of his life
that "I have often felt much difficulty about the proper application of
the terms, will, consciousness, and intention."[11] Rather Darwin tended
toward a common-sense use of such words as "mind" as applying "to
every manifestation occurring in living matter to which any, even the
most rudimentary form of consciousness could be ascribed."[12] What
mattered more to Darwin was that consciousness was part of his larger
theory of evolution that proposed a continuity of mind from lower to
higher organisms—a difference in degree, not kind.

Darwin's theory of evolution embedded humans inextricably within
nature. We were different, perhaps, but not separate. We were akin to,
not opposed to, the other living creatures of the world and it was not
clear where that kinship stopped, if it did. Evolution, not the Bible, told
the story of creation and its incremental development through time. As
he fully expected, Darwin's views drew fire from all sides. Despite the
ground laid by precursors of evolutionary thought like Georges-Louis
Leclerc, Comte de Buffon, and Jean-Baptiste Lamarck in the preceding
century, the orthodox science, philosophy, and theology of Darwin's
time still clung tenaciously to the Christian/Cartesian view of the immu-
tability of species and a difference in kind, not degree, between human
and non-human animals. The orthodox view that non-human animals
were driven by instinct and humans by reason merely restated the old

---

10. Ibid., 75.
11. Marion Hamilton Carter, "Darwin's Idea of Mental Development," *The
American Journal of Psychology* 9, no. 4 (July 1898): 540.
12. Ibid., 543.

Cartesian divide. Additional resistance to Darwin's sympathetic and humbler views of an indelible bond between humans and non-human animals arose in America where they ran counter to overweening desires that needed nature to be separate, amoral, and providentially given for human use and exploitation.

The firestorm around Darwin's evolutionary theory regarding consciousness focused on the mental continuity from non-human to human animals and the idea that humans' mental capacities had evolved over time. In an attempt to counter the criticisms, the anecdotal movement arose among Darwin and his contemporary followers, most notably George Romanes. The anecdotal method was based on Darwin's theory of the continuity of mental states and on introspection by analogy, that is, the assumption that the same mental processes that occur in the human mind also occur, albeit in differing degrees, in the minds of non-human animals. Said Romanes:

> Starting from what I know subjectively of the operations of my own individual mind, and the activities which in my own organism they prompt, I proceed by analogy to infer from the observable activities of other organisms what are the mental operations that underlie them.[13]

By collecting stories of purportedly human-like capabilities of the "higher" animals, the anecdotalists attempted to narrow the gap between the mental capacities of non-human and human animals. Unfortunately, they also claimed that the purported animal-like behaviors of "savages" and prehistoric humans showed that they were more evolutionarily connected to the so-called higher animals than to modern humans. Romanes was convinced that through such anecdotal evidence:

> [I]t may be safely promised, that when we come to consider the case of savages, and through them the case of prehistoric man we shall find that, in the great interval which lies between such grades of mental evolution and our own, we are brought far on the way

---

13. George Romanes, *Animal Intelligence* (London: Kegan Paul, Trench & Co., 1982), 1–2.

towards bridging the psychological distance which separates the gorilla from the gentleman.[14]

The anecdotalists fell easy prey to charges of anthropomorphism and sentimentality. In reaction to the anecdotalists, a more scientific, systematic approach to comparative psychology arose in the late nineteenth century. This new movement emphasized greater precision in observation and increased use of carefully controlled experiments, often within laboratories. It was deeply suspicious of anecdotal evidence and what it considered to be anthropomorphic analogies. More than anything else, the movement wanted to establish comparative psychology as a science worthy of the name.

Perhaps the most influential figure in the experimental period was Conwy Lloyd Morgan. He emphasized careful observation and experimentation and penned perhaps the most famous sentence in all of comparative psychology as an antidote to the perceived excesses of the anecdotalists. The "Morgan Canon" stated:

> *In no case may we interpret an action as the outcome of the exercise of a higher psychical faculty, if it can be interpreted as the outcome of the exercise of one which stands lower in the psychological scale.*[15]

There has been much discussion and disagreement over what Morgan meant by "higher" and "lower" psychical faculties, but the general consensus is that "higher" means more human-like in terms of reason while "lower" implies more animal-like in terms of instinct. In between, Morgan postulated various levels of "intelligence." This kind of grading of psychical faculties was seen especially in Romanes, and Morgan used similar terms despite his rejection of Romanes' anecdotal style.

The Morgan Canon puts the burden of proof on those claiming that a particular behavior implicates or infers conscious activity of a higher order to show that the behavior cannot be explained by something lower. This should not be taken to mean, however, that Morgan was averse to the idea of higher-order consciousness in non-human animals. Rather

---

14. George Romanes, *Mental Evolution in Man: Origin of Human Faculty* (London: Kegan Paul, Trench & Co., 1988), 439.

15. Conwy Lloyd Morgan, *An Introduction to Comparative Psychology* (London: Walter Scott, Ltd., 1894), 53.

he asked for a systematic, non-anthropomorphic approach to animal psychology. In a plea to his readers he asked them

> to be good enough to credit me with an unbiassed desire to interpret the phenomena of animal psychology without exaggeration, either in the direction of excess or defect of mental power and differentiation. As an evolutionist who believes that the whole range of the mental faculties have been developed by natural processes, the tendency of my bias would assuredly not be in the direction of setting a gulf between the faculties of animals and the faculties of man. My sole aim is to endeavour to reach by legitimate process of scientific induction the most probable interpretation of zoological psychology, and by comparing this with the psychology of man to ascertain by what steps the lower faculties of animals may have passed by natural process of development into the higher faculties of man.[16]

Morgan was emblematic of a strong movement that "was characterized in terms of physics envy."[17] This group wanted to establish comparative psychology as a rigorous, experimentally based science on par with other "hard" scientific fields. Despite this desire, the old orthodoxies that we reviewed in the previous chapter persisted and held sway, and, just as in the seventeenth and eighteenth centuries, "Commitments that were explicitly or essentially theological made many naturalists reluctant to embed their own species [i.e., human] within the system of animal connections."[18] Moreover, the experimentalists struggled to break free from the intuitive appeal of the anecdotal period and its reliance on introspection by analogy and inference as ways of establishing at least a common-sense acceptance of the "higher faculties" of non-human animals. What was needed by the experimentalists was a way to expel these "non-scientific" approaches.

The answer came in epiphenomenalism. Descartes had considered non-human animals to be non-conscious automata, mere machines, and that they were thereby distinguished from humans, who were con-

---

16. Ibid., 124.

17. Harriet Ritvo, "Animal Consciousness: Some Historical Perspective," *American Zoologist* 40, no. 6 (December 2000): 852.

18. Ibid., 850.

scious. Thomas Huxley took a view that was at once more inclusive and extreme—he considered non-human animals and humans to be both conscious *and* machines. Building on earlier materialistic views such as those of Julien Offray de La Mettrie and Pierre Jean Georges Cabanis, Huxley asserted that all mental states were caused by physical events in the brain. This causal relationship was one-way—Huxley claimed that mental states had no effect on physical behavior. Instead, neural events within the brain cause both the physical behaviors and their accompanying mental states in both non-human animals and humans. Note the sequence—neural events, physical behaviors, and then mental states. Thus, mental states do not affect behavior—mental states might be *correlated* with behavior, but they are not *causative* of that behavior:

> The consciousness of brutes would appear to be related to the mechanism of their body simply as a collateral product of its working, and to be as completely without any power of modifying that working as the steam-whistle which accompanies the work of a locomotive engine is without influence upon its machinery. Their volition, if they have any, is an emotion indicative of physical changes, not a cause of such changes.[19]

And lest there be any doubt that this view applies to humans:

> It is quite true that, to the best of my judgment, the argumentation which applies to brutes holds equally good of men; and, therefore, that all states of consciousness in us, as in them, are immediately caused by molecular changes of the brain-substance. It seems to me that in men, as in brutes, there is no proof that any state of consciousness is the cause of change in the motion of the matter of the organism. If these positions are well based, it follows that our mental conditions are simply the symbols in consciousness of the changes which takes place automatically in the organism; and that, to take an extreme illustration, the feeling we call volition is not the cause of a voluntary act, but the symbol of that state of the brain which is the immediate cause of that act. We are conscious automata...[20]

---

19. Thomas H. Huxley, *Method and Results: Essays* (London and New York: Macmillan, 1904), 240.
20. Ibid., 243–44.

Other favored similes of nineteenth-century epiphenomenalists for the relationship between mental states and physical behavior were that mental states are like a melody, the notes of which follow temporally and melodically without causing the melody (Shadworth Hodgson), or a shadow following a moving object (Théodule Armand Ribot), or the foam on the crest of a wave (Hodgson).[21] William James, decidedly not an epiphenomenalist, described the theory as saying that feeling

> is a mere collateral product of our nervous processes, unable to react upon them any more than a shadow reacts on the steps of the travel-ler whom it accompanies. Inert, uninfluential, a simple passenger in the voyage of life, it is allowed to remain on board, but not to touch the helm or handle the rigging.[22]

Epiphenomenalism, apart from being counterintuitive to a com-mon-sense view that mental states can affect and cause behavior, also ran aground with evolutionary theory. If mental states had no effect on behavior, then it was not clear how they could have adaptive value and so would seem to have no place within evolutionary change over time. Nonetheless, some experimentalists readily adopted the theory as a way to move forward that, in their view, freed them from the constraints of anthropomorphism and the anecdotalist's introspection by analogy. For those who wanted to reduce behavior to learned responses to stimuli, two philosophical avenues were now offered—they could either claim that consciousness existed but did not matter, or they could claim that at least non-human animals were not conscious at all. John Watson, the leading proponent of behaviorism, added a third way—simply define psychology in a manner that left out any consideration of mental states.

In 1913, Watson published his "Psychology as the Behaviorist Views it," and made clear his position:

> Psychology, as the behaviorist views it, is a purely objective, experi-mental branch of natural science which needs introspection as little

---

21. Citations in Victor Caston, "Epiphenomenalisms, Ancient and Modern," *The Philosophical Review* 106, no. 3 (July 1997): 311 n.4. Caston also points out that Huxley never used the terms "epiphenomenal," or "epiphenomenalism." Their most likely first use was by William James in his *Principles of Psychology*.

22. William James, "Are We Automata?" *Mind* 4, no. 13 (January 1879): 1.

as do the sciences of chemistry and physics. It is granted that the behavior of animals can be investigated without appeal to consciousness. Heretofore the viewpoint has been that such data have value only in so far as they can be interpreted by analogy in terms of consciousness. The position is taken here that the behavior of man and the behavior of animals must be considered on the same plane; as being equally essential to a general understanding of behavior. *It can dispense with consciousness in a psychological sense.* The separate observation of 'states of consciousness,' is, on this assumption, no more a part of the task of the psychologist than of the physicist. (Emphasis added.)[23]

By putting non-human animals on the same theoretical footing as humans, Watson paved the way for laboratory experimentation that used small animals, primarily laboratory rats and birds, whose findings could then be extrapolated to humans. Behaviorists rejected introspective methods and instead insisted that all behavior resulted from learning through interaction with the environment. Early behaviorists such as Watson and Ivan Pavlov focused on respondent conditioning that operated without regard to mental states. B.F. Skinner later extended behaviorism's reach by accepting the existence of mental states while insisting that they could also be conditioned to respond to stimuli (operant conditioning).

The early part of the twentieth century saw the field of animal studies divide. In America, comparative psychology became dominated by laboratory-based behaviorism while in Europe field-based ethology developed, especially in the mid-twentieth century. Classical ethologists such as Niko Tinbergen, Konrad Lorenz, and Karl von Frisch considered ethology to be a part of biology, not psychology, and emphasized observation of animals in natural settings instead of the contrived settings of the laboratory. (Tinbergen, Lorenz, and Von Frisch were jointly awarded the Nobel Prize in Physiology or Medicine in 1973 for their work.) Unlike the behaviorists that focused on learning, ethologists were interested in "naturally occurring behavioral patterns that are dis-

23. John Watson, "Psychology as the Behaviorist Views It," *Psychological Review* 20, no. 2 (March 1913): 176.

played by nondomesticated species behaving under natural conditions."[24] Ethologists also rejected the behavioristic approach of studying a limited number of species in favor of studying large numbers of species. But ethology nonetheless basically ignored mental states in non-human animals because it considered such states to be beyond the reach of science. It was one thing to have a conviction that non-human animals possessed subjective experiences, but because we did not have first-person access to them as with humans (because of a shared language), such subjective experiences were considered not amenable to scientific explanation.[25]

In the 1970s, a new approach to animal studies emerged that focused on the behavior of social groups of animals and the social structures within them using evolutionary theory as an explanatory tool. The resulting field received widespread attention in 1975 with the publication of E. O. Wilson's book *Sociobiology*.[26] In ensuing years, behavioral ecology developed to study behavior in terms of evolutionary adaptations to environmental pressures. Like classical ethology, these developing fields have for the most part set aside questions of subjective states of non-human animals.

This thumbnail sketch of religious, philosophical, and scientific views on non-human animal consciousness only scratches the surface of an extremely complex history.[27] It is often difficult to know how even to discuss the subject matter—what exactly do we mean by words like consciousness, awareness, mental states, subjectivity, emotional expressions, etc.? These definitional difficulties are compounded by the fact that reli-

24. Donald A. Dewsbury, *Comparative Psychology in the Twentieth Century* (Stroudsburg, Penn.: Hutchinson Ross Publishing Company, 1984), 10.

25. For a description of this tension in Lorenz's work, see Bernard E. Rollin, *The Unheeded Cry: Animal Consciousness, Animal Pain, and Science* (New York: Oxford University Press, 1989), 213-16.

26. Edward O. Wilson, *Sociobiology: The New Synthesis* (Cambridge, Mass. and London: The Belknap Press of Harvard University Press, 1975).

27. For more detailed histories, see Donald A. Dewsbury, *Comparative Psychology in the Twentieth Century*; Stephen Walker, *Animal Thought* (London: Routledge & Kegan Paul, 1983); Robert Boakes, *From Darwin to Behaviourism* (Cambridge: Cambridge University Press, 1984); Colin Allen and Marc Bekoff, *Species of Mind: The Philosophy and Biology of Cognitive Ethology* (Cambridge: The MIT Press, 1997); Rollin, *The Unheeded Cry*; and Warden, "The Development of Modern Comparative Psychology."

gious, philosophical, and scientific discourse often seem to delight in being obtuse and inaccessible to those not indoctrinated to their jargons, mores, and methods. Still, for our purposes, we can distill some general themes.

First is that discussions of animal consciousness are often a tangle of religious, philosophical, and scientific beliefs that interpenetrate and influence one another. Early philosophical and scientific views were thoroughly imprinted with religious beliefs and traditions. Later, claims of what it meant to be scientific, such as Watson's claim that only so-called objective behaviors were proper sources of scientific study, were merely circular proclamations of underlying philosophical beliefs. And what is particularly significant is that this entanglement is just as tightly knotted today as it was four hundred years ago.

Second, from the beginning of Western thinking on animal consciousness the overwhelmingly dominant view has been anthropocentric—non-human animals only matter insofar as they matter to humans and the degree to which they might be said to be conscious is to be determined in terms of human consciousness. Starkly put, non-human animals are either like us or not like us—they either share divinity (like us) or they are as insignificant as stones, they either have a soul (like us) or they are mere automata, they either are capable of feeling (like us) or they lack even the ability to feel pain, they either warrant a duty of moral decency (like us) or they are incapable of being mistreated, they are either capable of volitional acts (like us) or they are driven purely by blind instinct. And, even if it is allowed that such distinctions are not either/or but admit to some degree of variation, the consciousness of non-human animals will be described, defined, and determined in terms of the human mind. Although many comparative psychologists proclaimed the importance of studying non-human animal *behavior* apart from its significance to humans, when the turn is made to considering whether non-human animals think or feel they must do so on our terms and according to standards derived from human consciousness.[28]

---

28. Dewsbury states that "the vast majority of comparative psychologists study animals without direct application to problems of human behavior as their primary concern." *Comparative Psychology*, 333. Although arguably true of classical ethology, such was certainly not the case for behaviorism: "Give me a dozen healthy infants, well-formed, and my own specified world to bring them up in and I'll guarantee

Third, except for the brief period between Darwin's *The Descent of Man* (1871) and Morgan's *Canon* (1894) the steady trajectory in Western thought has been to deny, discredit, ignore, or define away the potential or relevance of non-human animal consciousness. It is difficult to think of another area where intransigence in the face of common sense has been so dogmatic. Theologians, philosophers, and scientists have maintained their positions against non-human consciousness with remarkable, and indefensible, certainty. As the extraordinary animal behaviorist Donald Griffin noted, "When scientists consider conscious mental experience, they exhibit an almost irresistible tendency to assert definite conclusions, even though the available evidence is crude and inadequate."[29]

Traditional Western views on non-human animal consciousness have shown themselves to be muddled, self-centered, and close-minded. Nowhere are these tendencies clearer than in the alleged taboo of anthropomorphism. Bernard Rollin points to an inherent contradiction in the allegation that anthropomorphism is a fallacy by way of pain research using non-human animals:

> [S]uch research presents a dilemma for the common sense of science: either animals are experiencing pain (unpleasant subjective sensations) or they are not. If they are, and they are valid 'models' for human pain, that commits one to the presence of a human (or human-like) mental state in the animal and renders one liable to the conviction of having committed the fallacy of anthropomorphism. If they are not, animals have nothing like experienced pain, in which case there is no point to such research, since one cannot model the human situation on it. [30]

The alleged fallacy of anthropomorphism rests on the assertion that humans are projecting thoughts and feelings onto non-human animals. This assumes, in classic Western style, that human and non-human

---

to take any one at random and train him to become any type of specialist I might select—doctor, lawyer, artist, merchant-chief and, yes, even beggar-man and thief, regardless of his talents, penchants, tendencies, abilities, vocations, and race of his ancestors." John B. Watson, *Behaviorism* (New York: W.W. Norton, 1925), 82.

29. Donald R. Griffin, *The Question of Animal Awareness: Evolutionary Continuity of Mental Experience* (New York: The Rockefeller University Press, 1976), 10.

30. Rollin, *The Unheeded Cry*, 26.

animals are qualitatively different, that the only relevant standard for thoughts and feelings are human, and that we already know that non-human animals are incapable of thoughts and feelings.[31] But what if anthropomorphism is not a projection? What if it is an attempt, given our anthropocentric limitations of thought, feeling, and language, at recognizing consciousness in non-human animals? Can we not imagine, as did Darwin, that the differences between us and non-human animals are of degree, not kind? A dog does not have to be happy in the same manner that a human is happy for the word "happy" to make sense when applied to a dog. Whatever inaptness might appear in the word is our problem, not the dog's. It is we who are struggling to give voice to a direct and tacitly grasped awareness of a conscious state in a fellow creature. From this perspective, anthropomorphism is not a projection but a concession, a confession of the limitations of our methods and terminology, and of our inability to meet non-human animals on their terms.

By the 1970s there had been decades of observation of non-human animals by researchers from various disciplines. At the same time, the repression of research into even the possibility of consciousness in non-human animals was reaching a breaking point. A catalyst appeared in 1974 when Thomas Nagel published "What Is It Like to Be a Bat?" In that article, Nagel maintained that the question of consciousness could be stated as "an organism has conscious mental states if and only if there is something that it is like to *be* that organism—something it is like *for* the organism."[32] Nagel concluded that because of the limitations of human thought and imagination we simply are unable to know "what it is like for a *bat* to be a bat."[33]

---

31. For a careful analysis, and refutation that anthropomorphism is always a categorical fallacy, see John Andrew Fisher, "The Myth of Anthropomorphism," in Marc Bekoff and Dale Jamieson, eds., *Readings in Animal Cognition* (Cambridge, Mass.: The MIT Press, 1999), 3–16. "Without a plausible argument that ascribing mental states to non-human animals is a categorical fallacy the most basic assumptions of critics of anthropomorphic thinking is seen to be untenable" (ibid., 15).

32. Thomas Nagel, "What Is It Like to Be a Bat?," *The Philosophical Review* 83, no. 4 (October 1974): 436.

33. Ibid., 439.

Nagel's article attracted the interest of many, perhaps most notably Donald Griffin, whose 1976 book *The Question of Animal Awareness*[34] kindled widespread interest in what has come to be called cognitive ethology. Marc Bekoff, a leading scholar in the field, defines "cognitive ethology" as

> the evolutionary and comparative study of nonhuman animal... thought processes, consciousness, beliefs, or rationality... Because behavioral abilities have evolved in response to natural selection pressures, ethologists favor observations and experiments on animals in conditions that are as close as possible to the natural environment where the selection occurred, and because cognitive ethology is a comparative science, cognitive ethological studies emphasize broad taxonomic comparisons and do not focus on a few select representatives of limited taxa.[35]

Griffin embraced the challenge posed by Nagel and maintained that the goal of cognitive ethology is "to reopen the basic question of what life is like, subjectively, to nonhuman animals."[36] For Griffin, there are philosophical, ethical, and scientific reasons why the study of consciousness in non-human animals is significant:

> The philosophical importance of animal consciousness lies in its relevance to the general question of other minds and to the difficult questions of how to define and identify consciousness. The ethical importance lies in the widespread belief that causing pain and suffering to a conscious creature is morally wrong in an important sense not applicable to an unfeeling mechanism. And the scientific importance lies in our interest in animals as such. We want to understand what the lives of these other creatures are like, to them.[37]

---

34. Donald R. Griffin, *The Question of Animal Awareness: Evolutionary Continuity of Mental Experience* (New York: The Rockefeller University Press, 1976).

35. Marc Bekoff, "Cognitive Ethology and the Explanation of Nonhuman Animal Behavior," in *Comparative Approaches to Cognitive Science,* ed. Herbert L. Roitblat and Jean-Arcady Meyer (Cambridge, Mass.: The MIT Press, 1995), 119. Available online at *http://cogprints.org/157/1/199709002.html*

36. Donald R. Griffin, *Animal Minds* (Chicago and London: The University of Chicago Press, 1992), 3.

37. Ibid., 233.

Returning to Nagel's critique, Griffin argues that Nagel did not deny that "partial understanding and significant, though incomplete, information about the behavior of bats or other animals can be deduced from their behavior."[38] Although it may be true that humans can never have a precise and complete understanding of what it is like for a *bat* to be a bat, Griffin rejects the idea that "the content of animal thinking is hopelessly inaccessible to scientific inquiry."[39]

Griffin's work has been highly influential and sparked an explosion of research into various aspect of consciousness in non-human animals.[40] Of course, there are those who continue to insist that cognitive ethology is simply a return to the anecdotal anthropomorphism of Romanes, or who deny outright that consciousness of non-human animals can or should be studied at all. Bekoff calls these detractors "slayers," with other people being "skeptics" and "proponents."[41] But despite the critics, the fact remains that the field of cognitive ethology is a testament to scientific open-mindedness. After literally millennia of disregard and disrespect, non-human animals are finally getting the attention and study they deserve.

What this revolution is also teaching us is the degree to which humans are unconscious of our prejudices and limitations when it comes to our relationship to non-human animals, even when we are overtly well-intentioned. In his aptly named book *Are We Smart Enough to Know How Smart Animals Are?*,[42] Frans de Waal recounts a common experiment with chimpanzees involving their ability to use tools. Food will be placed out of their reach, but a stick will be left where they can reach it. The question is whether they will then use the stick as a tool to reach the food

---

38. Ibid., 237.

39. Ibid., 260.

40. For just a sample of the available literature, see Colin Allen and Michael Trestman, "Animal Consciousness," in *The Stanford Encyclopedia of Philosophy* (Winter 2017 Edition), edited by Edward N. Zalta. Available online at *https://plato.stanford.edu/archives/win2017/entries/consciousness-animal/*

41. Bekoff, "Cognitive Ethology," 120.

42. Frans de Waal, *Are We Smart Enough to Know How Smart Animals Are?* (New York and London: W. W. Norton, 2016).

and pull it to them. The result is that they excel at such a task, suggesting problem-solving capability as well as tool use.

A similar experiment was designed for elephants. Food was suspended above their reach and a stick was provided just like with the chimpanzees. But the elephants didn't seem to make the same mental connection that had been made by the chimpanzees. They didn't try to use the stick to reach the food. Did that mean that elephants weren't as "smart" as chimpanzees and lacked the ability to mentally solve the same problem? No, the problem was the design of the experiment itself. Elephants rely on their exceptional sense of smell and touch and have relatively poor eyesight. Picking up a stick with its trunk blunted the elephant's ability to smell and use its trunk.

In a modified experiment, researchers placed a cube within the elephant's reach. The elephant retrieved the cube, pushed it underneath the dangling food, and then used the cube as a stepping stool to reach the food. The elephant was as adept as the chimpanzee in problem solving and tool use. The lacking was in the researcher's failure to take into account the differences between elephants and chimpanzees.

In 1970, Gordon Gallup developed the mirror self-recognition (MSR) test. First, chimpanzees were introduced to mirrors and over a period of days it appeared that they comprehend that they were looking at their own bodies. They would use the mirrors for grooming parts of their bodies that they could not otherwise see, they would pick food from their teeth using the mirrors, make faces at the mirrors, etc. Then, the mirrors were removed, the chimpanzees were anesthetized, and small red dots were placed on the upper eyebrow ridge and the top of the opposite ear. After the animals were fully recovered from the anesthesia, the mirrors were reintroduced. The question was whether the animals would recognize the dots as being on their bodies by looking at their reflection in the mirrors. The animals almost immediately began touching the red dots with their fingers. Based on this test, Gallup surmised that "self-recognition of one's mirror image implies a concept of self."[43] Later in

---

43. Gordon Gallup Jr., "Chimpanzees: Self-Recognition," *Science* 167, no. 3914 (January 2, 1970): 87.

his life, Gallup extended his view, suggesting that "species that pass the mirror test are also able to sympathize, empathize and attribute intent and emotions in others—abilities that some might consider the exclusive domain of humans."[44]

Following Gallup's initial experiment, the MSR test was given to a wide range of species. At first it seemed like only some of the great apes and humans were able to pass the test. Today it is known that at least a handful of species can pass the test, including bottlenose dolphins, Asian elephants, and Eurasian magpies. It is also possible that cleaner wrasses are also capable of self-recognition in mirrors.[45] But the MSR test should not be considered binary, as if to pass the test means that an animal is self-aware, and to fail the test means that an animal is not self-aware. Indeed, there is no consensus on what it even means to say an animal is self-aware. Bekoff and De Waal argue for a "gradualist" approach where an animal's cognition of itself as an entity existing in relation to other entities occurs along a continuum.[46]

I worry that efforts to identify "self"-awareness in non-human animals can too easily perpetuate an underlying belief in human exceptionalism. We, of course, are taken as the epitome of self-awareness, we give one another names, feel empathic bonds with one another and other species, reflect on our own identities, etc. We become the measure by which other animals are evaluated and judged. But there are many ways to be in the world. Animals make judgments all the time that implicate an awareness of their capabilities and limitations. Will that branch support me, am I strong enough to win a fight with a competitor, does that other entity pose a danger, etc.

The moral of the story is that to learn more about how other animals think and feel, humans need to find ways to more fully appreciate the capabilities and differences of animals on their terms. By rejecting

---

44. Gordon Gallup Jr., "Can Animals Empathize? Yes," *Scientific American* 9, no. 4 (Winter 1998): 66.

45. Frans de Waal, "Fish, Mirrors, and a Gradualist Perspective on Self-Awareness," *PLOS Biology* 17, no. 2 (1994): 1–2.

46. Marc Bekoff and Paul W. Sherman, "Reflections on Animal Selves," *Trends in Ecology & Evolution* 19, no. 4 (April 2004): 176–80; De Waal, *Are We Smart Enough*, 243; De Waal, "Fish, Mirrors," 1–2.

anthropocentrism and attempting to learn about other animals in their own right, humans may come to have a better understanding not only of how they are like us, but how we are like them. Even more importantly, we can learn to appreciate the wondrous differences between the many things of the world and to recognize the essential, life-sustaining importance of those differences.

In 1934, Jakob von Uexküll coined the term *Umwelt* [environment] to describe a species-specific subjective world formed by an organism's perceptual and cognitive capabilities and its interaction with the environment. As he put it, "everything that a subject perceives belongs to its *perception world* [*Merkwelt*], and everything it produces, to its *effect world* [*Wirkwelt*]. These two worlds, of perception and production of effects, form one closed unit, the *environment*."[47] Thus, for von Uexküll, there are as many *Umwelten* as there are organisms, each perceiving and understanding the world in its own way, and each altering that world through its interaction with the world.

Umwelt is often explained in terms of differing perceptual capabilities – the bat's use of echolocation instead of sight, the ability of birds to see ultraviolet wavelengths, the communication by elephants through infrasonic rumbles undetectable by humans, etc. But in the conclusion of his book, Von Uexküll applies the term to the differing worlds of the astronomer, deep-sea researcher, atomic physicist, a researcher of airwaves, a sensory physiologist, and a musicologist. Each perceives the world differently through their perspectives and how they imagine the world through the lenses of their respective interests and ideas. Although as humans they share certain perceptual capabilities, they nonetheless inhabit different *imaginal Umwelten*. Despite what Watson believed, human talents are not fungible and interchangeable. I might be able to imagine to some degree what it is like to be an atomic physicist, but I will never be able fully to know what it is like for an *atomic physicist* to be an atomic physicist.

---

47. Jakob von Uexküll, *A Foray into the Worlds of Animals and Humans,* translated by Joseph D. O'Neil (Minneapolis and London: University of Minnesota Press, 2010), 42.

Nagel wrote that we cannot fully know other minds because "every subjective phenomenon is essentially connected with a single point of view."[48] Perhaps, but that does not mean that every subjective phenomenon is *only* connected with a single point of view. In Greek myth, a given story might accentuate the acts of a particular god, but the rest of the pantheon was always present by implication. All things are full of gods. So, we do not have to imagine subjectivity as singular, isolated, or impervious, or as taking place only within an individual. Instead of defining *Umwelt* as a closed world comprising perception and production of effects, we add a third factor—imagination. From this perspective, the many things of the world present themselves as images, each image a precisely given display implicating the other images with which it is given, even if those accompanying images are not readily apparent. Perception and the production of effects rely on imagination as their animating (ensouling) force. C. G. Jung wrote that "psyche *is* image,"[49] and Hillman has said that images are "the psyche itself in its imaginative visibility."[50]

This "imaginative visibility," which should not be confused with literal visibility, is given by beauty. Whether a fox in a field or a black snake in a dream, it is beauty that provides the animating context that allows for perception to occur within and through imagination and that gives form to how images interact (behave) with one another. Beauty, then, is what makes *Umwelts* possible. Again, in myth, it was Aphrodite, goddess of beauty and either consort or mother of Eros, god of love and desire, that made the world, including the gods, visible. "She was more than an aesthetic joy; she was an epistemological necessity, for without her, all the other gods would remain hidden, like the abstractions of mathematics and theology, but never palpable realities."[51] *The sensate availability of the world, and its inherent sensibility, belong first to beauty.*

---

48. Nagel, "What Is It Like to Be a Bat," 437.

49. *Collected Works of C. G. Jung,* vol. 13: *Alchemical Studies,* edited and translated by Gerhard Adler and R. F. C. Hull (Princeton, N.J.: Princeton University Press, 1970), par. 75.

50. James Hillman, "Image and Soul: The Poetic Basis of Mind," in *Uniform Edition of the Writings of James Hillman,* vol. 1: *Archetypal Psychology* (Putnam, Conn.: Spring Publications, 2013), 17.

51. James Hillman, "The Practice of Beauty," *Sphinx: A Journal for Archetypal Psychology and the Arts* 4 (1992): 20.

By taking *Umwelt* imagistically, we avoid reducing so-called subjectivity as taking place solely within an observer. Rather subjectivity and observing are themselves seen within the context of beauty and imagination. "The *Imagination*," said Darwin, "is one of the highest prerogatives of man. By this faculty he unites *former* images and ideas, independently of the will."[52] (Emphasis on *former* added.) Images come first, prior to and independent of the will, and afford the potential for observation and appreciation. Darwin further comments on the autonomy of imagination by quoting the poet Jean Paul Richter as saying that the poet "who must reflect whether he shall make a character say yes or no—to the devil with him; he is only a stupid corpse."[53] Darwin says that dreaming gives us the best example of the independence of imagination, again citing Richter who said that "the dream is an involuntary act of poetry."[54] And Darwin does not hesitate to assert that animals "have vivid dreams [as] shewn by their movements and sounds uttered" and so "we must admit they possess some power of imagination."[55]

By observing how non-human animals present themselves and interact within their natural environments we learn how to become more attuned to discerning relationships and correlations. We learn *from them* how to notice subtleties and nuances within their precisely given contexts. They *teach us* to forestall the epistemological goals of understanding and explanation to focus on the immediacy of recognition, awareness, and appreciation. By opening our senses through careful imagining we increase our ability to grasp the beauty of our fellow inhabitants of a shared world.

This leads us to another point drawn from our review of the history of human ideas about non-human animal consciousness. We have seen that until recently any appreciation of consciousness in non-human animals was simply ruled out, dismissed, or ignored. It is indeed remarkable that so many smart people could be so wrong for so long. But it is the dismissiveness that is particularly galling. What is missing is respect. We have seen in our discussion of nature and now again in our discussion of our

---

52. Darwin, *The Descent of Man*, 74.
53. Ibid.
54. Ibid.
55. Ibid., 74–75.

relationships with non-human animals that lack of respect leads to eco-logical atrocities and barbarism. To disrespect something is to refuse to regard it, to refuse to look at it again (*re*: "back" + *specere*: "to look at"). This refusal results in the repression of beauty. As Hillman puts it:

> [B]elow the ecological crisis lies the deeper crisis of love, that our love has left the world; that the world is loveless results directly from the repression of beauty, its beauty and our sensitivity to beauty. For love to return to the world, beauty must first return, else we love the world only as a moral duty: clean it up, preserve its nature, exploit it less. If love depends on beauty, then beauty comes first, a priority that accords with pagan philosophy rather than Christian. Beauty before love also accords with the all-too-human experience of being driven to love by the allure of beauty.[56]

Franz de Waal writes that "the maestro of observation, Konrad Lorenz, believed that one could not investigate animals effectively without an intuitive understanding grounded in love and respect."[57] More, this call to empathy "is not self-focused but other-oriented. Instead of making humanity the measure of all things, we need to evaluate other species by what they are."[58] When beauty returns, we are at once humbled and inspired. Humbled because we come to see ourselves within the broader tapestry of imagination and to recognize the limitations of human intro-spection and self-reflection. Inspired because with beauty comes love, a love that both re-grounds us amidst the many things of the world while also awakening our desire for them. We no longer want to care for the other things of the world out of a sense of duty but rather as an expres-sion of love and delight in their possibilities. Rilke said that the highest task of a bond between two people was to "stand guard over the solitude of the other,"[59] and I would extend this to our relationship with the many things of the world. This is the way of beauty, a protective embrace that does not restrain, a respectful appreciation that asks nothing more than for things to be as they are, each thing beautiful in itself.

---

56. Hillman, "The Practice of Beauty," 17.

57. De Waal, *Are We Smart Enough*, 19.

58. Ibid., 275.

59. *Letters of Rainer Maria Rilke 1892-1910*, translated by Jane Bannard Greene and M. D. Herter Norton (New York: W.W. Norton, 1945), 65.

FOUR

A Taſte for the Beautiful

Animals are always doing something. They are constantly interacting with their surroundings and with other living creatures, they hunt for food and search for water, they mate and reproduce, they construct all manner of nests and lodgings, they fight, they sleep, they play. They always seem so direct and purposive in their actions, so certain of the world they inhabit and their place in it; they might appear to ponder or consider, but they don't seem to doubt.

Before 1859, the common explanation among biologists for such behaviors was that they were the result and enactment of God's design. God had created each animal as it was, fully formed and endowed with its precise characteristics. Animals acted as they did because God intended them to act that way. They had no independent agency and were capable of only robotic decisions programmed by God. To study animals, then, was to study the mind of God and through animal behavior we could discern divine intentionality. All of Nature (note the "capital-N") was given as a piece, self-contained, unchanging through time, and undeviating in its processes. From such a perspective, biology was a subset of natural theology.[1]

But then there were the fossils. How to explain these curiosities that seemed to show animals that were similar to existing animals but no longer extant? And why were there gaps in the fossil record? One answer, popular in the nineteenth century around the same time the idea of "extinction" was becoming more accepted, was the theory of catastrophism that posited there had been a series of godly creations and erasures.

---

1. The following account of pre-Darwinian biological views is based on Robert Trivers, *Social Evolution* (Menlo Park, Calif.: The Benjamin/Cummings Publishing Company, 1985), 9–10.

God made a world and then destroyed it, repeating this process until finally arriving at our current world, which was taken (hoped!) to be the final iteration of God's creations. The things of nature did not change in themselves; it was God that changed the things of nature. Later creationist theories have attempted to explain the fossil record by postulating a great flood that wiped out all of the prior animals and somehow deposited their remains in an apparently orderly fashion within geological strata such that they give the appearance of change over time. But this appearance is only an illusion to the limited mortal mind that cannot comprehend God's Plan.

Given the religious bias within the larger community of biologists during Darwin's time, it is little wonder that his idea of "evolution" was so vehemently rejected. Darwin theorized that living organisms changed over time and that existing organisms had descended from now extinct predecessors. This view was rejected by many biologists because it was contrary to their belief that biology had to rest on the religious view that Nature was static unless or until it was catastrophically changed by divine intervention.

In 1859, Darwin published *On the Origin of Species by Means of Natural Selection, or the Preservation of Favoured Races in the Struggle for Life*. As the title of this remarkable work suggests, Darwin believed that natural selection was the primary process for evolutionary change. For Darwin, natural selection combined three interrelated factors. First, that within a given species variation occurs among individuals, and that some of this variation is heritable ("heritable variation"). Second, that within a given species some individuals are more successful at reproduction than others ("differential reproductive success"). Third, that most offspring die before reaching reproductive age ("pre-productive mortality").[2] Taken together, Darwin theorized that:

> As many more individuals of each species are born than can possibly survive; and as, consequently, there is a frequently recurring struggle for existence, it follows that any being, if it vary however slightly in any manner profitable to itself, under the complex and sometimes varying conditions of life, will have a better chance of

---

2. Ibid., 12.

surviving, and thus be *naturally selected.* From the strong principle of inheritance, any selected variety will tend to propagate its new and modified form.[3]

Natural selection therefore referred to individuals, not species or groups, and it favored individuals with heritable variations that increased their reproductive success, both in terms of number of offspring and the survivability of those offspring. Naturally selected variations, or "adaptations," occur within and in response to an individual organism's particular environment, the "the complex and sometimes varying conditions of life." Because most adaptations are environmentally contingent, there are few if any adaptations that would be selected for all environments. The coat of a polar bear would hardly be suitable for the tropics.

We must keep in mind that Darwin was working prior to an understanding of genetics. Within the modern context, natural selection is a process by which some individuals in a species are more likely to out-reproduce other individuals within that species across generations, due in part to genetic differences.[4] The observable characteristics of an organism ("phenotype") result from the interaction of the organism's genetic constitution ("genotype") with its environment. An organism's phenotype includes, among other things, its physical form and structure ("morphology"), behavior, and the extended products of its behavior such as nests or dens. Natural selection favors phenotypes that are better adapted to survive within a given environment, and individuals having such a phenotype will produce more offspring that have a better chance of surviving, thereby passing on the adaptive phenotype to their offspring. Through this process, the genes associated with the phenotype are perpetuated over generations. Darwin, however, had no recourse to this genetic model, and he struggled to find a sound basis for his theory of natural selection.

In the years after *On the Origin of Species,* even as Darwin's general idea of evolution became more accepted by biologists, the process of natural

---

3. Charles Darwin, *On the Origin of Species by Means of Natural Selection, or the Preservation of Favoured Races in the Struggle for Life* (London: John Murray, 1861), 4–5.

4. This formulation from Dr. Jill Mateo in conversation with the author.

selection remained problematic. As a result, various alternatives were proposed. Theistic evolution attempted to couch evolution within a religious context, claiming that God, not natural selection, intervened to push evolution along by supplying species with beneficial variations.[5] Neo-Lamarckism insisted that acquired traits were more influential in evolution than random variations.[6] Orthogenesis theorized that variation was not random and that evolution was propelled by ingrained developmental forces moving in a linear march toward perfection.[7] And saltationism posited that evolution proceeded not through gradual and incremental change but through large jumps fed by spontaneous mutations, sometimes creating a new species in a single leap.[8] Such alternative views created considerable resistance to natural selection during the "eclipse of Darwinism"[9] that lasted until the early twentieth century. Beginning in the 1920s, however, the "modern synthesis" began to combine Gregor Mendel's understanding of heredity, the study of genetic variations within populations, and Darwin's views on natural selection. Once natural selection found its genetic footing it became widely accepted as the primary evolutionary process.[10]

While scientists grappled with Darwin's ideas of natural selection in the years after *On the Origin of Species,* Darwin was occupied with what he thought were limitations to his own theory. In *On the Origin of Species,* Darwin had confronted the difficulty of how natural selection could lead to "organs of extreme perfection and complication," taking as an example the human eye:

> To suppose that the eye, with all its inimitable contrivances for adjusting the focus to different distances, for admitting different

5. Edward J. Larson, *Evolution: The Remarkable History of a Scientific Theory* (New York: Random House, 2006), 126; Peter J. Bowler, *Evolution: The History of an Idea* (Berkeley: University of California Press, 1989), 222–26.

6. Larson, *Evolution,* 126–27; Bowler, *Evolution,* 257–68.

7. Larson, *Evolution,* 126–27; Bowler, *Evolution,* 268–70.

8. Larson, *Evolution,* 127–28.

9. The phrase was used by Julian Huxley to describe the status of evolutionary theory "before genetics and selectionism were combined to give the modern synthesis.'" Bowler, *Evolution,* 246.

10. For much more on this complicated and fascinating topic, see Larson, *Evolution,* 221–43; Bowler, *Evolution,* 307–32.

amounts of light, and for the correction of spherical and chromatic aberration, could have been formed by natural selection, seems, I freely confess, absurd in the highest possible degree...Reason tells me, that if numerous gradations from a perfect and complex eye to one very imperfect and simple, each grade being useful to its possessor, can be shown to exist; if further, the eye does vary ever so slightly, and the variations be inherited, which is certainly the case; and if any variation or modification in the organ be ever useful to an animal under changing conditions of life, then the difficulty of believing that a perfect and complex eye could be formed by natural selection, though insuperable by our imagination, can hardly be considered real.[11]

Despite his conviction in the essential truth of natural selection, Darwin was nonetheless aware that there were many variations in animals that not only did not enhance their survival but indeed appeared to hinder them. He was especially troubled by one such example—the extraordinary beauty of the peacock's huge tail that, although beautiful, also hindered the peacock by making it slower and more vulnerable to predators. How could natural selection possibly lead to an apparently detrimental trait or explain its exquisite detail and beauty? For Darwin, this example was even more difficult than the "perfect and complex eye," and he wrote of this conundrum to his friend, the Harvard botanist Asa Gray, in 1860:

> It is curious that I remember well time when the thought of the [human] eye made me cold all over, but I have got over this stage of the complaint, & now small trifling particulars of structure often make me very uncomfortable. The sight of a feather in a peacock's tail, whenever I gaze at it, makes me sick![12]

Darwin struggled with this question for years before taking it head-on in his *The Descent of Man and Selection in Relation to Sex*. But the kernel of his answer was already there in *On the Origin of Species*:

---

11. Darwin, *On the Origin of Species*, 204–5.

12. Letter to Asa Gray, April 3, 1860. Darwin Correspondence Project, "Letter no. 2743," available online at *https://www.darwinproject.ac.uk/letter/DCP-LETT-2743.xml*

I can see no good reason to doubt that female birds, by selecting, during thousands of generations, the most melodious or beautiful males, according to their standard of beauty, might produce a marked effect. I strongly suspect that some well-known laws, with respect to the plumage of male and female birds, in comparison with the plumage of the young, can be explained on the view of plumage having been chiefly modified by sexual selection, acting when the birds have come to the breeding age or during the breeding season; the modifications thus produced being inherited at corresponding ages or seasons, either by the males alone, or by the males and females; but I have not space here to enter on this subject.

Thus it is, as I believe, that when the males and females of any animal have the same general habits of life, but differ in structure, colour, or ornament, such differences have been mainly caused by sexual selection; that is, individual males have had, in successive generations, some slight advantage over other males, in their weapons, means of defence, or charms; and have transmitted these advantages to their male offspring.[13]

Although Darwin recognized in *On the Origin of Species* that sexual selection was different from natural selection, the latter of which he also referred to as "ordinary selection,"[14] he nonetheless seemed to subsume sexual selection under natural selection (he introduced the idea of sexual selection in his chapter on natural selection). His primary examples for sexual selection referred to variations associated with direct male-male competition for females such as antlers and spurs.[15] Although not directly tied to matters of survival, such variations were nonetheless useful because better armed or protected individuals could be expected to mate more and leave more offspring.

And yet not everything came down to sword or shield. "The rock-thrush of Guiana," wrote Darwin, "birds of Paradise, and some others, congregate; and successive males display their gorgeous plumage and perform strange antics before the females, which standing by as spec-

---

13. Darwin, *On the Origin of Species,* 94.
14. Ibid., 144, 174, 176.
15. Ibid., 93.

tators, at last choose the most attractive partner."[16] There was something else going on here beyond battle, something just as inexplicable as the beauty of the peacock's tale. Darwin already saw in *Origin* that this aspect of mate choice could not be neatly subsumed under the utilitarian assumptions of natural selection. "The effects of sexual selection, when displayed in beauty to charm the females, can be called useful only in rather a forced sense."[17]

In *The Descent of Man,* Darwin set forth the revolutionary idea that sexual selection was a separate process from natural selection. He said that sexual selection operates in two ways. The first is the "law of battle" of male-male competition for females, which Darwin theorized led to larger body size and strength in males, the development of weapons like horns, antlers, and spurs for fighting, and prehensile organs for holding females (this kind of sexual selection is sometimes referred to as "intrasexual selection"). The other mode ("intersexual selection") operates through the subjective choice by an individual, usually the female, of a mate based on aesthetic appeal alone. While natural selection favors traits that enhance survival and/or reproductive success, sexual selection favors traits that lead to success in obtaining mates and increasing reproductive success. Unlike natural selection, which takes place within and in response to a specific environment, sexual selection is an independent process that takes place among animals relating to one another. In intersexual selection, said Darwin, the selection of mates is based on a "taste for the beautiful."[18] Sexual selection took place within an environment, but was not responding to the environment. Instead, "animals had evolved to be beautiful to *themselves.*"[19]

Darwin used language to describe the process of intersexual selection, which is most commonly a matter of female choice, that many biologists found difficult to accept, and indeed many still do. He described females as having an "aesthetic faculty,"[20] and that males attempt to "charm

---

16. Ibid., 93–94.
17. Ibid., 219.
18. Darwin, *The Descent of Man,* 92.
19. Richard O. Prum, *The Evolution of Beauty: How Darwin's Forgotten Theory of Mate Selection Shapes the Animal World—and Us* (New York: Doubleday, 2017), 23.
20. Darwin, *The Descent of Man,* 93.

the females by love-dances or antics."[21] He used words like "appreciate," "admire," and "love":

> With the great majority of animals, however, the taste for the beautiful is confined, as far as we can judge, to the attractions of the opposite sex. The sweet strains poured forth by many male birds during the season of love, are certainly admired by the females, of which fact evidence will hereafter be given. If female birds had been incapable of appreciating the beautiful colours, the ornaments, and voices of their male partners, all the labour and anxiety exhibited by the latter in displaying their charms before the females would have been thrown away; and this it is impossible to admit.[22]

Darwin attributed all of this to animals having a "sense of beauty":[23]

> When we behold a male bird elaborately displaying his graceful plumes or splendid colours before the female, whilst other birds, not thus decorated, make no such display, it is impossible to doubt that she admires the beauty of her male partner. As women everywhere deck themselves with these plumes, the beauty of such ornaments cannot be disputed. As we shall see later, the nests of humming-birds, and the playing passages of bower-birds are tastefully ornamented with gaily-coloured objects; and this shews that they must receive some kind of pleasure from the sight of such things.[24]

Sexual selection thus operated on aesthetic choices that brought pleasure to the female, and the pleasing traits were there solely to be appreciated. Darwin made this latter point clear when writing about the extraordinary beauty of the Argus pheasant, saying that "it affords good evidence that the most refined beauty may serve as a sexual charm, *and for no other purpose.*"[25] (Emphasis added.)

Richard Prum points to two other distinctive features of Darwin's theory of sexual selection. First is that it is "coevolutionary."[26] The idea here is that the preference for a given trait and the trait itself reinforce

21. Ibid., 496.
22. Ibid., 92.
23. Ibid.
24. Ibid.
25. Ibid., 400.
26. Prum, *Evolution of Beauty,* 26.

one another and are both passed to offspring—future males will inherit the pleasing trait and future females will inherit the preference for the trait. Second is that Darwin observed that in the most highly ornamented species it was almost always the female's aesthetic preferences that drove sexual selection. "Ultimately," says Prum, "it is female sexual autonomy that is predominately responsible for the evolution of natural beauty."[27]

Darwin's choice of using language that assumed subjective states in animals was part and parcel of his larger goals in *The Descent of Man*. Although he had mostly dodged the issue of the evolution of man in *The Origin of Man*, in *The Descent of Man*, Darwin explicitly made the case that humans had descended from earlier animals. The point that humans and non-human animals differed in degree and not kind was integral to his theory. For Darwin this included subjective and cognitive traits, and by using words like "appreciate" and "taste" he intentionally implied that human experiences of beauty and pleasure could be compared to those of non-human animals.

Not surprisingly, such ideas were too much for most of Darwin's Victorian-age readers. Even among those who accepted the general idea of evolution and the process of natural selection, the idea that "brutes" could possess the cognitive ability to make aesthetic discernments was beyond the pale. Worse still was the idea that females could be the drivers of evolution through mate choices based on aesthetic preferences. Although the law of battle appealed to Victorian patriarchal traditions, Darwin's idea of aesthetic evolution for its own sake was soundly rejected.[28] Ares was okay, but Aphrodite went too far.

The law of battle idea was also readily accepted because, contrary to Darwin's own view, it was relatively easy for critics to describe it as a subset of natural selection. Weapons and protections against weapons could be explained in terms of functionality and usefulness. But Darwin's foes had a harder time with the idea of aesthetic choice because if they rejected it, then they had to find some other way to explain the extraordinary proliferation of beauty within the animal world. That task was taken up most vociferously by Alfred Russel Wallace.

---

27. Ibid., 27.
28. Ibid., 28–31.

Wallace, who is commonly credited as co-discoverer along with Darwin of evolution through natural selection, was strident in his belief of "the overwhelming importance of Natural Selection over all other agencies in the production of new species."[29] Prum suggests that perhaps Wallace was so vehement in rejecting sexual selection because it violated his religious conviction that only humans had been created by God with the necessary abilities to make aesthetic judgments.[30] For whatever reason, Wallace was absolute in his conviction that natural selection "acts perpetually and on an enormous scale," such that it would "neutralise and destroy any influence that may be exerted by female selection."[31] As for the proliferation of beauty among animals, Wallace leveled his devastating response to Darwin. The plumage and colors of animals might be beautiful to humans, said Wallace, but not to animals. Instead, Wallace declared that such traits were utilitarian and were chosen by females because they were "strictly correlated with [a male's] health, vigour, and general fitness to survive."[32]

As Prum so forcefully argues, the idea that ornaments are signals or indicators of fitness became the prevailing and orthodox view of biologists and remains so today. It is a way of ignoring Darwin's own views on sexual selection as an aesthetic activity by simply proclaiming that sexual selection is a handmaiden to natural selection. Indeed, Wallace went so far as to proclaim that by rejecting sexual selection he was "the advocate of pure Darwinism."[33] According to Prum, the "Darwin we have inherited, through the filter of Wallace's outsized influence on evolutionary biology in the twentieth century, has been laundered, retailored, and cleaned up for ideological purity."[34] The ideology to which Prum refers is "the belief that adaptation by natural selection is a uni-

29. Alfred Russel Wallace, *Darwinism: An Exposition of the Theory of Natural Selection With Some of Its Applications* (London: Macmillan, 1889), vii.
30. Prum, *Evolution of Beauty*, 32.
31. Alfred Russel Wallace, *Natural Selection and Tropical Nature: Essays on Descriptive and Theoretical Biology,* 2nd ed. (London: Macmillan, 1895), 378.
32. Ibid., 379.
33. Wallace, *Darwinism*, viii.
34. Prum, *Evolution of Beauty*, 35.

versally strong force that will *always* be predominant in the evolutionary process."[35] Thus the proponents of such an ideology claim to be more Darwinian than Darwin!

Wallace's critique, along with the general inability of biologists to seriously entertain the idea that animals had the ability for aesthetic choice, or that females could play so powerful a role in evolution, resulted in Darwin's idea of aesthetic mate choice being ignored for over a hundred years. It got a small boost in 1915 and 1930 through the work of Ronald Fisher, who provided a verbal genetic model that supported Darwin's theory of aesthetic mate choice (Fisher was a mathematician but never provided a mathematical model for his theory). Fisher asserted that although the initial preference for a trait might arise from natural selection, it was possible for the preference and associated trait to become separated from the pressures of natural selection and to begin to operate solely on an aesthetic basis. The trait would then become attractive in and of itself without need of expressing any kind of utilitarian benefit. Similarly, the preference for the trait would evolve as a preference based solely on the taste for the beautiful in the selecting mate.[36]

Fisher's knowledge of genetics gave him an advantage over Darwin. Fisher theorized that the genes associated with the preference and the appealing trait would co-evolve through genetic linkage. Moreover, when females chose a trait in a male, the females were also indirectly selecting on the preference for that particular trait because the mothers of the males likely also had a preference for that trait. This coevolving reinforcement of preference and trait Fisher called a "runaway process."[37] It was a runaway process because it would continue to evolve the trait, for example a long tail like the Argus pheasant, until the sexually selected trait became so disadvantageous that it was halted by natural selection and an equilibrium was established between the two processes.

Fisher's idea also explained the potential evolutionary benefit of aesthetic choice for the female. If a female chooses a particular attractive

35. Ibid., 34.
36. Ibid., 36.
37. Ibid., 37.

trait, her male offspring are more likely to have that trait. If we assume that other females will also prefer that trait, her sons will end up being more attractive to other females and will therefore have greater reproductive success. This results in a wider propagation of the female's genes. The benefit does not directly benefit the female in terms of her survivability or reproductive success, but rather is an indirect, genetic benefit arising from the reproductive success of her sexually attractive sons. In modern parlance this is called the "sexy son hypothesis."[38]

What is significant about Fisher's model is that even though he believed the initial preference might be tied to natural selection, the runaway process depended on the independent process of sexual selection based on aesthetic choice alone. Confirming Darwin, Fisher insisted that traits arising from this selection were "arbitrary," by which he did not mean accidental or random, but rather that they did not convey information of a utilitarian nature. They were not signals or indicators of fitness as asserted by Wallace, but rather were chosen because the female found them appealing according to her standards of beauty and for no other purpose.

Fisher's theory fell into the same void as Darwin's views on sexual selection for the next fifty years. A standard textbook first published in 1978 states that "[t]hese are exciting and challenging days for students of sexual selection. From Darwin's time until the 1960s, with the notable exception of R. A. Fisher and Julian Huxley's work in the 1930s, the subject [of sexual selection] lay dormant."[39] Prum suggests that perhaps the burgeoning women's movement led to a more receptive atmosphere for the idea of female autonomy and mate choice.[40] For whatever reason, the reemergence of sexual selection brought with it the enduring split between the aesthetic Darwinian/Fisherian approach and that of neo-Wallacean adaptationists.

On the Darwinian/Fisherian side, Prum emphasizes the work of mathematical biologists Russell Lande and Mark Kirkpatrick in the

---

38. Ibid., 39.

39. Paul H. Harvey and Jack W. Bradbury, "Sexual Selection," in J. R. Krebs and N. B. Davies, eds., *Behavioural Ecology: An Evolutionary Approach*, 3rd. ed. (Oxford: Blackwell Scientific Publications, 1991), 203.

40. Prum, *Evolution of Beauty*, 41

early 1980s who independently confirmed with mathematical models Fisher's earlier verbal theory. According to Prum, both men showed that preferences and traits can coevolve solely on the advantages provided by sexually attractive offspring ("sexy sons") and that display traits evolve through a balance between natural and sexual selection.[41]

Although Lande and Kirkpatrick were directly influenced by Darwin and Fisher, Prum argues that the "neo-Wallacean" tradition had to be "reinvented from scratch" because nobody remembered Wallace's own theory of adaptations as being signals or indicators of fitness.[42] Unlike Wallace, modern proponents of the view that all adaptations arise through natural selection did not reject sexual selection, they merely redefined it as a subset of natural selection. According to this view, sexual selection operates by selecting adaptive traits that signal or indicate benefits of two kinds. Direct benefits accrue to the female choosers themselves and serve to increase their health, survival, or fecundity. This could include choosing a mate that provides relatively large prey items to the chooser during courtship ("nuptial gifts"), that provides better protection from predators, a better territory with more food or better nesting sites, fewer or no parasites or diseases, or a better ability to provide parental care.[43]

Indirect benefits come through the "good genes" model. According to this theory, females choose mates having good genes that are then passed on to the female's offspring. "Good genes" are "good" because they increase the survivability and fecundity of the female's offspring by positively adapting them to their particular environment, for example through superior foraging skills or the ability to repel predators. This is similar to Fisher's sexy son hypothesis in that good genes indirectly benefit the female through increased propagation of the female's genes. But under the good genes model, it isn't the attractiveness of the female's offspring that matters, but that they are better at surviving and reproducing.[44] Because the good genes are different from the genes that pro-

41. Ibid.

42. Ibid., 44.

43. Lee Alan Dugatkin, *Principles of Animal Behavior,* 2nd ed. (New York: W.W. Norton, 2009), 194–96; Prum, *Evolution of Beauty,* 45.

44. But see, Hanna Kokko, "Fisherian and 'Good Genes' Benefits of Mate Choice: How (Not) to Distinguish between Them," *Ecology Letters* 4, no. 4 (July 2001):

duce the desirable trait, which is taken as only an indicator of fitness, the benefits of the good genes can be passed on to both male and female offspring.[45]

Both direct and indirect benefits result from a female choosing a mate based on a preference for an observable trait in the male that is correlated with increased survival and fecundity, either directly for the female or indirectly through her offspring. The question, then, is how does this happen? What is the process connecting the observable trait and its additional benefits?

One answer to this question came from Amotz Zahavi and his "handicap principle." Zahavi started from the view that "sexual selection is effective because it improves the ability of the selecting sex to detect quality in the selected sex. The selecting sex benefits because it can be assured of the quality of its mate, while the selected sex benefits because it can better advertise its quality and thus probably acquires more or a better mate."[46] Here Zahavi was reiterating Wallace's view that certain traits were attractive because they were indicators of good qualities. But then Zahavi added a twist—the reason an attractive trait indicates good qualities is because the trait lowers the survivability of its possessor, i.e., it is a "handicap." The very fact that an individual organism has survived with this handicap shows it is of higher quality than individuals lacking the handicap.

> It is possible to consider the handicap as a kind of test imposed on the individual. An individual with a well developed sexually selected character, is an individual which has survived a test. A female which could discriminate a male possessing a sexually selected character, from one without it, can discriminate between a male which has passed a test and one which has not been tested. The more developed the character the more severe was the test.[47]

322–26, where she argues that mating success should be included as indicators of "good genes." Under this model, Kokko says that "Fisherian only processes ... may be considered unlikely, when mating success of male offspring is included in studies of sexual selection." Ibid., 325.

45. Dugatkin, *Principles,* 196–98; Prum, *Evolution of Beauty,* 45–46.

46. Amotz Zahavi, "Mate Selection—A Selection for a Handicap," *Journal of Theoretical Biology* 53 (1975): 207.

47. Ibid.

As with Fisher's runaway process, the handicaps will continue to elaborate until an equilibrium is reached between its sexual advantage and its detrimental impact on survivability.

Direct benefits, good genes, and the handicap principle are the main explanatory models for mate choice used by modern biologists. Notably they are all variations on Wallace's basic attack on Darwin's view of aesthetic mate choice because they all assume the trait chosen by the female is indicative of fitness. None of these models accept the possibility that a trait can be chosen solely because it is aesthetically pleasing to the female.

A variation on the utilitarian understanding of mate choice is known by various names—sensory exploitation, sensory bias, or preexisting bias. Under this view, females have a preexisting preference arising through natural selection that males then exploit to their benefit of being chosen as a mate. For example, if red berries are the preferred food source for a blue-feathered species of birds, a preference for red will become, through natural selection, part of the neurobiology and psychology of the species. Should an individual male within that species happen to develop red feathers instead of blue, a female would prefer that male because of the female's neurological predisposition in favor of red.[48] Unlike the other utilitarian models that seek to explain the underlying process of mate choice, sensory bias attempts to explain the origin of male characteristics, the evolutionary history of traits and preferences, and why females have the preferences.

In a 2004 paper that remarkably parallels Prum's efforts to resuscitate Darwin's theory of aesthetic mate choice, Wolfgang Welsch describes two trends among biologists who view sexual selection as a form of natural selection. One, the minority view, is that the female's choice is in fact based on an aesthetic preference but that the underlying process is ultimately utilitarian. The second, majority view is that females are not perceiving beauty at all but only indicators of fitness. "They are direct decoders of the beautiful appearance. What to us looks like perception of beauty and an aesthetic judgement is in truth nothing but the decoding of fitness."[49]

---

48. Dugatkin, *Principles*, 205–6.
49. Wolfgang Welsch, "Animal Aesthetics," *Contemporary Aesthetics* 2, no. 2 (2004).

The extent and fervor of the rejection of even the possibility that animals are capable of aesthetic judgment is reminiscent of the rejection of animal consciousness generally. Sexual selection as broadly presented almost always leaves out Darwin's insistence on the possibility of aesthetic choice based on arbitrary traits that are pleasing in and of themselves. Indeed, not only is Darwin's view rejected, it is also at times denigrated:

> The flavor of Darwin's argument for female choice may represent one of the largest shortcomings of his treatment of sexual selection because it gave the impression that animals would need a human-like sense of aesthetics for sexual selection to operate...[I]n the midst of Darwin's tremendous insights pertaining to sexual selection, the suggestion that a sense of aesthetics is necessary for sexual selection to operate may have been his most significant shortcoming. It can be argued that it took almost 100 years for the study of sexual selection to overcome this erroneous view of mating preferences.[50]

Similarly, reviews that reject Prum's attempt to have Darwin's view of sexual selection taken seriously as a distinct process from natural selection tend to amount to little more than claims that Prum is simply wrong.[51] What is especially notable is the dismissive tone of such reviews that tends to reinforce Prum's point that sexual selection based on aesthetic choice of arbitrary traits has been largely defined out of evolutionary theory.

Prum suggests an intriguing explanation for the resistance to even considering Darwin's view that sexual selection is a separate evolution-

Available online at *https://digitalcommons.risd.edu/cgi/viewcontent.cgi?article=1026&* *context=liberalarts_contempaesthetics*

50. Adam G. Jones and Nicholas L. Ratterman, "Mate Choice and Sexual Selection: What Have We Learned Since Darwin?" *Proceedings of the National Academy of Sciences* 106, Supplement 1 (June 16, 2009): 10002. Available online at *https://doi.org/10.1073/pnas.0901129106*

51. See, e.g., Jerry Coyne, "An Evolutionary Biologist Misrepresents Sexual Selection in *The New York Times*," available online at *https://whyevolutionistrue.com/2017/05/08/an-evolutionary-biologist-misrepresents-sexual-selection/*. See also, e.g., Gerald Borgia and Gregory F. Ball's review in *Animal Behavior* 137 (2018): 187-88 (available online at *https://science.umd.edu/biology/borgialab/Animal%20behavior%20review%20of%20Beauty.pdf*); and Gail L. Patricelli, Eileen A. Hebets, and Tamra C. Mendelson's review in *Evolution*, 73, no. 1 (2019): 115–24.

ary process than natural selection. Prum points to a "belief that conceptual unification is a general scientific virtue," such that science prefers "singular theories, laws, and frameworks."[52] This effort to find a single, all-encompassing theory is derailed by Darwin's claim that sexual selection is a separate process. Prum concludes:

> Of course, many of Darwin's Victorian antagonists were recent converts from religious monotheism to materialist evolutionism. Their historic monotheism might have predisposed them to adopt a powerful new monoideism; they replaced a single omnipotent God with a single omnipotent idea—natural selection. Indeed, contemporary adaptationists should question why *they* feel it is necessary to explain all of nature with a single powerful theory or process. Is the desire for scientific unification simply the ghost of monotheism lurking within contemporary scientific explanation?[53]

With this last idea we find ourselves on unfortunately familiar ground. We saw both in our discussion of the alienation of the human from nature and in the stubborn denial of animal consciousness that it is the monotheistic cast of mind that so greatly contributes to the problem. Christian monotheism, *as a style of imagining,* continues to permeate how people, including scientists, think about the relationship between humans and the other things of nature. There is a repeated fall into fundamentalism, whether it is insisting that humans are divinely separated from nature, or that non-human animals are mindless automata, or that there can only be one process of evolution that "acts perpetually and on an enormous scale" (Wallace). The mistake is the same. Although the extraordinary diversity of form and appearance in the natural world suggests that we need approaches of like diversity that would respect this multiplicity, we remain wed to an unconscious drive to impose uniformity and singularity.

Let's remember White's point that we do not have to be Christians as a matter of personal faith, or profess personal belief in one omnipotent god, to nonetheless perpetuate the monotheistic cast of mind. As we have seen repeatedly, the ideas and theories of philosophers and scientist

---

52. Prum, *Evolution of Beauty,* 52.
53. Ibid., 52–53.

proclaiming to follow the strictest standards of rationality and objectivity can nonetheless remain caught in the singular, sweeping current of monotheism. It seems ironic that those who so strongly profess open-mindedness can at the same time be fundamentalists, but a closer look shows that it is not irony at all.

Although we usually think of fundamentalism solely within a religious context, it is important, as noted earlier, that fundamentalism is more properly thought of as a variety of *rational* experience. Creationists mount arguments that they conceive as being *rational* responses to counter the claims of evolution. Deniers of anthropogenic climate change assert counterfactual arguments of cyclical variations in weather and climate as proof of their position ("we just had the coldest April on record so there is no global warming"). And people who consider the novel coronavirus pandemic a hoax point to mortality statistics to argue, wrongly, that COVID-19 is no worse than the flu. Setting aside the absurdity of such claims, the point is that they are all presented in terms that the fundamentalist conceives as being rational. Fundamentalists do not *believe* they are correct, they *know* they are correct, and it is this obstinate certainty that is the hallmark of the fundamentalist perspective.

Fundamentalism is the expression of monotheism's single-mindedness dressed in rational garb. And so, fundamentalism begins with premises taken as fact and then relies on a familiar supporting cast of ideas such as a preference for overarching, universal explanations, the positing of either/or oppositions (good/bad, heaven/hell), intolerance of differing views (there is only "one true God"), a preference for hierarchy, and a positing of transcendence as the path to enlightenment to reach its "logical" conclusions. It is notable that "theology" belongs to monotheism, while polytheistic and animistic traditions are content with myth, poetics, and ritual. Monotheism wants to know God; polytheism and animism tell stories about the gods.

Returning to the Darwin/Wallace debate, it is telling that Darwin felt no need to declare that sexual selection was the only evolutionary process or to deny the existence of other evolutionary processes. Darwin was not a fundamentalist; Wallace was. Indeed, Darwin's flexible mind was content to admit that various evolutionary processes would often intertwine and that sometimes it "is impossible to distinguish between the effects of natural and sexual selection."[54] Nonetheless, he was firm in his conviction that the proliferation of beauty was an end unto itself. It is as if beauty exists to elaborate, proliferate, and to appear in relationship with other things. Darwin's views maintain the passion that is so obviously present whenever we speak of beauty. He refuses to reduce beauty to cold utilitarianism and instead insists on a beauty of rapidly beating hearts, rapturous dances, and excited anticipation. This is an Aphroditic view of evolution, driven by the power of female desire and pleasure, and held in the embrace of appreciation and aesthetic display.

Although sexual selection is usually driven by female choice, aesthetic appreciation is not limited to females. Consider male bowerbirds who construct and decorate elaborate bowers to entice females to mate. The males go to great efforts to create beautiful bowers and to decorate them in a manner pleasing to the females. Individual males will pick certain colors and textures to ornament their bowers and they are extremely particular in their arrangements. If researchers move a pebble or flower from where the male put it, the male will notice and replace it to its proper place. In this instance, *it is the male who is making aesthetic judgments* in selecting materials, manners of construction, and modes of decoration. The critical point, however, is that the male's selection of ornaments *is not itself sexual*—the adornment of the bower and its surroundings rely on choices that are purely aesthetic. It may be that the intent of the male is to create a bower that is pleasing to the female, but the construction of the bower and the selection and arrangement of its ornaments are being made according to the *male's* taste for the beautiful. Similarly, when a female makes an aesthetic judgment in choosing among the available bowers, the ultimate result might be copulation with the male, but the proximate act of aesthetic choice cannot properly be said to be sexual in nature. Aesthetic choice might lead to mate choice, but it cannot be reduced to mate choice.

Whether it is a male bowerbird collecting moss and trinkets to decorate his bower, or a female manakin choosing her mate because of his love antics, it comes down to preference. The male bowerbird chooses this flower and not that one and puts it here and not there because that

---

54. Darwin, *The Descent of Man*, 210.

is how he prefers it. Although a given species or a population within a species might have common standards of beauty—some species of bowerbirds, for example, seem to prefer certain colors over others—the final preference for one thing over another is always individual. The preference is directed in response to the beauty of a particular thing—this red berry—that stands out from others.

So instead of drawing a line between sexual selection and natural selection, between beauty and utility, perhaps we can look at things a bit differently. Whether an individual says "look at me, I am so beautiful," or "look at me, I am so strong," or "look at me, I have such a large territory," it all begins with "look at *me*." The things of the world are first and foremost appearances. (I am using here the sense of sight, but of course there are many other ways to perceive and be perceived.) Even in the context of mate choice, a male is asking to be seen as different, apart, unlike the other males. As such we can imagine that an individual's morphology and behavior show its uniqueness in ways that extend beyond matters of sex or fitness. It is not only what is shown but *how* it is shown that differentiates an individual's particular way of being in the world that is unlike all other ways of being. It is this immediate presence of a thing, its individualized presentation as an *image,* that impresses itself on the imagination of others, allowing others to appreciate it as it is. This image, says Hillman, is *"the complete how of a presentation."*[55]

This unique "how of a presentation" is what a mentor sees in the student who seems to stand apart from others. It is not just raw ability but a peculiar eccentricity that makes the student unlike the rest. The "how of a presentation" is what we perceive, even though we cannot identify what we perceive, when we read the emotions of a face, the cadence of a walk, the inflection of a word. Ask any parent if they still see mannerisms and traits in their grown children that were already there in the cradle. Ask any person who has loved what it was about that particular one that set them apart from all the rest. Ask yourself what we mean when we say, "it was love at first sight." Here I part company with Heraclitus who said,

---

55. James Hillman, *The Soul's Code: In Search of Character and Calling* (New York: Random House, 1996), 123.

"nature loves to hide."[56] Instead I say that nature loves to be seen in all of its incredible diversity and particularity; it is beauty that matters most, and where there is beauty there is love, and where there is love there is psyche.

The Swiss zoologist Adolf Portmann maintained that animal forms exist to be seen. Although convinced of the fact of evolution, he nonetheless cautioned that by interpreting animals only through the principles of adaptation and fitness we risk missing a fuller appreciation of them. He draws our attention to the aesthetic power and significance of the manifest living form, a power and significance that can be overlooked in pursuit of hidden meaning. He urged that the "preservation of both individual and species preserves precisely the rich existence of manifold forms, and all of them are, without exception, more than bare carriers of preservative functions."[57]

For Portmann, the morphology of an individual gave visual form to an individual's inwardness, which he called an individual's unique "self-presentation."[58] He urged us not to move too quickly beyond appearance in search of hidden causes and effects:

> We shall perceive that the appearance that meets the eye is something of significance and shall not allow it to be degraded to a mere shell which hides the essential from our glance. We would not wish to be like grubbers after treasure who have no suspicion that the really valuable things can be found anywhere but hidden away deep in dark places.[59]

According to this view, an animal's essence is right there in front of us, asking to be seen as more than a façade. The furs and plumage, the faces and carriage, are "all a coat which raises its wearer to a place apart."[60] To think, then, that beauty is only skin deeps denigrates the power of

---

56. Heraclitus, fr. 17, in Philip Wheelwright, *Heraclitus* (Princeton, N.J.: Princeton University Press, 1959), 20.

57. Adolf Portmann, *Essays in Philosophical Zoology,* translated by Richard Carter (Lewiston: The Edward Mellen Press, 1990), 154.

58. Ibid.

59. Adolf Portmann, *Animal Forms and Patterns: A Study of the Appearance of Animals,* translated by Hella Czech (London: Faber and Faber, 1948), 35.

60. Ibid., 25.

what we are actually being shown by the skin, which is a palette show-ing the fullness of a thing's being. Beauty is not shallow or passive, it is revelatory of intrinsic value.

Portmann made another contribution that directly pierces attempts to reduce beauty to mere utilitarian significance. This was his insistence that not all aspects of a living organism can be reduced to self-preser-vation or reproduction. Rather there is another dimension to the mani-fest appearance of organisms, and that is self-expression. Indeed, said Portmann:

> The more closely we look at those phenomenal aspects of life whose sole purpose it is to serve self-expression and not self-preservation, the more evident it becomes that those forms on which technical thought prefers to fasten are merely the most obvious. We begin to realize that the vast majority of living forms cannot be explained in terms of technical or preservation effects alone, but that they must be evaluated first and foremost in terms of self-expression.[61]

To drive this point home, Portmann distinguishes between "addressed" phenomena, whose significance depends upon the presence of a specta-tor to whom the presentation is addressed, and "unaddressed" phenom-ena that is "directed neither at the eye of a sexual partner nor that of an enemy, phenomena whose sole purpose is to express the phenomenal essence of an animal or plant."[62] Addressed phenomena fall easily into the tradition of indicators and signals, and so can be analyzed in terms of survival and reproduction. But unaddressed phenomena suggest the pre-sentation of patterns and forms for no other reason than for the aesthetic power of presentation. According to this remarkable view, *beauty exists without need of a beholding eye.* Portmann gives as an example for unad-dressed phenomena the thousands of different forms of leaves. They all have the same functional task, and yet the proliferation of diversity in shapes, sizes, and outlines outstrip any reduction to this utilitarian func-

61. Adolf Portmann, *New Paths in Biology*, translated by Arnold J. Pomerans (New York: Harper & Row, 1964), 99.
62. Ibid., 100

tion. Instead, much in the shape and outline of a leaf "is not adaptation to the environment but pure self-representation."[63]

For Portmann, it is quite possible that self-expression involves manifest structures and patterns whose complexity cannot be reduced to survival mechanisms. "[S]uch structures are not occasional exaggerations, but the fulfillment of an important demand of life [i.e., self-presentation]. An examination of our own existence leads to a similar conclusion: our actions often go far beyond the demands of mere survival."[64] It is important here to note exactly what Portmann means by the "self" that presents itself to us in so many different ways. It is not the secret-self of so much of modern psychology, but rather is a "living form that not only maintains its life and propagates its kind, but one that also manifests its special manner of existence."[65] Portmann's "self" is not secret, but *apparent* and exists in ways that might serve, but cannot be reduced to, survival and reproduction. By focusing solely on the functional aspects of visible form (and he also gives examples of acoustical phenomena that are both addressed and unaddressed) we risk missing the greater part of life beyond the merely functional.[66] "Whenever we forget that scientific statements have a limited scope, we necessarily reduce life to the level of our technical grasp."[67] This in turn can lead us to getting our priorities skewed:

> Metabolism may serve the survival of the individual, but however important it is, we must remember that the individual is not there for the sake of its metabolism, but rather that metabolism serves manifest individual existence. That is why the special structures, which we call this plant or that animal, are much more than organized complexes of survival mechanisms.[68]

---

63. Ibid., 101.
64. Ibid., 151.
65. Ibid.
66. Portmann gives an example of a garden warbler who repeats its "mating" call in the autumn when all sexual activity has ceased, and even when kept in complete solitude. "This song is therefore the bird's acoustical means of self-expression—no less so than the characteristic coloration of its plumage." Ibid., 152–54.
67. Ibid., 158.
68. Ibid., 152.

Portmann thus picks up the discussion on the proliferation of beauty that Darwin began and that Welsch and Prum have so well-revived in our day. But Portmann takes us beyond swords, shields, and sex to suggest that beauty exists in animal forms simply because animals are beautiful and for no other purpose. So,

> while it is true to say that all flowers serve the reproduction of their kind, this statement fails to explain why a given flower should have one form rather than another. In the current view, the structural function alone is considered, and the structural plan is ignored. However, before it can serve any function, *the plan itself must be there*...[69] (Emphasis added.)

I ask that you keep this last emphasis in mind when you read the next chapter about Hillman's idea of "mythical certitude" and the formative, epistemological, and ontological power of myth.

The idea of unaddressed phenomena is a difficult one for us precisely because "[w]e cannot speak of the world, or of awareness, of inner responses, or of phenomena, without ourselves and our own experience becoming the presupposition of any statement we make. In short, we cannot imagine phenomena apart from a seeing eye."[70] Despite our difficulty, the fact is that many unaddressed phenomena "have existed before the emergence of the first eye, and yet were examples of self-expression."[71] Here again, Portmann emphasizes the importance of self-presentation as necessary and sufficient unto itself. The manifest forms of the many things of nature exist because it is their nature to be exist, and it is through their manifest appearance that they reveal their self-expression.

> Even the "liveliest" robot has the arbitrary form that its constructor has chosen for it, and obeys [the constructor's] will...The most modest plant, however, expresses its independent being in the form of its leaf, flower, and fruit, as does the butterfly in its larva, pupa, and imago. Those marine snails which are seen by no eye except that of the occasional human explorer, express their essence in a

---

69. Ibid., 152.
70. Ibid., 154.
71. Ibid.

host of splendid forms and colors—each according to its kind. Their appearance speaks a language of which we suspect we can grasp a few words, and gives evidence of a hidden power of life, that goes far beyond the needs of mere self-preservation.[72]

The physicist Werner Heisenberg said that "what we observe is not nature in itself but nature exposed to our method of questioning."[73] So, too, we must be mindful of the manner of our observing. We must beware the conceit that to look at something with a cold eye yields some kind of objective truth when in reality the coldness is already a methodological stance of disengagement. It simply is not possible to appreciate the "complete how of a presentation" dispassionately. Rather, as Portmann puts it, "to observe means to study every detail lovingly, to dwell upon these minute structures, not to be rushing from one thing to another with a hasty glance as it catches the eye."[74] Remember that Lorenz, the "maestro of observation," too, insisted that love and respect were *methodologically* essential.

When the great cellist Jacqueline du Pré was four years old, she was listening to a BBC radio program about orchestral instruments with her parents. When she heard the cello, she told her mother, "I want make that sound."[75] It was that particular sound that awakened her genius in the old meaning of that word as a tutelary spirit. The sound of the cello educated her taste for the beautiful by giving aesthetic, worldly form to what was before only an unheard, latent potential, an invisible preference waiting to be called forth. The cello made the life she led possible, and her life and talent elaborated the aesthetic possibilities of the thing that called to her at age four.

It is the things of the world that lead our talents and capabilities outward such that they, too, become things of the world, our once unformed potentials finding expression and taking form through their encounters

---

72. Ibid., 159. For a discussion of "those marine snails," see ibid., 119–29.

73. Werner Heisenberg, *Physics & Philosophy: The Revolution in Modern Science* (New York: Harper & Row, 1962), 58.

74. Portmann, *Animal Forms,* 23.

75. Carol Easton, *Jacqueline du Pré: A Biography* (London: Hodder & Stoughton, 1989), 26.

with other worldly things. Is that not the point of education, which etymologically means "to bring or lead out?" We study the world and in so doing it reveals our preferences and inclinations, allowing us to discover what was already there waiting to meet its kindred spirits, waiting to find its mates.

Here, then, is another way of imagining sexual selection. When we find our calling or our "true love" we embrace them with passion. It is difficult to say whether we picked them, they picked us, or, as we often say when speaking of love, we found one another. An Aphroditic view of evolution sees the world as a place where selections are made through desire called forth by beauty. Sometimes selection leads to a coming together that produces offspring, be it a child, a song, or an idea. There are many ways that beauty and desire proliferate to adorn and elaborate the many things of the world. But, in the beginning, there is beauty that shows a particular "complete how of a presentation" that steps forward out of all other things, drawing our gaze and taking our breath, leaving us to whisper, "I want that one."

A final consideration. At least within the context of non-human animals Darwin posits two limitations on the taste for the beautiful. One is that any appreciation for beauty is within a given species. The other is that appreciation for beauty takes place with regard to sex and reproduction. Indeed, these two limitations are linked given that if beauty and its appreciation are limited to mate choice then it would not make sense from an evolutionary perspective for one species to have a cross-species "standard for beauty." A female Argus pheasant would therefore not find anything attractive or pleasing about a male bowerbird's bower.

On the other hand, Darwin goes to great lengths to maintain that there is a continuity between the "mental powers" of humans and non-human animals—a difference of degree, not kind, he said. He readily attributes pleasure, happiness, wonder, curiosity, attention, and imagination to non-human animals.[76] In the previous chapter we saw how egregiously wrong humans have been about the capabilities of non-human animals.

---

76. Darwin, *The Descent of Man,* 69ff.

Indeed, it seems that every attempt to draw a stark line between "us" and "them" eventually falls under the weight of additional observation honestly and lovingly given. We would do well, then, not to rule out the possibility that non-human animals are capable of appreciating beauty beyond the bounds of sex, reproduction, or conspecifics.

A true story:

> Seeking a brief respite from months of continuous chimpanzee following, I took a rare day off to climb one of the steep ridges leading upward to the high rift escarpments that demarcated the eastern boundary of the park. As I sat alone at the crest of a grassy ridge watching a spectacular yet common sunset over the silvery waters of Lake Tanganyika in wonderful solitude and silence, I suddenly noticed two adult male chimpanzees climbing toward me on opposite slopes. They saw one another only as they topped the crest, just yards from my seat beneath a tree, whereupon both suddenly stood upright and swiftly advanced as bipeds through waist-high grass to stand close together, face to face, each extending his right hand to clasp and vigorously shake the other's while softly panting, heads bobbing. Moments later they sat down nearby and we three watched the sunset enfold the park. When dusk fell my two companions went off to build platform nests high in the trees of the valley. Nevermore, I realised as I hastened homeward to my own bed (a lower platform) at the field station before darkness fell, would I regard chimpanzees as "mere animals." On that singular eve, which also marked the twilight of my youth, I had seen my species inside the skin of another.[77]

Another researcher tells the story of Zuma, a female orangutan, who would gather salad and cabbage leaves, place them on her head, and then go to a mirror to look at her head covering, straightening and squashing it a bit while she looked at her reflection.[78] Still another tells of an orangutan

---

77. Geza Teleki, "They Are Us," in Paola Cavalieri and Peter Singer, eds., *The Great Ape Project: Equality Beyond Humanity* (New York: St. Martin's Griffin, 1994), 297–302. Another researcher tells a similar story of a chimpanzee watching a particularly beautiful sunset for a full fifteen minutes, retiring to the forest only after it got so dark that he didn't get a chance to pick a pawpaw for his evening meal. Adriaan Kortland, "Chimpanzees in the Wild," *Scientific American* 206, no. 5 (May 1962):128–140.

78. De Waal, *Are We Smart Enough,* 245.

stringing and wearing a bead necklace that no one had taught her how to make.[79] Such stories are of course open to charges of anthropomorphism— that we are assuming aesthetic appreciation because we see in non-human animals behaviors similar to our own. We have already shown the weakness of such objections. Better to give our fellow animals the benefit of the doubt and to recognize behaviors that suggest at least the possibility of aesthetic appreciation unbounded by sex or reproduction.

We must also keep in mind the limitations of our methods of observation and experimentation. We do not know how other species might exhibit aesthetic appreciation or even if there would be any associated observable behavior at all. When I appreciate a beautiful sky while on a walk it is often taken in stride—I do not always stop and gaze nor do I always make mention of it. Not all aesthetic pleasures lead to observable behavior. There simply is no reason to deny non-human animals the capacity for aesthetic appreciation outside of sex and reproduction. If humans possess the obvious ability to appreciate beauty outside of our species, in ways unconnected to sex or reproduction, and in non-organic created works, there is little reason to doubt that at least some other animals have this capacity. To say otherwise is yet another repression of beauty.

We know that birds sing to attract mates, to establish territories, and to warn off competitors. But are we really willing to stop there? Do we really want to close the door on the possibility that they also sing just to sing? We might hear their songs in a way far different than how they hear them, but the joy and beauty of their songs make it difficult not to imagine that they, too, delight in a pure note, a clever arrangement, and a lilting refrain.

79. Carl Safina, *Beyond Words: What Animals Think and Feel* (New York: Henry Holt and Company, 2015), 56.

FIVE

An Ecology of Imagination

A seven-month old baby crawls across the floor. A foal, an hour into its new life, wobbles up on spindly legs. A fledgling, two-weeks old, takes flight. In each case, the animal relies with certainty on the mediums of its environment, the baby secure on the floor, the foal on firm ground despite shaky legs, the fledgling held aloft by invisible air. How is it that animals move so surely through their (our) world without forethought nor impeded by doubt?

There is something remarkable in the most mundane of animal actions because they are not based on reflection or suppositions about how things are. Animal actions instead proceed as embodied movements engaged with a world that is directly perceived as available to and supportive of those actions. The animal moves with certainty because its movement takes place outside of demands of truth or veracity. Hillman calls this "mythical certitude" and locates it within myth:

> We may not *know* things, the truth of them or of ourselves, but we are nonetheless certain while perceiving and behaving that we are and they are. The actions of our immediate life express this certitude because these actions are embedded in myth. If myths are founding our perceiving, dealing and believing, then only in action with the world do we recover myth and become certain.[1]

Here Hillman is using "myth" in a manner that is unfamiliar to most of us. He is not talking about the stories of mythology, the *logos* of *mythos,* but rather of myth as the imaginal foundation that is given with and makes possible all perception or action of any kind. "The very certainty ... of any stance," says Hillman, "is mythically founded, and ... the

---

1. James Hillman, "On Mythical Certitude," *Sphinx: A Journal for Archetypal Psychology and the Arts* 3 (1990): 230.

myth in any action, is precisely what gives action its certitude."[2] This harkens back to my earlier comment that all animals enter a world already underway. *"The plot of things, the way in which the world appears and we are in its images, is myth."*[3] In other words, the experience of life proceeds in and through images and the imagination in a manner that is not dependent upon reflection or analysis. We can rely on the many things of world because they *are* reliable, and we grasp this reliability without need of intellectual validation—*mythos* precedes and makes possible *logos.*

But Hillman's goes farther to insist that *mythos* does not require *logos,* that is, myth cannot be reduced to or equated with the stories and accounts of mythology. Instead, he points to other etymological connotations of myth as "mute, mum, mumble, mutter, cognate with *myein,* closed as mystery, as the eyelid closes."[4] This has implications for our interest in the certainty of animal actions because it takes myth out of the world of language. The examples I gave of baby, foal, and fledgling do not belong to the world of language or even, indeed, to the world of thought. They result directly from the animal's quiet, inalienable faith in the world.

To understand Hillman's point, it helps to follow a distinction that he makes between *verum* and *certum.* For our purposes, we can talk about this distinction as that between *veracity* and *certainty.*

Veracity has to do with truth (verity) as logically conceived and postulated. Veracity belongs to the realm of philosophy, law, science, and rationality. Veracity is determined—verified—by evidence and proofs that are acceptable to standards established by the rational mind. This circularity is one of rationality's defining characteristics; it plays only by its rules and excludes other perspectives as incapable of providing truth or certainty. From the perspective of *verum,* then, "mythical certitude" is an oxymoron. *Verum* refuses to separate *mythos* from *logos,* demanding instead that myth remain bound to language, and, if so, then myth must be making claims that are subject to being verified by standards accept-

---

2. Ibid., 226.
3. Ibid., 230.
4. Ibid., 224.

able to *verum.* And, of course, this myth cannot do, and so it is declared false (*verum*'s only alternative to truth) and ends up on the same heap as all other things that cannot meet *verum*'s standards. For *verum*, myth is merely an attempt by unsophisticated people to explain things clearly beyond them, couched in terms of whimsy, fable, and fantasy. "The philosopher's business is to dispel the veil of myth and penetrate to the 'nature of things,' a reality satisfying the requirements of abstract thought."[5] The irony is that although myth includes the rational mind as a legitimate mode of mythical thinking, rationality excludes myth as a legitimate mode of thinking. Rationality is blind to its own mythical stance, which makes it vulnerable to fundamentalism as we noted in the prior chapter.

Certum, on the other hand, "precedes *verum* as the [6]concrete engagement with the world precedes what we make of this engagement." Mythical certainty coexists with perceiving and acting, a kind of certainty that takes place outside the realm of *verum.* Animals, including humans, perceive and act without need of knowledge or truth, or, better said, knowledge and truth exist within and are expressed by the animal's perceptions and actions. Mythical certainty is embodied and direct, unlike abstract thought that pretends to exist apart from the body. As the anthropologist Tim Ingold puts it,

> Western thought...whose penchant for constructing dichotomies is one of its main defining characteristics, has given us a distinction between intellect (as a property of mind) and behaviour (as bodily execution)...We may of course describe as "intelligent" an animal whose actions manifest certain sensitivity and responsiveness to the nuances of its relationships with the components of its environment. But it is quite another thing to attribute that quality to the operation of a cognitive device, an "intelligence," which is somehow *inside* the animal and which, from this privileged site, processes the data of perception and pulls the strings of action...[C]ognition is an accomplishment of the *whole animal,* it is not accomplished by a mechanism interior to the animal and for which it serves as a vehicle. There is

---

5. Francis M. Cornford, *Principium Sapientiae: The Origins of Greek Philosophical Thought* (Cambridge: Cambridge University Press, 1952), 145.
6. Hillman, "Mythical Certitude," 229.

therefore no such thing as an "intelligence" apart from the animal itself, and no evolution of intelligence other than the evolution of animals with their own particular powers of perception and action.[7]

Moreover, mythical certainty is specific and particular, just as all images are particular and precisely given. *Certum* situates the animal in a specific context in which the animal's perceptions and actions are realized in a manner that could not be otherwise. The certainty of animal perceptions and actions cannot be separated from the perceptions and actions themselves, just as an animal's perceptions and actions cannot themselves be separated or attenuated over space or time as if one precedes or causes the other. An animal perceives the world as it moves within the world, and it moves through the world in step with its perceptions. "If myths return us to the styles of our actions," says Hillman, "these actions themselves stamp facts with certitude. So certitude results from myth, is dependent on it."[8]

Myth, then, does not belong to the abstracting mind but rather appears within the direct, inherent intelligibility of the world as sensate, sensual, and sensible. The physicality of the world, its immediate facticity and intelligibility, and the participatory, embodied action of animals go together because they appear as images within the context of imagination guided by myth. The world appears animated because it *is* animated, alive with images presented by beauty and contextualized by myth. And so just as the black snake slithers surely through the dream, so, too, the baby crawls upon the floor graced by mythical certitude. It doesn't matter whether we ever read the stories of mythology or recognize the presence of the gods in what we do. The power of myth lies in part of its invisibility and how it sustains and supports animal action. The baby does not think about the floor, the foal stands without contemplation, and the fledgling does not need to see the air. Myth does not need our belief because it precedes our mentation; the sense that we make out of things is possible because things *are* sensible, and that sensibility is given by myth.

---

7. Tim Ingold, "Tool-Use, Sociality and Intelligence," in Kathleen Gibson and Tim Ingold, eds., *Tools, Language and Cognition in Human Evolution* (Cambridge: Cambridge University Press, 1993), 430–31.

8. Hillman, "Mythical Certitude," 231.

This direct engagement of animals with the world through imagination and myth I consider to be essentially aesthetic. The many things of the world appear as they are, how they are, through the powers of beauty, that "seizing upon the senses and imagination, captivate the soul, before the understanding is ready either to join with them, or to oppose them."[9] Here, too, just as with imagination, I refuse to attribute or confine aesthetic appreciation first to an isolated mind, but rather claim that aesthetics is embodied, given with the animal as animal, inherent in its perceptions and actions, present in its form and the very muscularity of its behavior. If beauty is that which makes the many things of the world apparent and available to one another then it is also beauty that grants the foal its unmediated, direct faith to stand up and the fledgling to take wing.

Although these ideas are difficult to articulate, the realities they address are present with every life experience. The eyes open after sleep to see the world is still there. We step back from the curb as a bus approaches a bit too close for comfort. A fish leaps into the air and is not surprised to fall back into the sea. Like Zeno's paradox that would make the arrow's flight impossible, the notion that thought must proceed action would leave animals frozen in place, unable to move until the next doubt is dispelled. Instead, action is given with life and may even be synonymous with life, for all living things move in their own manner.

I have taught hundreds of people how to sail and there is something unusual that happens with almost every single student. The boats that I teach on are mid-sized cruising sailboats with steering wheels instead of tillers and when a student is driving the boat in the harbor for the first time and they need to turn the boat into a channel or slip they almost always ask me "When do I start turning?" It sounds like a perfectly reasonable question, but the problem is that with sailboats there is no hard and fast answer as to when to start turning. A sailboat is on a moving medium—water—and is affected by natural forces like currents and wind. Also, sailboats don't make sharp-angled turns like a car but continue to move forward as they turn. The speed of the boat also affects when and how turns are made. All of these factors have to be taken into

---

9. Edmund Burke, *Philosophical Enquiry into the Origin of our Ideas of the Sublime and Beautiful* (London: A. Robertson & Co., 1824), 185.

consideration when turning a sailboat; there is no abstract answer as to when to start turning or how to turn. My answer to my students, then, is: "Let your hands do it. Make the turn when your hands want to make the turn." At first, of course, this is not a satisfactory answer, but over time they come to see that it is the only answer.

An extension of this comes as students start to learn to sail. I have seen countless times that a student's hands will start to do the correct thing – reach for a line to trim a sail, tie a knot, or turn the boat into the wind in a gust – only to stop mid-action because their mind interferes with their hands. Over and over, I tell students to "trust your hands," "follow your hands," "let your body do it," "don't think about it too much." It is as if the skills they need are already there and I just have to find a way to get their mind out of the way so their body and hands can take over. Their bodies know; their minds doubt.

There is nothing mystical about this. Well, maybe a little mystical. But what I think is going on is that the students' bodies are trying to realize an existing, intimate connection with the sailboat and the act of sailing that is being thwarted by an interfering mind. Their hands and bodies want to be educated by the boat, but they are frustrated by habits of the mind that insist they must know before they act. Sailing, I tell them, is an aesthetic act that depends more on sensual appreciation and appropriate response than analytic understanding.

If someone hands us a tool that is unknown to us, we can ask what it is and learn its name. We can ask what it does and what it is for and be given descriptions and explanations. But only when we begin to use the tool does its design and shape begin to take full form. The tool helps the hand to imagine things more fully, feeling how the tool works, how it turns a screw or tightens a bolt. Tools also teach us their limitations; it is unfair to criticize a pair of pliers for not floating or a wrench for being inept at driving a nail. Each tool has its place and its purpose and through them they teach us about the necessity of relationships and context.

To teach us about themselves tools must also teach us about the things they are designed to address. Nothing exists in isolation, and so tools teach us about how various things respond to one another's presence. A knife teaches about cutting and slicing and the possibilities of sharpness. A piece of leather responds to a knife in one way while paper responds in quite another. Through these various interactions we learn about the qualities of the materials involved. We might even imagine that tools delight in their interactions with the things they serve, a screwdriver snugging a screw into place, a socket matched appropriately to the head of a bolt. A needle must learn how to adapt to soft cloth or tough canvas, and the fingers that use that needle must likewise learn how to handle the needle when addressing different materials.

A wrench will teach an observant user how to use a wrench. Its shape and design will suggest its purpose and through practice the hand will learn how to hold and maneuver the wrench to best advantage in different applications. But the wrench also teaches about the nature of nuts and bolts, the suitability of joining certain things together in certain ways, the advantages and mathematics of leverage, the limitations of space, and the importance of proper dimensions that suit hand and job. Stripped threads teach us about the nature of tolerance and the relative hardness of different metals. A sheared bolt teaches about torque, stress, and the weak points in things otherwise strong. Skinned knuckles teach about what happens when you move too fast in the wrench's world, or over-reach, or start too soon, or press too hard. Much finesse is required in tightening and loosening. The wrench lives in a hard world and can teach hard lessons but it also teaches that there are all kinds of hardness, that hardness is full of grades and combinations, and that things can be hard in some ways and not in others, each hardness having its own peculiar strengths and weaknesses.

When we pick up a tool it becomes an extension of our hands, offering new and better ways to connect us with the things that we are working on. Tools make such good teachers because they show us how to appreciate each thing in its own context. We learn about tools from using tools, each tool teaching us about its particular use and about the nature of usefulness in general. But to learn from tools we have to pay attention as we use them, trusting our hands to feel through the wrench when the bolt is tight enough. Tools teach the hands and hands teach the mind. As the neurologist Frank Wilson writes in *The Hand,* "the hand speaks to the brain as surely as the brain speaks to the hand."[10]

What is true of tools is true of the many things of the world in general. James J. Gibson came up with an especially nice way of talking about how animals interact with their environment, including other animals and among themselves, through his idea of *affordances*:

> The *affordances* of the environment are what it *offers* the animal, what it *provides* or *furnishes,* either for good or ill. The verb *to afford* is found in the dictionary, but the noun *affordance* is not. I have made it up. I mean by it something that refers to both the environment and the animal in a way that no existing term does. It implies the complementarity of the animal and the environment.[11]

For example, Gibson describes a horizontal, flat, extended surface of sufficient size and rigidity, both relative to the size and weight of a given animal, as affording support to the animal. Such a surface might be a ground or a floor, in which case Gibson says it is "stand-on-able" or "walk-on-able," or like a ledge or chair, in which case it is "sit-on-able." Other terrestrial surfaces can be "climb-on-able," "fall-off-able," "get underneath-able," etc.[12] A tree branch of appropriate size, then, can afford a squirrel a place to jump from or to, while a branch that is too small or weak for a squirrel could nonetheless afford a bird a place to land.

For Gibson, the "composition and layout of surfaces *constitute* what they afford."[13] This is a critical component of Gibson's idea. Affordances are given with the substance and form of the thing itself and *are not dependent on the animals who take advantage of what the thing affords.* (Note here the similarity between Gibson's idea of the independence of affor-

---

10. Frank R. Wilson, *The Hand: How Its Use Shapes the Brain, Language, and Human Culture* (New York: Vintage Books, 1911), 291. Wilson goes on to write: "Self-generated movement is the foundation of thought and willed action, the underlying mechanism by which the physical and psychological coordinates of the self come into being. For humans, the hand has a special role and status in the organization of movement and in the evolution of human cognition."

11. James J. Gibson, *The Ecological Approach to Visual Perception* (Hillsdale, N.J.: Lawrence Erlbaum Associates, 1986), 127.

12. Ibid. 127–28.

13. Ibid., 127.

dances from needing animals to make use of them with Portmann's idea of unaddressed phenomena that exist without need of a receiving eye.) There was ground before there were feet to walk upon the ground, ledges before there were things to sit on them. On the other hand, with the appearance of animals the affordances of things become realizable. This is what Gibson means by the "complementarity" of the animal and the environment.

> [A]ffordances...are in a sense objective, real, and physical, unlike values and meanings, which are often supposed to be subjective, phenomenal, and mental. But, actually, an affordance is neither an objective property nor a subjective property; or it is both if you like. An affordance cuts across the dichotomy of subjective-objective and helps us to understand its inadequacy. It is equally a fact of the environment and a fact of behavior. It is both physical and psychical, yet neither. An affordance points both ways, to the environment and to the observer.[14]

Because the composition and surface of a thing constitutes what they afford, Gibson asserts that "to perceive them is to perceive what they afford," and that an affordance's "values" and "meanings" are directly perceived, and are "external to the perceiver."[15] Gibson saw affordances as a way out of the Cartesian dualism of object and subject because affordances cannot be understood without the complementarity of the thing's affordance and the animal's perception and reliance on what is afforded. "When we consider the affordances of things," says Gibson, "we escape [Descartes's] philosophical dichotomy."[16]

Another important aspect of Gibson's theory of affordances is that things provide affordances in accord with the scale and abilities of the animal. Stairs afford nothing to a crawling infant but afford an adult a way to climb. Animals themselves are affordances and offer different possibilities for different animals, for example a given animal can be both prey and predator depending upon the circumstances. So, too, affordances offer different possibilities according to the perceptual capa-

---

14. Ibid., 129.
15. Ibid., 127.
16. Ibid., 41.

bilities of animals—a human and dog going on a walk are afforded very different experiences along the way.

Gibson differentiates between "environment," "habitat," and an "ecological niche." Environment is the broadest of terms and means the surroundings of any animal, including other animals, plants, and non-living objects such as rocks or buildings. Gibson's somewhat idiosyncratic meaning of "environment" requires the presence of an animal to be surrounded. For him, a world imagined without animals is not an environment but simply a physical reality. In a sense, then, all animals share a common environment, but at some point "environment" becomes so abstracted that it loses specificity and context in relation to particular animals in particular places.

"Habitat" refers to where particular animals live and is therefore more limited than "environment." Different animals prefer and are adapted to different habitats, and these habitats provide animals the resources they need for survival, e.g., food and shelter. Habitats also provide threats to survival, e.g., predators, diseases, competitors for resources.

If habitat refers to *where* animals live, an ecological niche refers more to *how* an animal lives. An animal's ecological niche includes its behavior in relationship to its specific localized habitat and also how the presence of the animal in turn affects its ecological niche. For Gibson, an ecological niche is a set of affordances. "The niche implies a kind of animal, and the animal implies a kind of niche."[17] Thus, an animal's ecological niche includes all of its interactions of whatever kind with its biotic and abiotic community. Here, again, Gibson emphasizes the complementarity of an animal and its ecological niche just as with an animal and an affordance. In both cases it is impossible to conceive of the animal as separate from its relationships to the various affordances provided within its ecological niche and to the affordances the animal offers others within its ecological niche. Every animal begins its life already placed within a specific ecological niche. Although its perception and behavior might change over time, it nonetheless perceives and behaves in accordance with what its ecological niche affords. "The awareness of the world," says Gibson, "and of one's complementary relations to the world are not separable."[18]

---

17. Ibid., 128.
18. Ibid., 141.

Here we return to the beginning of this chapter. The floor affords the baby crawling, ground affords the foal standing, and air affords the fledgling flight. Per Gibson, floor, ground, and air pre-exist baby, foal, and fledgling, and the composition and form of floor, ground, and air constitute what they afford. With the appearance of the animals, these affordances become realizable. The mysterious part has to do with how the animals recognize and respond to the affordances. This is where Hillman's idea of mythical certitude comes in. I maintain that the floor, ground, and air offer *aesthetic affordances* that provide appropriate animals the opportunity for an imaginative, embodied awareness that imbues perception and supports behavior. Affordances are *mythically constituted* and contain within themselves a latent intelligibility that is realized in the complementarity between them and the animals that recognize and respond to them. The affordance of a branch to a squirrel is perceived by the squirrel as coincident with the branch itself. This intelligibility of the branch to the squirrel is not the result of thought or reflection but appears in the squirrel's jump, or, put another way, the jump *is* the meaning of the branch to the squirrel.

An ecological niche, then, can be imagined as a set of complementary images in which animals perceive and relate to the niche, including one another, through imagination. Taken as an image, each animal is a "complete how of a presentation" that includes all of its interactions of whatever kind with the other images within its niche. From this perspective, the many things of the world exist as an aesthetic array where each individual presents itself as itself through its unique presentation, its unique way of being in the world, within the context of myth and imagination.

I am suggesting here an *ecology of imagination* in which the many things of the world appear as images in relationship to other images. Hillman wrote that an image implicates "a precise context, mood and scene."[19] Not only are the many things of the world given as precisely qualified images in themselves, they also are always present in a broader, complex milieu of other images. It is this network of interrelated images that I

---

19. James Hillman, "An Inquiry into Image," *Spring: An Annual of Archetypal Psychology and Jungian Thought* (1977): 62.

am referring to as an ecology of imagination that is both inhabited by and constituted by its resident images. This further implies that images recognize and relate to one another through aesthetic appreciation; the "use" of an affordance is inseparably bound with an embrace of the affordance that recognizes and relies on its inherent sensibility through mythic certainty.

"Oecologie" was introduced by the German zoologist Ernst Haeckel in 1866, and he specifically intended the meaning of the Greek *oikos,* our "eco," as "household," suggesting that "ecology" refers to a household of organisms, including their relations to one another and their abiotic surroundings.[20] This meaning is significant because for the ancient Greeks a "household" included the resident invisibles that came with and were part of the household. All things were full of gods, and it was this invisible presence that provided the very possibility of a household because there was no being without the gods. If an ecological niche is taken as a household of images, then it is myth and imagination that support and make possible the niche in all of its aspects. The appearance of the biotic and abiotic members of the household, their perceptual realities and capabilities, the certainty of their behaviors, the varied and particularized natures of their reliances and relationships, all comprise the complete how of the household's presentation and are all made present and available through the revelatory power of beauty and the inherent intelligibility given by myth.

If we go back to Hillman and the black snake in a dream, we can now see it as part of an ecology of imagination and as inhabiting a household of images. The black snake cannot be separated from the totality of its relationships within the dream. Our observation of the snake includes its interactions with the other images within the dream and it cannot be abstracted or interpreted into a symbol or meaning without us losing the snake. The snake in the dream is active and animated, and it is doing something very particular in relationship to the other inhabitants of the dream.

---

20. Astrid Schwarz and Kurt Jax, "Etymology and Original Sources of the Term 'Ecology,'" in Astrid Schwarz and Kurt Jax, eds., *Ecology Revisited: Reflecting on Concepts, Advancing Science* (Dordrecht: Springer, 2011), 145.

It slithers through the dreamscape with mythical certitude, secure in the relative confines of its ecology of imagination, its imaginal niche.

This is an imagistic naturalism, an aesthetic ethology based on observation taking place in the wilds of imagination, seeking not to interpret, analyze, or explain but rather to attend and appreciate. Hillman suggested a *"poetic basis of mind,"* to which I add an aesthetic basis of nature, where "nature" is not an overarching concept but rather refers to an ecology of imagination presented by the many things of the world as animate displays, each complete with aesthetic affordances, and each perceiving and acting within their own imaginal niche.[21]

Jung said that "psyche [soul] *is* image. Another way of saying this is that *"anima* is image." Can we take the next step and say that *"animal* is image"? Here the animal, and we will have more to say about non-animal things later, is taken as an imaginal presence. Following Portmann and Gibson, we refuse to fall into the trap of asking what the animal *really* is, in terms that would appease materialistic and positivistic habits of mind, but rather are content with how it appears and acts, and how it is experienced directly by and among the other things of the world through its form and behavior and style. An aesthetic ethology, then, depends on appreciating animals as images, where animals are perceived and imagined at the same time because there is no perceiving without imagining. From this perspective, all experience begins with an appreciation of the aesthetic affordances of the many things of the world that appear to us because beauty shows them to us. Aphrodite is always present to make things sensately and sensually available, perceptible, drawing us out into the world by showing us what is possible, educating our preferences and inclinations, revealing our individuality through the things that call to us, like little Jacqueline wanting the thing that made that noise.

An ecology of imagination thus avoids the reductivism of Cartesian subjectivity by maintaining that there is no experience of existence other than that which is given by and through the complementarity of

---

21. James Hillman, *Re-Visioning Psychology* (New York: Harper and Row, 1975), xi: "Here I am suggesting both a *poetic basis of mind* and a psychology that starts neither in the physiology of the brain, the structure of language, the organization of society, nor the analysis of behavior, but in the processes of imagination."

things taken as images. So, for example, a person's individuality is realized through his or her form, behavior, and relationships and cannot be reduced to a secret self that is available only through introspection. The other things of the world perceive what we afford, and it is through our relationships with them that we come to learn about the possibilities of our own individuality. Our fellow inhabitants know at least as much, if not more, about us than we do about ourselves because only they can observe us as a unique image within our imaginal niche. We cannot imagine or perceive ourselves as fully realized just as a mirror's reflection cannot present us as embodied and substantial. We cannot witness our own lives, which is why it is important to take seriously how others see us instead of trusting only the voices that seem to abide privately in our minds. Hillman said that "only in action with the world do we recover myth and become certain." We can now extend this to say that only in action with the world do we recover myth and become who, what, and how we are. We greet one another by asking "how are you" but the truth is that we are the least likely to know how we are. When we are asked that question, we retreat to our subjectivity—"I'm fine." But when we turn our attention to asking how a tiger is, we answer in terms of its form and behavior—it is prowling, hunting, resting. An ecology of imagination response to "how are you," might be: "I'm heading to the grocery store, and before I left the house Jill told me about a new bird she saw this morning, and she was wearing a forest-green shirt that really set off her dark hair and brown eyes, and these new shoes I'm wearing have very soft soles but are rubbing the back of my heel a bit, and the air feels heavy and smells like rain."

An ecology of imagination suggests that each of us plays a complementary role in the individuality and uniqueness of others. The aesthetic affordances that constitute them and are given with their uniqueness are not dependent upon us for their presence, but those affordances are realized by, through, and with us. And because we, too, are unique, and because we, too, afford other people possibilities that are not otherwise available to them, we co-constitute one another's individuality. This interdependence is perhaps what makes both individuals and society possible and gives rise to an ethical claim based on the reciprocity of aesthetic appreciation. We are responsible for others because we aid in their begetting. This is what I think Rilke meant by the duty to "stand guard over the solitude of the other."

The depth and range of affordances that we receive, and offer, to other animals, including other people, is almost endless. The immediate recognition of the forms that are presented to us come complete with their significance (Gibson's "values" and "meanings")—a cat's purr, a flirtatious wink, a casual touch that lingers just a little too long—such things are perceived and understood directly and simultaneously because their form and their meaning are inseparable. An image cannot be broken into pieces but must inhere to itself, each aspect of the image being appreciated in terms of its imaginal niche, its particular style of being (its "how"), and the relationships it occasions with its fellow inhabiting images. "Behavior affords behavior," says Gibson.[22]

For Gibson, affordances offer things that are either useful or harmful to an organism, utilitarian or deleterious. Nonetheless, affordances are first perceived and appreciated (at the same time) aesthetically. As we saw in the last chapter, beauty does not require any purpose beyond itself and cannot be reduced to the eye of a beholder. We can be stopped in our tracks by a sunset or the scent of our lover's hair and there is nothing useful being offered beyond the experience itself. But beauty also shows the hand how to use a wrench and the squirrel how to jump. We must avoid equating beauty with prettiness. So, too, we must avoid the temptation to follow Santayana in limiting beauty to "pleasure objectified."[23] Yes, beauty has the power to elicit pleasure and ignite desire, but its primary power is revealing the immediate psychic facticity of the many things of the world in all of their particularity and diversity.

The foundational importance of beauty has been misplaced, indeed repressed, by philosophy's persistent and tired dichotomy of subject/object. The subjectivists insist that beauty is in the mind and eye of the beholder, that it is humans that create beauty by declaring things to be beautiful. They support this view by arguing that if two people disagree over what is beautiful then the determination of beauty must therefore

---

22. Gibson, *The Ecological Approach*, 135.

23. George Santayana, *The Sense of Beauty: Being the Outline of Aesthetic Theory* (New York: Charles Scribner's Sons, 1896), 52.

belong to a purported inner subjectivity. But disagreements over what is beautiful are to be expected because even within a given species, individuals will perceive aesthetic affordances differently. The complementarity between an individual and an affordance is itself unique, given with the uniqueness of the pairing. Appreciation of an aesthetic affordance will vary precisely because appreciation is not a function of subjectivity, not perceived by the mind but rather encountered in embodied action. The poet Adrienne Rich captures this idea when she writes that a poem is "not a philosophical or psychological blueprint; it's an instrument of embodied experience."[24]

On the other hand, objectivists insist that beauty belongs to an object or thing itself and is not determined by subjective evaluation. Classically this view divides along two lines. For Plato, beauty belonged to the ideal world of Forms, and so particular things could be said to be beautiful only to the extent they conformed with this ideal. For Aristotle, beauty is defined by characteristics of an object, such as symmetry, order, balance, and proportion. According to such objectivist views, beauty exists apart from subjective judgment and belongs instead to conceptual formalisms.

Beauty in my meaning exists outside of such theoretical conundrums. "Suppose we were to imagine," writes Hillman, "that beauty is permanently displayed, inherent to the world in its data, there on display always."[25] Beauty is not a formal property of an object because without beauty there would be no object; beauty is found in the world because beauty is foundational of the world, it is the aesthetic power inherent in images. Note the word "data" in Hillman's statement. By "data" he means the "given world." and this world does "not just appear as simple inert facticity, but as images of intelligibility."[26] Moreover, the intelligibility of images is not subjective, "it occurs with the world itself as the mode by which the given world (data) is intelligible, how it presents itself as immediately credible."[27] This is what I am calling the immediate psychic facticity of the many things of the world as given by beauty, a

---

24. Adrienne Rich, *What is Found There: Notebooks on Poetry and Politics* (New York: W.W. Norton, 1993), 13.
25. Hillman, "Mythical Certitude," 230.
26. Ibid.
27. Ibid.

facticity that is not inert but *animated*. Instead of speaking only about living organisms as being animate, we now can see that the many things of the world are all animate because they are presented by beauty as images that are "immediately credible."

By grounding experience in beauty, we release beauty from the enclosures of the art gallery and the extravagances of the sublime. Aphrodite "was more than an aesthetic joy, she was an epistemological necessity."[28] Without her the many things of the world, including the gods, remain hidden, and through her the world is made manifest in its particularity and diversity. We come to know the world through beauty, through how it looks, smells, sounds, tastes, and feels. Other animals have other ways of sensing the world, but for all of us the many things of the world educate our senses, drawing us into relationships, teaching us how to distinguish among things. The landscape architect James Corner describes how the many things of the world impress themselves upon us:

> Materials in the landscape radiate a host of sensory stimuli that are deeply registered by the sentient body: the aroma of material; the feeling of humidity or dampness; the intensity of light, dark, heat and cold. Different woods burn in different ways. They give off varying flame patterns—some crackle, some hiss, their embers may glow, sparkle, or smoke. As living trees, the same woods are known to us in significantly different ways. In the pine stand the wind whispers and whistles; in the snarled oak forest it broods and wallows; in the aspen grove it rustles. Things and places become known to us because of what they impart to our senses through the very organization of their sensible aspects. The significance of anything encircles and permeates tangible matter.[29]

Animals move through the world with certainty because beauty and myth give them a world that is sensate, sensual, and sensible. The many things of the world are intelligible in the first instance not to the mind but rather are discovered through the certainty of embodied actions—

---

28. Hillman, "The Practice of Beauty," 20.
29. James Corner, "Representation and Landscape: Drawing and Making in the Landscape Medium," *Word & Image: A Journal of Verbal/Visual Enquiry* 8, no. 3 (1992): 250.

the tiny fledgling taking that first wing into air. They "become known to us because of what they impart to our senses through the very organization of their sensible aspects." This inherent intelligibility given with the many things of the world as images is, I think, what Hillman calls myth, and what Portmann had in mind when he said that before a manifest form can serve any function, *the plan itself must be there.*[30] The "plan" is not teleological but mythical.

Although minds befuddled by purported subjectivity might say otherwise, the fact is that we do know our place in the world and this knowledge is displayed in our unmediated actions among the many things of the world. We are always placed, present, and accounted for despite what our doubting minds might say. Descartes became so lost in thought that he forgot that he was already there before the thinking began, that he appeared to the other things of the world and they to him before he ever had a chance to conjure a meditation, and that, despite his rigorous doubting, when he took a walk at day's end, he did so with a certainty that required no thought to be.

---

30. Portmann, *New Paths in Biology*, 152.

SIX

Animal Mundi

In the previous chapters we have seen how we have repressed beauty through a monotheistic cast of mind that spawns false dichotomies such as human/nature, mind/body, and subject/object. We have repressed beauty with slanders and sleights against our fellow worldly inhabitants, especially the animals, erecting ourselves as both the judge of their abilities and as the measure by which their abilities are to be judged. We have repressed beauty by decreeing, in the name of a single god, be it religious or economic, that the many things of the world are there for us, under our dominion and subject to our exploitation. And we have repressed beauty by insisting that beauty is but a handmaiden of natural selection that must be pressed into the service of utilitarian ends if it is to have any worth whatsoever.

When we ask, "are humans part of nature," or "what is my place in the world," we give voice to the lonely arrogance wrought by the repression of beauty. The first question posits a separation by its very asking, as if it is up to humans to determine whether we are "part" of an already abstracted "nature" that could even be conceived in terms of separateness; monotheism is the invisible questioner here. The second question could not be more forlorn. A person who asks this question has lost sight that the question itself is coexistent with the person's place in the world, i.e., their place in the world is that of a person who asks such questions and anticipates that such questions can be satisfactorily answered; here the *cogito* lodges the inquiry. Although both questions are posed as questions, they are also assertions, creatures of method, which to say they are mythical acts, images that reveal through their ideational styles their place in an ecology of imagination. Their context is disenchantment, their mood displaced confusion, and their scene a laboratory removed from the wilds of imagination, a laboratory where such questions are treated seriously and given credence, as if they can be answered with verifiable truths.

We have seen that the repression of beauty takes place primarily through bad ideas, and that these ideas have consequences that are both personal and planetary. The symptoms of soul that plague us as individuals also plague the planet, and, as Chapter Five suggested, we cannot be sure where one ends and the other begins. Even with today's heightened awareness of anthropogenic climate change and a more honest acceptance, at least by some, of the atrocities visited upon the earth, air, and water by the rapacious acts of one species alone, there remains a basic disconnect between the musings of the gaming mind at play and the mundane, irreducible facticity of everyday, animal life.

When soul symptoms are experienced by humans, we habitually take them as subjective, either as arising either within our own individual "self" (and I set that word off in quotes to protect against its infectious nature), or perhaps as between persons, particularly partners, mates, or family. Some now even take the next step and accept that such symptoms might be reactions to degradations of the larger environment, that the conditions of our lived ecologies might affect our psychic conditions, might even be causative of our subjective sufferings. But even here the old divide remains. We might accept that the many things of the world can contribute to our subjective sufferings, but what about *their* suffering? So long as we locate soul within the limits of human subjectivity, we leave out the greater part of soul that lies beyond the human. I have argued that all things are animate, ensouled, full of gods. If so, then we must find a way to address the symptoms of soul in the greater world beyond our postulated subjectivity. This "shifting of the center of gravity of consciousness from the cosmos around him into the personal human being," what Barfield called internalization, is responsible for much of the repression of beauty. This move inward is nothing less than monotheism subjectivized, where it continues its aesthetic oppression under the guise of human secularism.

If the COVID-19 pandemic can be said to have had any positive effect it has forced us into new ways of appreciating the ecology of imagination and the mythical extent of our households. It did not take us long, when suddenly locked within our literal households, to begin to recognize through our isolation that our households could not be literally so confined. We began to long for our friends, our family, our hangouts, habits, and habituations. We began to see that our households extended far beyond the walls and rooms of our homes. Facial coverings revealed to us the importance of faces and their extraordinary range of expression; we became more adept at reading the eyes of others even as we longed for the simple beauty of a smile, Aphrodite's gift. We missed dressing up and going out, seeing and being seen, and having a night on the town. Many people were surprised to discover the natural beauty of their surroundings and began to see, many for the first time, the birds and other animals that are our fellow inhabitants, long-time neighbors who had gone unseen because we were too busy to look.

Meanwhile the invisibles that we usually so blithely ignore became frighteningly present, in the air we breathed and the things we touched. All things became alive, animated, with every tabletop, carton of milk, and doorknob a potential deathtrap. Because we have for so long denied the invisible powers inherent in all things, we were especially traumatized when reminded so terribly of their presence. Having followed Newton and Descartes in declaring the many things of the world dead, we were doubly shocked when those very things became active carriers of death. Perhaps most frightening, we became aware that we, too, could be silent carriers of the invisibles and that our breaths and our bodies could make others sick even if we personally felt no symptoms.

When faced with such realities we, or at least some of us, became acutely aware that we are responsible to one another for our mutual well-being and took steps to protect and care for one another. Meanwhile, others refused to acknowledge the inherent morality of shared life, and in their refusal, they showed us what fundamentalism looks like, how when a mind is inflated by hubris it actually shrinks within itself because it loses the greater world of which it is a part and to which it is responsible. The denial by some of their mutual responsibility to others revealed the ugliness of detached, heartless individualism.

And yet, despite the damage we have caused to the many things of the world, both by direct abuse and through our neglect, beauty remains. The many things of the world still shine around us, still afford us the mythical certainty of our animal lives that we take daily for granted.

Beauty offers us so much in every moment, even if we fail to recognize its offerings. Although we might feel our everyday world as ordinary and dull, it remains ready at any moment to show us its wonder and radiance; "there is much beauty everywhere," said Rilke.[1] The baby's crawl, the foal's standing, the fledgling's flight could not be more commonplace, nor more wondrous.

Beauty can sometimes surprise us by showing us the ordinary in a new light. Sunlight falls upon a familiar house plant in a certain way and suddenly it appears like a new plant, the sunlight revealing lustrous green leaves that draw our eyes and focus our attention. We take a visitor around town to show them the sights and they perceive beauty in things that we have lost sight of because we have come to take them for granted. Things become ordinary when we cease to engage with them, and it is only when we lose interest in them that they fade into a backdrop of regularity. But then beauty steps in to awaken us from our slumber so that we may see things anew. Or, sometimes, sadly, we don't awaken in time and only come to appreciate what beauty has offered to us until it is too late. There is no pain like beauty lost.

When I began this book, I wanted to explore how we have repressed beauty and how we might encourage the return of beauty. But I now see that beauty has never left. The many things of the world, and especially the other animals, have not lost beauty, have not become detached from one another, have not been dulled in their senses or displays. No, it is not the return *of* beauty that we seek but the return *to* beauty. As Jonathan Rosen says, the blindness is of our own making. The question is how to stir from our slumber, how to reawaken our senses, how to clear the anesthetizing fog to once again see, touch, smell, and hear, how to appreciate our bodily intelligence, the sensuality of time and space, and to become alert once again to the many eyes that look upon us.

Let us begin by removing the blinders of subjectivity. Not introspection, but extrospection, not looking within but looking around. What we find there, when we look around, are the many things of the world. But, here, too, let us press for a better word. Like "capital-N" "Nature,"

---

1. Rainer Maria Rilke, *Letters to a Young Poet,* translated by Reginald Nell (London: Sidgwick and Jackson), 25.

which is an inflated concept lacking particularity, so, too, the word "world" has to the modern mind an all-encompassing meaning. It is precisely this inflation that I have tried to avoid by insisting on "the many things of the world." But even here the many things are subsumed under the broader, categorical term "world."

Hillman has suggested the Greek word *kosmos* as an alternate way of imagining the many things. *Kosmos,* from which we get our *cosmos,* was for the Greeks an aesthetic term that meant "fitting order." It was also a moral term, meaning "good order, good behavior, decency." Other meanings are becomingly, duly, decently, form, fashion, ornament, decoration, embellishment, and dress. *Kosmos* was also "descriptive of sweet songs and ways of speech." The verb *kosmos* meant "to arrange, adorn, furnish."[2]

Notably, none of these meanings have the all-enveloping connotation of our "world." Indeed, the word *kosmos* did not mean "world" for the early Greeks, but rather referred to the "general arrangement of things."[3] The particularity inherent in the early Greek usage of *kosmos* can be contrasted with the later Roman translation of *kosmos* into *universum,* meaning "turning around one or one turn or turned to one (*unusverto*)."[4] This step from the particular to the all-embracing, of course, is exactly the step that we do not want to take. "Universe" evokes grand unified theories of everything, Big Bangs, infinite space and limitless time. The mundane, the particular, and the simple facts of things are not good enough to keep company with such ever-expanding concepts. In the universal realm, particulars become parts whose significance matters only in terms of the relationships and interactions that constitute the whole. Only the whole can provide meaning, completeness, and coherence; things in themselves are insufficient and so require theories and explanations *to be applied to them* because from a universal perspective

---

2. James Hillman, "Cosmology for Soul," *Sphinx: A Journal for Archetypal Psychology and the Arts* 2 (1989): 21.

3. Aryeh Finkelberg, "On the History of the Greek κοσμοσ," *Harvard Studies in Classical Philology* 98 (1998): 119. Finkelberg is compelling in his argument that the imposition of "world" onto *kosmos* is a later occurrence and that there was no such correlation among the early Greeks.

4. Hillman, "Cosmology for Soul," 21.

parts cannot be wholes, meaning cannot be inherently intelligible, and completeness cannot exist in the apparent, manifest forms of things.

The corruption of "cosmos" into "universe" reappears in our "cosmology" and "cosmogony," where the particular, sensate adornments and ornamentations of the general arrangement of things are turned into "a vast gas bag, outer, empty, spacey, and cold, while the *logos* of the cosmic is without sweet song."[5] But just as we saw earlier that *mythos* does not have to rely on *logos,* so, too, *kosmos* exists independently from *logos.* The many things of the cosmos exist apart from mentation, theory, origins, reflections, or what we have to say about them. Rather *kosmos* arises within a polytheistic context where things are revealed through their individual presentations among other things. Their apparent, animate natures are given with and by their form (Portmann) and are directly perceived as images within an ecology of imagination. As Henri Frankfort writes with regard to ancient Egyptian polytheism: "Powers confront man wherever he moves, and *in the immediacy of these confrontations the question of their ultimate unity does not arise.*"[6] (Emphasis added.) Cosmos is not a projection; universe is.

So, too, *kosmos* is perceived instantaneously in and through images, each thing a *kosmos,* fittingly ordered, becoming, contained, *"not a universe but a unity."*[7] Particulars, not parts, are made coherent not by an over-arching theory but by the fitting order given with each thing, the inherent intelligibility of things as they are, immediately available in the mythic certitude of each event, each thing specifically placed among others, arranged as a bouquet or a concerto is arranged, their sensibility not held in an idea but through the integrity of the image as such. "Cosmos," says Hillman, "does not present itself as an all-embracing whole but as the appearance of fittingness of each thing as and where it is; how well, how decorously, how appropriately it displays. *And its beauty is that very display*; cosmos in each, as each, grain of sand."[8] (Emphasis added.)

---

5. Hillman, "Cosmology for Soul," 21.

6. Henri Frankfort, *Ancient Egyptian Religion: An Interpretation* (New York: Harper Torchbooks, 1961), 4.

7. Hillman, "Cosmology for Soul," 23.

8. Hillman, "Practice of Beauty," 23.

If *kosmos* is revealed by beauty in the display of each thing, then the immediate, unmediated experience of *kosmos* is aesthetic. Our word "cosmetics," with its aesthetic relation to adornment and ornamentation, shading and blushing and coloration, especially of the face and eyes, is much closer to the early Greek meaning of *kosmos* than are the grand theories of cosmology and cosmogony. "Aesthetic" also comes to us from the Greeks. *Aisthesis* goes back to *aiou* and *aisthou* that both mean "to perceive" and have the root meaning of "taking in," "breathing in," "gasp," and "struggle for breath."[9] Although modern translators equate *aisthesis* with "sense-perception," that meaning "cannot be understood without taking into account the Greek goddess of the senses [Aphrodite] or the organ of Greek sensation, the heart, and the root of the word—that sniffing, gasping, breathing in of the world."[10]

This root meaning of aesthetics suggests an embodied appreciation of things—the instinctive gasp, the *ahh* that we experience when we encounter a fox in the woods, or round a curve on a fall day in Vermont to confront a living color field of maples ablaze, or unexpectedly see a friend in a crowd when we are far from home. For that instant, beauty stops us, we gasp and beauty "takes our breath away." But there is another breathing in, too, the breathing in that comes with intimacy, that is indicative of place, and that abides in memory. The grassy smell of a spring rain, the salty brine of the seashore, the familiar fragrance of a lover's hair—think how we stop and linger to breath it in, taking it into our lungs, into our chests, into our hearts. Onians reminds us that in the Upanishads speech, sight, hearing, and mind were knows as breaths (prāṇa).[11] Does this perhaps suggest that all of the various ways by which we perceive beauty end up affecting us close to the heart, that organ that for many cultures is the place of meaning and the pulsing source of eros?

The historian of science Alexandre Koyré wrote that the scientific and philosophical revolution of the sixteenth and seventeenth centu-

9. Richard Broxton Onians, *The Origins of European Thought: About the Body, the Mind, the Soul, the World, Time, and Fate* (Cambridge: Cambridge University Press, 1988), 74.

10. James Hillman, *The Thought of the Heart and the Soul of the World* (Thompson, Conn.: Spring Publications, 2021), 35.

11. Onians, *The Origins of European Thought*, 75.

ries "can be described roughly as bringing forth the destruction of the Cosmos."[12] The way to reconstitute our connection to the cosmos, then, will not be through philosophy or science but through beauty. The more we abstract, idealize, explain, and theorize the more distant we become from the simple act of appreciation. Things do not ask in the first instance to be understood, much less explained; they ask to be seen, because, as Berkeley reminds us, *esse est percipi,* to exist is to be perceived. Things exist because they stand out, presenting their interiority in display (Portmann), the being of each thing "revealed in the display of its [image]."[13]

In his *Anatomy of Melancholy,* Robert Burton wrote: "It is most true, *stylus virum arguit,* our style bewrayes us."[14] I would extend that to the many things, each thing being what and how it is according to the style that reveals it. Note that style in this context has nothing to do with subjective choice, rather it is style that constitutes things and affords the possibilities of choice. *Things are before they decide to be,* and it is this immediate presence that is revealed, presented, and perceived in and by style. In an aesthetic cosmos, it is style that sets each thing before many eyes, showing it for what it is. Style reveals a thing's uniqueness, and through its many revelations style creates a becoming and welcoming cosmos in which each thing has its place.

When guided by style, aesthetic concerns become paramount. Style goes untouched by concepts and explanations that turn our attention away from the sensate and sensual presence of things and asks instead for a more carefully differentiated appreciation. Just think of how we are offended when others attempt to analyze or explain us. We feel both diminished and disrespected because we *are* being diminished and disrespected. Things are always so much more than any explanation can provide. "Instead of inquiry; interest, respect, welcome, praise—even attachment. To greet each event with desire, wanting it to stay so as to

---

12. Alexandre Koyré, *From the Closed World to the Infinite Universe* (Baltimore: The John Hopkins University Press, 1979), 2.

13. Hillman, *The Thought of the Heart,* 33.

14. Robert Burton, *The Anatomy of Melancholy* (London: Thomas Tegg, 1840), 8.

give all the attention is claims—is this love?"[15] Remember how Lorenz believed that one could not properly observe animals without an intuitive understanding grounded in love and respect. And remember, too, Portmann's call to dwell on "every detail lovingly." It is enough for style to be present in the most beautiful and appropriate manner possible, where beauty refers not to the pretty or cute but to the presence of a thing appearing as it is. Socrates, for example, was said to be beautiful not because of a handsome visage but because he was as he appeared to be. He was at home in his style.

An aesthetic cosmos displayed in and by images provides another way into the old idea of *anima mundi*—the "soul of the world" or "world soul." As a philosophical or religious idea, *anima mundi* becomes either transcendent ,"above the world encircling it as a divine and remote emanation of spirit," or immanent, "within the material world as its unifying pan-psychic life principle."[16] But *mundus,* from which we get *mundi,* did not only mean "world" as a transcendent or unifying whole. It also has meanings of order, to adorn, neat, and clean. Thus, it is closer to cosmos than to universe. An ensouled cosmos, then, would imply neither transcendence nor immanence, both of which assert something separate from things, one outside and beyond, the other within and contained, but rather would appear aesthetically, the soul of each thing given by the beauty of its presentation, "that particular soul spark, that seminal image, which offers itself through each thing in its visible form."[17] Plotinus said that Aphrodite means soul (*Enneads* 3.5.4), and in Apuleius's tale, Psyche (soul) is known first and foremost for her physical beauty, her radiance causing others to liken her to the Goddess of Beauty herself (*The Golden Ass,* Book 4). This intimate connection between soul and beauty reaffirms that soul is not limited to living creatures but rather is the animated and animating potential of each thing that is revealed in its display, its interiority present in its form. Beauty overcomes our repressions and reveals soul in the mundane things of everyday life, at once ordinary and radiant.

---

15. Hillman, "Cosmology for Soul," 29.
16. Hillman, *The Thought of the World,* 61.
17. Ibid.

Although all things are ensouled, for humans it has always been the other animals that possess a special power to elicit our wonder. Perhaps it is because animals are so mythically certain, their morphology and behavior presented at once in their image, their physiognomy inseparable from how they behave, how they move, and how they look, where "how they look" is always a double entendre meaning both the manner of their appearance and the manner of their perceiving. Animals give living form to cosmos, to the inherent patterning and order that comes with each individual as image, each animal an image and each image an animal alive in an ecology of imagination. Was it the inherent intelligibility of animals as images that allowed Adam to name the animals, because their characters were apparent in their bodies and behaviors, each one sensate, sensual, and sensible?

Stories from indigenous peoples all over the world tell of animals revealing cosmic truths to humans, of imparting divine wisdom. Indeed, in polytheistic and animistic cultures, animals themselves are often divine. Despite their evolutionary changes over time, within the context of direct human interaction animals seem permanent and unchanging, their presence seemingly given with the earth itself, intrinsically grounded, timeless. Frankfort writes of the "underlying religious awe felt before all animal life," and that for ancient Egyptians "the *animal as such*...seems to possess religious significance."[18] Ancient Egyptians perceived animals as divine because of "their inarticulate wisdom, their certainty, their unhesitating achievement, and above all in their static reality. With animals the continual succession of generations brought no change...The animals never change, and in this respect especially they would appear to share—in a degree unknown to man—the fundamental nature of creation."[19] Animals seem, too, to share with the gods a kind of intelligence that escapes the human mind, a kind of knowledge that seems unhesitating and certain because it is unmediated and direct. Animals "do not need the mediation of reason because they immediately perceive, and thus know."[20]

---

18. Frankfort, *Ancient Egyptian Religion*, 9.

19. Ibid., 13.

20. Hillman, "Cosmology for Soul," 27.

How unlike the Western traditions that we have reviewed that would deny consciousness to animals! By denigrating the manifest as but a façade for a hidden world of particles, physics, and mathematical truths, and by declaring that hidden world as superior to animal styles of consciousness that remain grounded in the manifest, we have made a cosmic error. It is animal consciousness, what Santayana referred to as "animal faith," that directly and correctly perceives the cosmos.[21] It is their style of consciousness that most adheres to the root meaning of "conscious" as to "to know with." Our human style of consciousness sets us apart from things because it wants to have knowledge *of* things; animal consciousness cannot be separated from their knowledge *with* things. Perhaps this is why animals can appear to us as both strangely familiar and yet totally other. We see in them, dimly, what we ourselves embody even if our modern minds deny it—they remind us of our animal faith. At the same time, "their inarticulate wisdom, their unhesitating achievement, and above all their static reality," outstrip our longing for a Unified Theory or a True God that might provide us the Truth, or some Grounding Principle that would help us make sense of things. The other animals know what we no longer do, that the sense we seek is given by the very things whose manifest forms we deny, and the grounding principle that we pursue is in the very ground upon which we walk. The perceptions and actions of the other animals exhibit a direct connection to an ensouled cosmos that exists only in the eachness of things given by beauty, which is the only manner in which soul and cosmos ever appear. This aesthetic connection to the cosmos of each thing is what affords the other animals their wisdom, achievements, and faith—not only *anima mundi,* but also *animal mundi.*[22]

---

21. "Animal faith, being an expression of hunger, pursuit, shock, or fear, is directed upon *things*; that is, it assumes the existence of alien self-developing beings, independent of knowledge, but capable of being affected by action. While things are running on in the dark, they may be suddenly seized, appropriated, or destroyed. In other words, animal faith posits substances, and indicates their locus in the field of action of which the animal occupies the centre." George Santayana, *Scepticism and Animal Faith: Introduction to a System of Philosophy* (New York: Charles Scribner's Sons, 1923), 214.

22. The idea of the connection between *anima mundi* and *animal mundi* first appeared in James Hillman, "Image-Sense," *Spring: An Annual of Archetypal Psychology*

We can recall here two comments from our discussion about the purported separation of human and nature. First is from Purdy: "I wonder whether—to stay with the religious imagery for a moment—*a polytheist or animist image* wouldn't fit better today and going forward. It's just not true that Nature has a meaning, or that we have relations with it as a whole." (Emphasis mine.) He told us of the Athabascan peoples whose "relations are specific—not with Nature, but with the salmon, or a river, or a tree."[23] And then there was Lynn White: "... to make fundamental changes in our attitudes and actions affecting ecology. *The religious problem is to find a viable equivalent to animism.*"[24] (Emphasis mine.)

I take both Purdy and White not to be calling for a literal return to polytheism or animism in terms of religious belief but rather a psychological perspective that reanimates our respect for cosmos as it is presented in the display of the many things of the cosmos. Purdy urges a "polytheistic or animistic image" and White a "viable alternative to animism." Purdy could not be more correct in his use of the word "image" because it is in and through images and their places in an ecology of imagination where we regain this deep reattachment to the particular, sensate things that beauty presents to our aesthetic sensibilities. The religious aspect to which both Purdy and White allude, and what I have referred to as all things being full of gods, is given with the mythical certainty and inherent intelligibility of things. It is difficult to speak of beauty, soul, love, and cosmos without our words partaking in the divine, and to speak as did Santayana of animal *faith*. But the divine of which I speak is not literal and the gods in all things have no need for either belief or proselytizing. Rather the divine shines in the patterns and internal relations of each thing just as it is as given by beauty, and in the inherent intelligibility of the general arrangement of things given by myth. It is

---

and Jungian Thought (1979), 143. He returned to the idea in his "Back to Beyond: On Cosmology," first published in David Ray Griffin, ed., *Archetypal Process: Self and Divine in Whitehead, Jung, and Hillman* (Evanston: Northwestern University Press, 1989) and reprinted in *Uniform Edition of the Writings of James Hillman,* vol. 8: *Philosophical Intimations,* edited by Edward S. Casey (Putnam, Conn.: Spring Publications, 2016).

23. See Chapter Two, note 36, above.
24. See Chapter Two, note 32, above

no accident that when humans try to bring *logos* to *mythos* we inevitably end up telling stories of gods.

When speaking of images and divinity it is important to keep in mind Frankfort's comment that for the ancient Egyptians animals *as such* were considered divine, that is, they were not symbols or representations that pointed to a divinity removed from them but rather were divinities present in animal form. "For what else is an image," says Hillman, "but a psychic fact. Facts: hard, real, naked, true. Not metaphors or interpretations, not hints, auras, suspicions. To the animal there are only facts as the animal itself is a fact, and to be a fact is to be fully there, fully intelligible."[25] Thus, when we say that all things are full of gods, we are also saying that the gods are inseparable from the immediate facticity of images as ensouled presentations. So, for the ancient Greeks, the tip of a spear *was* Ares, just as the owl *was* Athena who was herself "owl-eyed"; the gods and the many things of the cosmos, especially animals, existed in and through one another. An animalized cosmos, an *animal mundi,* offers us a way to return to our animal faith, which is a faith that does not require belief. Indeed, belief is required only when we lose faith in our direct, aesthetic attachment to images within an ecology of imagination. When we lose faith in the psychic facts (images) that beauty provides, and when we grow suspicious of the mythic certainty that we so irrevocably display in each instant of our lives, we become disassociated and paranoid, our doubting minds running parallel to things but unable to re-enter their fitting order. Without the grounding power of images, and the inherent sensibility of myth, we remain aloft and aloof, unable to find our place in the general arrangement of things, that sense of place, and yes, purpose, that are directly provided to us by beauty.

---

25. Hillman, "Cosmology for Soul," 31.

SEVEN

An Eye Grafted on the Heart

B eauty reveals each thing as an image unto itself, each image a cosmos, precisely displayed to the senses, sensually contextualized, and
inherently intelligible. But "unto itself" here does not mean isolated.
Rather images appear in the company of other images, as part of a household, partaking in an ecology of imagination. I have argued that humans,
and likely many of the other animals at the very least, perceive images
aesthetically and that this aesthetic sense proceeds through an embodied
imagination. By embodied imagination I mean that our engagement with
the world is not dualistic but rather organic and holistic, and that our
imagination cannot be separated from our bodies but is given with and
by our bodies. When we, or any other living thing, moves, we do so with
mythic certitude, our bodies intrinsically relying on the world to support our actions. We are connected to myth through imagination, and so
when we move, we imagine, and when we imagine we move. One does
not come before the other, body and imagination are always together.
This reality is what we experience when we perceive animals as images
and images as animals, when we are struck by "their inarticulate wisdom, their unhesitating achievement, and above all their static reality"
(Frankfort). But I have also said that we humans have lost touch with
our animal faith, which in my meaning is the same as embodied imagination, through a blindness that we have made for ourselves (Rosen). In
the previous chapter we broached the idea of how we might regain our
animal faith and occasion a return to beauty. To this topic we now more
fully turn.

We have seen that a monotheistic cast of mind seems inevitably to
create a separation between humans and cosmos. In a religious context,
this separation takes on moral dimensions, with humans being declared
superior to and having dominion over the rest of God's creation. In

the context of secular humanism, this separation appears as Barfield's "internalization," the dual act of positing a private, subjective self and then "shifting of the centre of gravity of consciousness from the cosmos around him into the personal human being himself." And so religious monotheism elevates the human above the general arrangement of things through transcendence and hierarchy, while psychological monotheism collapses cosmos into the black hole of subjectivity. Curiously, and significantly, both posit psyche as belonging only to humans, the former making it a gift from God, and the latter translating soul into "self." More, both proclaim that any sense that we might have of an ensouled cosmos are merely projections that are unfit for proper consideration by educated people and belong instead to the undeveloped minds of children, so-called primitives, or the depraved and deranged minds of the sinner and the sick.

To overcome these traditions that separate us from aesthetically engaging an ensouled cosmos we need to get past a recurring dichotomy in our tradition of dichotomies. Modern thought tends to split how we think about things into two opposing camps, the poetic/mythical/imaginative on the one hand, and the rational/logical/scientific on the other. The former is said to belong to art and religion while the latter is the domain of philosophy and science. The poet and writer Elizabeth Sewell describes the former as "more closely knit with the body (witness its habit, in myth, of expressing all concepts in terms of bodies, of embodying its ideas, in fact, and the close connection of myth with rite or bodily action)"[1] The latter ways of thinking we associate with the "intellect" or "mind" and consider them to function through abstract, that is, disembodied, thinking that operates within the realm of formal concepts and laws.

Sewell disputes that these two styles of thinking are in fact in opposition with one another. "Science and poetry," she writes, "mathematics and words, intellect and imagination, mind and body: they are old, they are tidy, they are mistaken."[2] She urges, as have I throughout this book, a way beyond such divisions:

---

1. Elizabeth Sewell, *The Orphic Voice: Poetry and Natural History* (New York: The New York Review of Books, 2022), 19.
2. Ibid.

The human organism, that body which has the gift of thought, does not have the choice of two kinds of thinking. It has only one, in which the organism as a whole is engaged all along the line. There has been no progression in history from one type of thought to another. We are merely learning to use what we have been given, which is all of a piece. This means too that we have to admit and affirm our solidarity with the thinking of the child and the savage. All thinking is of the same kind."[3]

The embodied coherence and intelligibility that finds expression in *both* poetry and science lies "in those elemental times and places which...are not simply the dwelling places of humanity in earlier times *but the sources of our mental powers in their primary form.*"[4] (Emphasis mine.) I have been asserting that the sources of these "mental powers" are beauty, myth, and imagination, and that different ways of thinking are simply different ways of imagining thought. "All striving and learning," writes Sewell, "is mythologizing; and language is the mythology of thought and action, a system of working figures made manifest."[5]

It is worth pausing here to note the degree to which modern thought gets this last point completely wrong. Instead of recognizing myth as being constitutive of the mind in all of its variations, the modern mind defines "myth" as something that is only figurative, something invented by the mind as a fable or fiction. Myth is the opposite of what is real— a mythical being is not a real being, and a mythical event is one that never occurred. Myths are mere stories, usually told by pre-scientific cultures not yet capable of understanding things through the lens of reason. Myths do not describe actual things or events but are primitive attempts at explanations by those lacking the proper means for explanations. We insist on thinking that the mind makes up myths, thereby insisting that *mythos* must rely on *logos,* instead of seeing that it is myth that makes the mind possible in all of its variations.

---

3. Ibid., 19–20.

4. Elizabeth Sewell, "Bacon, Vico, Coleridge and the Poetic Method," in Giorgio Tagliacozzo and Hayden V. White, eds., *Giambattista Vico: An International Symposium* (Baltimore: The John Hopkins Press, 1969), 129.

5. Sewell, *The Orphic Voice,* 28.

Sewell rejects our common definition of myth. Instead, she refers to "language-as-poetry" and "language-as-science" as being two ways in which *mythos* is expressed in *logos*. Although their styles might differ, they both derive their form and intelligibility from their primary source in myth.[6] Despite their kinship, however, the two styles do differ radically in how they relate to one another. As we saw earlier in Chapter Five, the realm of *verum,* to which language-as-science belongs, cannot admit language-as-poetry into its perspective as an equal partner, and it certainly cannot accept language-as-poetry as a legitimate form of knowledge or as a method equal to that of rational inquiry. Sewell contrasts the "exclusive mythology" of language-as-science with the "inclusive mythology" of language-as-poetry. The latter does not exclude language-as-science but instead accepts it as yet another form of myth, an imaginative activity that is characterized in part by its inability to acknowledge itself as such.[7]

The difference between language-as-science and language-as-poetry is not strictly ideological but also points to the relationship of each mythical style in terms of its participation with and in the body. For Sewell, language-as-science is a "specialized form of mythologizing activity in which attention is not paid to the participation of the body, which is nonetheless, tacitly, part of the process and a vital part."[8] Language-as-poetry, however, "is prepared in varying degrees to admit the body, the notion of the organism as a whole, as a partner in that very odd operation known as thought."[9] This attempted disassociation from the body by language-as-science leads to the repression of beauty, because beauty is always found either in bodily display or in embodied images such as in poetry and music. Beauty implies and implicates the sensual, and any attempt to ignore, transcend, or abstract from the body leads to a repression of beauty. This is why I have been emphasizing the importance of embodied imagination. When we keep imagination and body together, recognizing that they are an organic unity, we embrace our animal faith and occasion the return to beauty.

---

6. Ibid., 6.
7. Ibid., 38.
8. Ibid.
9. Ibid.

It is indeed unfortunate that the modern mind continues to so often adopt a view that the rational/logical/scientific style of thinking is somehow superior to and indeed a progression from the poetic/mythical/imaginative style. This notion of a progression from the mythical to scientific, typified by Auguste Comte's "law of three stages," whereby society supposedly progresses from the theological, to the metaphysical, to the scientific stage has been quite tenacious. Quite apart from its historical inaccuracies, this view highlights the elitism that comes with an exclusive mythology—language-as-science is not content with being different, it must be better and must maintain its claim that it alone offers access to the true and the real. This elitism is a defense against the deeper workings of myth. In contrast, language-as-poetry accepts a poetic basis of the mind (Hillman) by which we would "affirm our solidarity with the thinking of the child and the savage" (Sewell). This latter view accepts and respects language-as-science but does not grant its claims of superior or special access to the true and the real.

The denigration of the poetic/mythical/imaginative contributes to our defensiveness against the power of images. When we try to abstract from an image or attempt to turn it into a symbol or define its meaning, we lose our immediate, aesthetic connection to the image and its inherent power. Once that connection is severed, we lose our ability to appreciate the image on its own terms. The art historian David Freedberg writes:

> [W]e in the West ... choose to ignore the kinds of response [to images] that transcend cultural and chronological differences, and we refuse to acknowledge those aspects of response that precede detachment and rational observation... *We* may be quite happy to believe that images in primitive cultures are felt to partake of the life of what they represent, or even the life of things other than what they represent. But we do not like to think of this of ourselves, or of our own society. *We refuse—or have refused for many decades—to acknowledge the traces of animism in our perception and response to images*; not necessarily "animism" in the nineteenth-century ethnographic sense of the transference of spirits to inanimate objects, but rather *in the sense of*

the degree of life or liveliness believed to inhere in an image.[10] (Emphasis other than "*We* may be quite happy" added.)

Thus, by ignoring our aesthetic responses that "precede detachment and rational observation" we deny both the embodied power of images, and our ability to perceive "within them their life and liveliness." Because our modern approach has elevated the literal and opposed it against myth, we remain trapped in our rational assumptions and thereby become detached from the inherent liveliness of an animated cosmos. The irony is that these rational assumptions are incapable of admitting that they themselves are thoroughly mythical. "Now, in order that nature may be peopled with spirits," observed Barfield, "nature must first be devoid of spirit; but this caused scholars no difficulty, because they never supposed the possibility of any other kind of nature."[11] This inability to suppose the possibility of any other kind of nature is a hallmark of what Sewell calls an "exclusive mythology."

The inclusive mythology of language-as-poetry recognizes that language-as-science is mythical both in its methods and intelligibility. Language-as-poetry respects the achievements of language-as-science, which are considerable, but is unwilling to grant its self-proclaimed superior status. Instead, an inclusive mythology says that myth imbues all things, including thinking of all varieties, with the coherence and intelligibility that allow them to proceed. There can be no perception of things, no interaction among things, and certainly no imagining or thinking (the latter of which I claim to be a style of imagining) without myth.

Another misconception that we must avoid is that thinking, of whatever style, is somehow "purely" intellectual, where "purely" implies a kind of disembodied activity along the lines of highly idealized mathematics or symbolic logic. This "purely" is Descartes's mind/body dualism slipping in through the back door while we wrestle to give voice to things that seem to always outpace our words—how difficult it is to say what we know! Sewell refutes this move, insisting that intellectual activity,

---

10. David Freedberg, *The Power of Images: Studies in the History and Theory of Response* (Chicago and London: The University of Chicago Press, 1989), 32.

11. Owen Barfield, *Saving the Appearances: A Study in Idolatry* (Middletown, Conn.: Wesleyan University Press, 1988), 66.

or indeed any "formal activity," can never be abstracted from the body or the images which myth affords the body:

> If, for the living individual, the body is the original generator of forms, first its own form in structure and behavior, then forms which are in varying degrees separated from itself and which accordingly offer the mind-body scope for its formalizing tendencies, it may be true to say that all formal activity in the human mind has its origins and roots always in the physical. The mind-body may generate forms as language or terms for metaphoric activity by which to understand itself and its experience; but *all form, not matter how apparently abstract and intellectual, may never lose its connection with, its message for, the body* …
>
> I do not mean that the body translates form, abstractly perceived, into pictures; rather that all form addresses itself no less to the body than the mind, the former perceiving it by virtue of its own formalizing tendencies and uniting with it. The body mates with forms no less than the mind does. The more abstract they are, the more specialized, rarefied, perhaps even concealed an image they offer to the body; *but that image is always there.*[12] (Emphasis added.)

By maintain the primacy of the embodied imagination, I join Sewell in insisting that myth, image, imagination, poetry, and the many ways in which they take shape, always remain connected to bodily, *animal* forms. As such, "poetry, metaphor, mythology are highly realistic and down to earth."[13] It is this point that language-as-science finds so difficult to accept because from its perspective myth must by definition be unreal. Mythical certitude, however, grants what *verum* cannot—a direct, realistic, embodied experience of the world revealed by beauty and perceived in the image's inherent intelligibility given by myth. It is not myth, but rather the exclusive mythology of language-as-science that imagines itself as abstract and disembodied that is fantastical and out of touch with reality.

If we are to reawaken our aesthetic sensibilities so as to return to beauty, then, we need to become more attuned and accepting of our

---

12. Sewell, *The Orphic Voice*, 36–37.
13. Ibid., 39.

bodily presence as animals within the context of myth. Our animal bodies, *which is the same thing as saying our imaginal bodies,* are capable not only of perceiving through our senses but also of *knowing* through our senses. The forms and behaviors of other animals, presented by beauty and made sensible by myth, can teach us how we might move beyond our habits of inquiry and understanding to the greater callings of interest, respect, appreciation, and attachment. So, too, we might challenge what we mean, *exactly mean,* when we speak of the literal, true, real, and factual, and ask what we leave out in our drive for definitions and explanations. To return to beauty means that we return to an ensouled cosmos full of gods, and the way back to that cosmos is through the tutelary powers of animals in all of their visceral reality, just as animistic and polytheistic traditions have been telling us for so long.

The move of becoming aware that we simultaneously exist bodily and imaginally within the context of myth is perhaps the most difficult for us as modern people. We are so hung up on the idea that *we* invent myth that it seems incredible to say that we exist within myth. But myth and imagination do not belong to or depend upon us. They are autonomous psychic activities that provide the inherent intelligibility that is apparent in animal form and behavior, that presentation of inwardness so brilliantly expounded by Portmann that allows animals to "read" one another without need of words or symbols. Humans make sense to one another and to non-human animals because we all inhabit and share a mythical, imaginal field. Indeed, other animals often read us better than we read them because they are not constrained by language or by beliefs that separate them from us. Anyone who has ever lived with an animal companion knows that they often know how we are before we do, directly sensing our emotional states or even presaging physical illness. The Romans called such animals "familiars," and so they are. Would it ever occur to us that a dog, cat, or bird who sees our suffering or elation is somehow "projecting" that feeling onto us from their inner subjectivity? And yet when we recognize such states in them, we call it anthropomorphism and further repress beauty.

That the other animals perceive us, and in so doing know us, indicates the mythic context of our bodily lives presented through and to imagination. We, too, are images that are perceived and attended to by other images, like treating like, as the old saying goes. And so, we would do well to try to shed the old skins of thought-before-action and self-knowledge that try to constrain us within conceptualized bodies that we constantly outgrow. We are known by the myths that we embody and enact through our presentation in display and behavior. Perhaps this is why we always are so concerned about our image and what kind of impression we make. Perhaps it is not vanity that drives such concerns but a deeper recognition that we cannot be separated from our image that is perceived and appreciated by others. It is said that when Pythagoras was deciding whether to take on a student, he observed their manners of speech and laughter, with whom they associated, what they did in their leisure time, and what brought them joy or grief. But just as importantly, "he likewise surveyed their form, their mode of walking, and the whole motion of their body. Physiognomically also considering the natural indications of their frame, he made them to be *manifest signs of the unapparent manners of the soul.*"[14] (Emphasis added.)

To learn how myth is embodied in our animal form and behavior we must rely on the animal perceptions of others. This point is made in a joke. A young man is arguing with his friend, and at one point the friend says, "You're being a jerk!" The young man protests, "No I'm not!" To which the friend replies, "It's not up to you!" The joke rightly says that the constitution of an individual belongs to the perceptions of others. This implies that the "I" who interacts with other humans and non-human animals is not the "I" that I think I know through introspection. We, quite literally, are not who we think we are. The mentor sees the student *before* the student ever comes to know what the mentor sees.

The word "constitution" as used in the above paragraph deserves a closer look. Our most common meaning nowadays refers to the organizing principles of a nation ("nation" having the same etymological root as "nature") or state as often embodied in a written instrument (a Constitution). However, the word has other meanings, including:

1. The physical makeup of the individual especially with respect to the vitality, health, strength, and appearance of the body

---

14. Iamblichus, *Life of Pythagoras,* translated by Thomas Taylor (London: J.M. Watkins, 1818), 36.

2. The structure, composition, physical makeup, or nature of something

3. The forming or establishing of something

4. A person's mental of psychological makeup

5. The mode in which a state or society is organized

These meanings all permeate one another and, taken together, suggest that a thing's "constitution" *appears* in its body and reveals its "vitality," "nature," and "psychological makeup." I am saying that the "forming or establishing" of this constitution is a function of myth. Put otherwise, *myth is soul-making,* which also then means that *soul-making is myth.* Myth as soul-making inheres in the structure and composition of images, providing their eachness and integrity. Myth both appears in the precise presentation of images in their context, mood, and scene, and resides in the mystery at the heart of every image:

> Mythological statements lead to questions. Then follows something rather strange, for to these questions only the story itself can make an answer. The myth turns back upon itself because it is a question that figures its own reply, and it is that inner movement or dynamic that makes it feel obscure. This kind of unclearness is not muddle or mystification, but an indication of method.[15]

It is this tension between what we are given and what we make out of what we are given that appears to others as our constitution. It is they who determine if we have fulfilled our calling, answered our destiny, or, conversely, have "failed to make the most of our talents" or not "lived up to our potential." We need only remember that we have been told *ad nauseum* by philosophy, at least since Descartes, that others cannot know our "inner" thoughts (self/other being yet another pointless dualism), but the point is they don't need to. Our inner thoughts about ourselves are mostly irrelevant to who and what we are because who and what we are only become apparent through *how* we are. And this how is revealed through our animal form and behavior, through how we present ourselves and through what we do. It is not a happenstance that the old sto-

---

15. Sewell, *The Orphic Voice,* 4.

ries of the gods and heroes always told of their *deeds*. It is difficult to imagine Hercules struggling with his identity. There were lions.

We still have ways of talking about the myths that we display through our deeds even if we don't recognize them as such. One is reputation, a qualitative appreciation of a person that lies completely beyond the control or influence of a person's self-reflection. Our reputation is formed by the consideration and estimation by others of our actions over time. Our reputation is not immediately apparent but is cumulative; it belongs to the stories and gossip that others tell about us, a kind of mythology of our deeds. Our reputation pertains to us and yet does not belong to us. And yet how violently we will protect our reputation if we feel it threatened or impugned. Libel! Slander! Duels! Although we are not its author, we nonetheless feel deeply that the reputation others ascribe to us is "ours," and equate it with "our good name," harkening back to the old idea that a name expresses the nature of its owner and controls the owner's destiny (one's "permanent record"). But what we also feel is our helplessness in protecting our reputation, because it is in fact *not* ours. We perceive its fragility because it is a gossamer web of all that we have done and are known by in the imagination and memories of others. We recognize that an attack on our reputation is an attack on our image within our ecology of imagination, an attempt to dislodge us from the niche that we feel we have earned in the general arrangement of things through our repetitious (ritual?) acts embedded in our daily lives. These actions are the embodiments of soul-making that appear in our individual mythologies. And the more these actions cohere, the more solid our reputation becomes.

Another recognition of myth comes in character, which for the Greeks first referred to an engraved, scratched, or stamped mark. A person's character is their appearance in the context of myth and imagination. Our character constitutes us and is given with our nature, and Vico reminds us that "nature" originally meant "birth."[16] Myth stamps our character from the beginning, casting an indelible die that endures over time as who and how we are. And character does seem to mark itself on

<hr />

16. *The New Science of Giambattista Vico,* translated by Thomas Goddard Bergin and Max Harold Fisch (Ithaca, N.Y.: Cornell University Press, 2015), pars. 147–48.

our bodies over time, doesn't it? Character is engraved in the wrinkles and furrows and scars that show what we have done, what we have been through, how we have lived. The smooth faces of youth are beautiful in their own manner, but part of that beauty is because we know that they presage the promise of what is to come, a character yet to unfold. The elder's wisdom is apparent to us, written in the mapping lines of the face that show us what their eyes have seen. There is a famous, possibly apocryphal, story that after Pablo Picasso painted a portrait of Gertrude Stein an observer remarked that the portrait did not look like Stein. Picasso purportedly responded, "it will."

Character, James Hillman once wrote to me, "reveals itself in style." Character reveals us in a manner that reputation does not. Reputation builds over time while character is given with us as our enduring image, or rather as a "complexity of images," instantly recognizable by imagination:

> If the character of a person is a complexity of images, then to know you I must imagine you, absorb your images. To stay connected with you, I must stay imaginatively interested, not in the process of our relationships or in my feelings about you, but in my imaginings of you. The connection through imagination yields an extraordinary closeness. Where imagination focuses intently on the character of the other—as it does between opposing generals, guard and hostage, analyst and patient—love follows.
>
> The human connection may benefit from exhortations to love one another, but for a relationship to stay alive, love alone is not enough. Without imagination, love stales into sentiment, duty, boredom. Relationships fail not because we have stopped loving but because we first stopped imagining.[17]

We speak of a person of character and comment on his or her standing or status among their peers, a pillar of the community we might call them. Their character reveals what constitutes them, what is given by their constitution. All of these meanings of character relate to the Latin *status* "a standing, position," which in turn is from the past participle

---

17. James Hillman, *The Force of Character and The Lasting Life* (New York: Random House, 1999), 185–86.

stem of *stare,* "to stand." Our character is how we stand, and, like reputation, we guard our standing with utmost concern. We know intuitively that our character and reputation are what remain after we our gone. Long after our private notions of who or what we are have returned to dust, it is our character and reputation that remain, fixed in time through the imaginations of others, like the Greek statues that were once painted in lively colors but now seem immortal in the whiteness of their enduring form.

If other animals help to constitute us through their imagination, so, too, we have a part in the soul-making of ourselves and others. We are part of an ecology of imagination and so are inextricably intertwined with other images. The animal sureness (Hillman's "mythic certitude") with which we move through our environs bespeaks the imaginative power of our bodies as images. "Our bodies are both anatomical and imaginative structures."[18] Images are not passive, and so our actions have cosmic affect, altering the general arrangement of things.

This embodied imaginative awareness precedes reflection or thinking of any kind. Even Immanuel Kant recognized that imagination is an "indispensable function in the soul, without which we should have no knowledge whatsoever, but of the existence of which we are scarcely ever conscious."[19] This is a key point. From a psychological perspective grounded in soul, knowledge does not have to be constellated in the mind. Psychological knowledge is imaginative, and thus is given with our immediate and unmediated encounter with images in and through the embodied imagination. "The aesthetic imagination is the primary mode of knowing the cosmos."[20] This aesthetic knowledge can never be separated from the bodily form of animal life and is not held in concepts but demonstrated through the actions afforded by images within an ecology of imagination.

Here we are back to my students wanting to know when to turn the boat. It is difficult for us to trust our bodies because we have been taught

---

18. Ibid., 184.

19. Immanuel Kant, *Critique of Pure Reason,* translated by F. Max Müller (London: Macmillan, 1881), 69.

20. Hillman, *The Force of Character,* 184.

that the body itself is incapable of knowledge. Only the brain knows, we are told, and from its pilot house it declares what is knowledge and directs all bodily activity. Perhaps, but that is not how it feels. The great guitarist Mark Knopfler, during a performance in London in 2009, told the audience as he began an improvisation while playing a version of *The Sultans of Swing,* "I don't know what any of this is going to be!"[21] I take Knopfler at his word. All of us know this reality. We drive a car, make coffee, type on a computer, all without conscious thought. Try an experiment—while doing one of those things, well maybe not while driving —try to make conscious every action that goes into what you are doing. You will find that the mind stumbles and the actions become disjointed. When the mind interferes with the body's knowledge, we become clumsy because we are removed from the aesthetic flux and fluidity of imaginal life. So, too, when we try to impose thought onto images through interpretation or meaning we sever the image from its grounding in imagination. This is why interpretations become so flighty and fickle; detached from the image they lose the gravitas that the image provides, the structured feeling of coherence given by the image's constitution and cosmos, the aesthetic order given by myth and revealed by beauty.

My wife is a professor, and one of the courses she teaches is animal behavior. As part of that course, she has her students create an "ethogram," which is "a complete inventory or descriptive catalog of the behavioral motor patterns displayed by a given species." So, for example, for a generic "bird" an ethogram might include behaviors such as wing flapping, pecking, scratching, or probing with the bill. The point of the assignment is to teach observation, and one of the slides she uses for this assignment includes a statement relevant for our work here: "If it seems really hard to be descriptive *without* interpreting the function of the behaviors, then you're doing it right!" To observe without interpretation. It sounds so easy, and yet once again it goes contrary to our usual mental habits.

One of our difficulties with imagination is that we try to place it alongside other mental faculties such as thinking, willing, believing, remem-

---

21. The performance is available online at *https://www.youtube.com/watch?v= leZ4T8kt-1o* (The comment comes at the three-minute mark.)

149

bering, etc. But imagination cannot properly be said to be a mental faculty because imagination precedes and makes possible mental activities. Imagination is never discerned operating on its own, but instead operates *"through, behind, within, upon, below* our faculties."[22] This suggests that imagination might be the ground for all mental activities of whatever sort. Despite this foundational importance, we find it difficult to take imagination seriously. Here, again, the traditions of Western culture impose themselves with the common refrain that imagination is of a lesser order than knowledge arrived at through rational means. And "rational means" must themselves lead to meanings couched in terms of ideas and concepts. So, allow me to enter this lion's den of idea and concept, not to slay the animal but to lie down beside it, adopting some of the conceptualizing style that we find so comforting to look more closely at "image" as used in this book. Perhaps we can find a way to see through the reifying lens of our concepts to a method based on a poetic basis of the mind and an aesthetic basis for nature that allows us to appreciate images more directly; to observe without interpretation.

We can begin by noting the peculiar double meaning of the word "sense," which can refer both to perceiving something concrete, physical, and tangible through our "senses," and to the meaning or significance of something. We can sense the rock as hard and the knife as sharp, and we can also make sense out of an argument or get some sense knocked into us. In our Western tradition, we have seen that "sense" in the first meaning is assumed to connect us to an actual, physical reality that we take to exist apart from our sensations or perception—the purely physical world imagined by Gibson before sentient beings appeared.

It is curious that we feel such a strong need to declare an "objective" world that is received through sensations that are then "decoded" through perceptions. Could it be that the power of this need comes from our unconscious desire to relinquish once and for all our purported ability to create reality within our minds and to then project that reality onto Descartes's dead and cold *res extensa*? Could our desire for a world existing unto itself reflect our longing for an ensouled world that is not of our making, a world that is not dependent upon us to animate it? Could it be

---

22. Hillman, "Image-Sense," 133.

that we want to throw off the claims and chains that we are more akin to God than to the animals? Could it be that we want to climb down from the top rung of nature's ladder to regain our proper place among the other animals and the general arrangement of things? What if we have known all along, in our bones, that the world does not need us, as shown by its radical independence from us? The animals and plants came back to Chernobyl once we left.

In this book I have argued that sensation and perception cannot be separated from one another nor severed from imagination and myth, which from an aesthetic perspective is within, behind, and underneath them as their epistemological and ontological ground and impetus. If so, then when we sense images, we need not make the step of declaring something as real beyond our imagining. Rather we recall that for the Greeks, the word "sense," *aesthesis,* meant both sensation and perception, and so an aesthetic approach to images keeps them both embodied and sensible, what we have been referring to as the inherent intelligibility of the image, while not falling prey to positivistic claims of external reality. This approach does not split the word "sense" into two meanings that are at odds with one another, but rather keeps the two meanings together as inhering and implicating one another. When we sense things, they also make sense.

If we unconsciously seek a more egalitarian relationship with the other animals, perhaps this desire is borne out by the nature of images themselves. As presented within an ecology of imagination, images are equals, no one image having a higher value or significance than any other image. Patricia Berry calls this "the full democracy of the image."[23] This approach is quite different from seeing images as symbols, where certain images can be abstracted out of their ecology and made to stand for other things. Breaking an image up into parts and then looking at some of those parts as symbols elevates some parts above others. A dove becomes the Holy Spirit, or a woman in a flowered dress becomes the Feminine or my blooming sexuality. A symbolic approach to image is

---

23. "An Approach to the Dream," *Spring: An Annual of Archetypal Psychology and Jungian Thought* (1974): 64. Reprinted in Patricia Berry, *Echo's Subtle Body: Contributions to an Archetypal Psychology* (Thompson, Conn.: Spring Publications, 2017).

thus anti-democratic because it relies on biases that declare some images better than other, more worthy of our attention, more deserving of promotion through interpretation.

Symbols are abstractions, they replace precisely qualified presentations with meanings—once we know that the dove represents the Holy Spirit, we no longer need the dove. By contrast, images are autonomous and cannot be captured in a concept. An image, as Hillman has told us, is particularized by a specific context, mood, and scene. Image precision can teach us much about how to appreciate images. An image is complete in itself and its presentation *is* its precision. We must not take precision literally as some kind of collection of high-resolution details. Sometimes images present themselves ambiguously or vaguely, and this, too, is part of their precision. An image presents what is necessary, which implies that what is necessary is presented.[24]

When we sense an image in terms of is sensate sensuality, we at the same time acquire its sense and sensibility. Image and meaning are identical, said Jung, and "as the first takes shape, the latter becomes clear...[an image] portrays its own meaning."[25] We again need to remind ourselves not to hear "meaning" in its common usage. An image does not have a meaning that can be defined or conceptualized. Rather the image's meaning is presented by the precise imaginal syntax of the image itself. Moreover, images cannot be resolved into a single, fixed meanings. Images are polysemous, having many meanings—*polysemous* coming from the Greek "of many senses." And then there is always as aspect of an image that remains beyond meaning, an abiding mystery that deepens with every encounter but is never resolved. That is why we can go back to an image again and again and always find something new amidst the familiar.

Although we lose images when we seek to interpret them, our strong, sometimes irresistible desire to interpret them points to their depth and fecundity. There is always more to see, more to appreciate in even the

---

24. For more on image precision, see Hillman, "An Inquiry into Image," 68–69.

25. *The Collected Works of C. G. Jung,* vol. 8: *Structure & Dynamics of the Psyche,* edited and translated by Gerhard Adler and R. F. C. Hull (Princeton, N. J.: Princeton University Press, 1969), par. 402.

most apparently mundane of images. Images are both evocative and pro-vocative, they call forth and spark emotions, thoughts, and associations. One of the most difficult aspects of appreciation is to not be distracted by or pulled into these detours that lead us away from the image. Instead, the idea is to stick to the image instead of getting side-tracked into what it means or signifies for us. All of those personal and subjective associations will happen anyway and in their own time, but appreciation is best understood as carefully attending to the intra-relatedness of an image, how it adheres, coheres, inheres. Barfield has a nice take on this when he says that people "do not *invent* those mysterious relations between separate external objects, and between objects and feelings or ideas, which it is the function of poetry to reveal. These relations exist independently, not indeed of Thought, but of any individual thinker."[26] I would restate this as the inherent intelligibility of an image that is given with its presentation, a sensibility that is not given *by* our appreciation but that is revealed *to* our appreciation by the revelatory power of beauty and myth as they precisely inhere in a particular image.

By encouraging us to forego personal emotions, thoughts, and associations that images spark in us, I am not suggesting that we should take a cold or disinterested approach to them. Indeed, appreciation of images is not possible without intense interest. It is difficult to imagine beauty without desire, and appreciation of beauty often brings with it strong feelings of attachment. Images draw us to them; they have the opposite effect of abstraction which serves to draw us away from things. But the interest and attachment we feel through appreciation is a function of the power of the image as it engages us and draws us toward it, into it. So, it is not a matter of what the image means to me, but rather of what the image means in itself as given by its presentation. Images teach us how to appreciate them through the manner of their presentation, through the "how" of their presentation in a precise context, mood, and scene.

This latter point is important. Images afford their own means of appreciation. Like myth, every image prefigures the appropriate responses to

---

26. Owen Barfield, *Poetic Diction: A Study Meaning* (London: Faber and Faber, 1928), 86.

the image as correlated with the image's presentation. This suggests that it might be better to speak of appreciations, plural, instead of appreciation because each image will require its own approach, its own method to be derived from its imaginal form. Picasso expressed this idea:

> When I have something to express, I have done it without thinking of the past or of the future. I do not believe I have used radically different elements in the different manners I have used in painting. *If the subjects I have wanted to express have suggested different ways of expression I have never hesitated to adopt them.* I have never made trials or experiments. Whenever I had something to say I have said it in the manner in which I have felt it ought to be said. Different motives inevitably require different methods of expression.[27] (Emphasis added.)

Note that the modes of expression are suggested *by the subjects* and that Picasso accordingly adopts those methods. This is a style of appreciation in keeping with a deep respect for the integrity and volition of the image. The manner of appreciation must be in accord with the manner of the image, like treating like.

If we try to adopt a single method of appreciation regardless of the image, we risk confusing one image with another. Although one could argue that my advocacy for observation without interpretation is a single method, in fact observation is necessarily multiple and pluralistic, as noted by Picasso above. Observing a bird in flight and a rock face are not the same because each requires a manner of observation that matches the particularity of that which is observed. Appreciation as observation takes effort as we refocus and realign our attention with the array of images present within our field of imagination. Think of how quickly we grow tired when we visit new places or stroll through a gallery. I sometimes think this is why we fall back so quickly on symbols when confronted with images; symbols provide the comfort of the known while images by their very nature disrupt our habitual approaches by their insistence that we respect them as individuals.

---

27. "Pablo Picasso: An Interview," in Robert Goldwater and Marco Treves, eds. *Artists on Art from the XIV to the XX Century* (New York: Pantheon Books, 1945), 418.

Other than being confused with symbols and denatured by interpretations, another misconception is to think of an image as a picture.[28] Because we tend to think of images primarily in visual terms, we easily lapse into thinking of images as pictures when images can also present themselves to and through any of the senses, or as ideas or feelings or intuitions, or as that strange hybrid that is the dream (Jung's autobiography is titled *Memories, Dreams, Reflections*).[29] But images do share some characteristics with pictures that can help us learn how to appreciate images as images. First, like a picture, an image is self-contained. An image has borders, so to speak, because it is presented in a specific context, mood, and scene. Like a picture, an image doesn't refer to anything beyond itself, that is, an image is not an image *of* something else. So, for example, a painting of a vase of flowers has its own integrity that does not rely upon or point to some other vase of flowers, even if the painter might have relied on a vase of flowers for the painting. "Images don't stand for anything."[30]

Like pictures, images are complete in themselves. Moreover, like a picture, within its boundaries an image's various characteristics are given simultaneously, that is, an image is not like a story that has a narrative. When looking at a painting, one cannot determine which brush stroke came before another, nor does it matter. So, too, an image is given all at once and is all of a piece. This simultaneity can be readily brought to mind if we think of dreams. When we are dreaming, we are within the dream and are part of its context, mood, and scene. As experienced while dreaming, dreams are multilayered, a-temporal. But when we wake up and try to relate the dream through language, we impose a narrative and temporality that were not given in or by the dream as an image. We can bring this same recognition into the dayworld, where our everyday actions do not feel ordered or story-like when they are happening. Only

---

28. For a full discussion of images and pictures, see James Hillman, "Further Notes on Images," *Spring: An Annual of Archetypal Psychology and Jungian Thought* (1978): 152–62.

29. For images in sound, see Thomas Moore, "Musical Therapy" and Paul Kugler, "Image and Sound: An Archetypal Approach to Language," both in *Spring: An Annual of Archetypal Psychology and Jungian Thought* (1978): 128–35 and 136–51.

30. Hillman, "Further Notes on Images," 172.

later, when reflected upon or recounted to others, do they take on a narrative temporality that is bestowed by hindsight. There is not a "before and after" in images; like a picture, all the elements of an image inhere contemporaneously. "There is no past or future in art," said Picasso.[31]

Like a picture, images hold our attention in stillness. Think of how we stand or sit, often silently, before a painting or a sculpture or a bird. Like a picture, an image requires focus, attending to, careful consideration, so that we might "study every detail lovingly" (Portmann). Even when an image is given in nonvisual form, we often adopt this same stance of quiet attention, the audience hushed as the Maestro raises her baton, the apprentice silently watching the chef's hands as they measure and cut, the connoisseur closing her eyes to better taste the wine.

This muteness occasioned by images we have seen before in our discussion of Hillman's mythical certitude. The muteness that exists in images and in our appreciation of images, is a function of myth. "In Greek the fable was also called *mythos,* myth, whence comes the Latin *mutus,* mute. For speech was born in mute times as mental [or sign] language, which . . . existed before vocal or articulate [language]."[32] Perhaps this is why we find it so difficult to talk about images, because by their very nature they seem to alter "our habitual mind's way of experiencing in language, that is in stories made up of sentences, strung out in time, based on words, letters, literal."[33] And perhaps, too, this is why abstract and conceptual discussions of aesthetics, *and of soul,* seem so singularly unattractive and inappropriate. Only images can respond to images, like treating like, which is why I have been encouraging moves that take us wholly into imagination, where body, sense (both kinds), perception, and meaning are all relocated to the imaginal *anima mundi,* where they are imagined instead of defined, appreciated instead of explained.

The relationship between image and picture, then, is that an image can be like a picture, but it is not a picture. The analogy between image and picture can help us by encouraging us to keep the image's presentational qualities intact. But the analogy falls down because to "see" an

---

31. "Pablo Picasso: An Interview," 418.
32. *The New Science of Giambattista Vico,* par. 401.
33. Hillman, "Further Notes on Images," 161.

image does not necessarily mean that we perceive it visually. "Seeing" as aesthetic appreciation is an imaginative act that crosses and confuses our normal ways of sensing and perceiving. When I say, "I see what you mean," what exactly am I saying? When I "see your bet" and raise you a dollar, what is it I am seeing? Within imagination, our senses become polysemous—I can hear a meadowlark's song or I can hear a call to action, I can taste salt on my tongue or have a taste for the beautiful, I can smell a rose or smell a rat, I can touch a woven mat or be touched by an act of kindness. This constant interplay between bodily sensation and poetic meaning is yet another example of embodied imagination.

We get our word "idea" from the Proto-Indo-European root *weyd-* or *weid-* ("to see"). This metaphorical connection between ideas and seeing is what allows me to "see your point" or "see what you are saying." Ideas, then, are themselves images given by imagination in conceptual style. It is the nature of ideas to think of themselves as existing within the mind, and to carry within them a kind of self-inflation. Thus, for Plato, ideas became Ideas, the capital-I suggesting an idealized world of pre-existing Forms that lay behind and beyond the mere appearances of everyday life. This conceptualizing style is simply the way in which ideas present and imagine themselves. They think they are abstract, separate, non-corporeal, but hidden in the way we talk about ideas is another meaning. Ideas are conceptions, they are conceived like a child is conceived; we talk about the difference between the conception of an idea and its implementation—its gestation and emergence, we "give birth" to ideas. Ideas originate more in the womb of imagination than in the synapses of the brain. Here we return to Sewell's seminal (inseminating) insight, that all thinking is of a piece, science a style of poetry and poetry a style of science. Both flow from the birthing powers of imagination, and both are devoted to "passionate powers of observation, penetration, discrimination, and exactitude."[34] Ideas, then, are just one more way in which the embodied imagination gives voice to myth's inherent intelligibility:

> The mind's relation to its structure or myth is inclusive and reflexive. It is not detached; the working mind is part of the dynamic of the system, and is united, by its forms, with whatever in the universe it

---

34. Sewell, *The Orphic Voice*, 355.

is inquiring into ... The body is an essential part of the method. The method bears a close relation to sex and fertility. Love is a necessary part of its working. Its aim is the discovery of the world, and it is this which gives it all the beauty it has. [35]

By locating imagination in the animal body and the animal body in imagination, we also proclaim that appreciation is an act of embodied imagination. Appreciation is a sensuous involvement with images and not something that can exist "only" in the mind as if the mind can be imagined as somehow detached from the body. Detachment is the antithesis of appreciation. Indeed, appreciation is a communion between two images, both partaking and imparting within a shared imaginal field.

Embodied imagination has led us to say that animals are images and images are animals because that is how animals and images present themselves. They are not mere fungible things but have inherent integrity, nobility, even divinity. This leads us further to refine a phrase I have used repeatedly throughout this book: "the many things of the world." We first revised this phrase by dropping the over-arching "world" so as to move from a general concept to speaking instead of imagistic particulars. This step allowed us to better appreciate the cosmos of each thing. Now we can refine further and replace "things" with "images," because from the perspective of imagination there are no things other than images. Beauty presents images as sensate, sensual, and sensible, and the muteness of myth gives breath to the inherent intelligibility of each image as its cosmos is particularized by its precise context, mood, and scene. In return, we respond by *aisthesis*—appreciating images through our own embodied imaginal senses and perceptions, breathing in their beauty and in so doing coming to know them. We are no longer separated from our fellow animals by God or by rungs on a latter but are re-placed in the general arrangement of images, sharing a common ecology of imagination:

> [I]mages as instincts, perceived instinctually; the image, a subtle animal; the imagination, a great beast, a subtle body, with ourselves inseparably lodged in its belly; imagination an *animal mundi* and an *anima mundi,* both diaphanous and passionate, unerring in its patterns and in all ways necessary, the necessary angel that make brute

35. Ibid., 404–5.

necessity angelic; imagination, a moving heaven of theriomorphic gods in bestial constellations, stirring without external stimulation within our animal sense as it images its life in our world.[36]

In this aesthetic world, gone is the abstracted world of symbols, the doubting of the obvious, and the paranoia that says what we perceive with our animal faith is not real. Gone, too, the constant quest for meaning, as if meaning is to be found elsewhere than where we are, like the idea of nature that excludes our presence. Maybe what that incredibly odd idea is really trying to tell us is that we are *not* needed by the other animals, that they can take care of themselves without our dominion. Maybe it is the autonomy and shared equality of animals as images that can finally release us from the bondage of hubris and the crushing duty to take care of the world as its keeper. The world does not need us! How blessed a thought. But that does not mean that we do not have a place here. An aesthetic life exists to appreciate the images that we inhabit, drawing closer to things, as happens in love, Eros unbound, free to land wherever he pleases. Appreciation leads us to care for the world out of love instead of duty, because "anything that's beautiful, you fall in love with and anything you fall in love with, you want to keep alive...You don't want to destroy what you love."[37]

Imagine moving quietly through the world, attentive to its sights and sounds, its smells, tastes, and textures, always alert for the beauty that might appear at any moment out of nowhere like a bird on the wing. I am not talking misty-eyed idealism but a clear-eyed practicality that *recognizes* the images of the world as they are. Imagine seeing each image as it is instead of as an example of something else. If we attend to the inherent integrity of images (Rilke's "guarding solitude"), we naturally become better worldly partners. Once you see and appreciate the animals you cannot help but see and appreciate where they live. And with that appreciation comes a desire to care for them and their (our) home.

Rodin said that for the artist "the only thing is to see... [with an] eye, grafted on his heart." Such an eye sees by and through images, and in so

---

36. Hillman, "Image-Sense," 143.

37. James Hillman interviewed by Joel Lang, in "The Wisest Man You've Probably Never Heard Of," *The Hartford Courant* (July 18, 2004).

doing "reads deeply into the bosom of nature."[38] This imaginal seeing is the seeing of our animal faith, robust, full-bodied, visceral. Without this manner of seeing, says Rodin, an artist's work remains "flat and without character."[39] An eye grafted on the heart sees the fullness of life, it apprehends and appreciates the character of things, and respects their mythic integrity.

As with art, so with life. An aesthetic life is a well-rounded life full of character and characters. We read the images that are given to us and so come to know the cosmos inherent in the particularity of each individual and how each individual relates to the other members of its ecological household. This knowledge is given to us by and through images. A life of appreciation does not have to search for meaning because, like beauty, meaning is everywhere, given with the images that *are* life. "It seems aesthetics is the *via regia*," says Hillman, "if we would restore our life in images."[40]

---

38. Auguste Rodin, in *Artists on Art,* 325.
39. Ibid.
40. Hillman, "Image-Sense," 143.

EIGHT

Terrible Beauty

Much has been written about the connection between beauty and pleasure. This is in keeping with how we usually imagine beauty, as if it's all about sunsets and pretty faces. But that is not the beauty of this book. For us, beauty has retained its psychological, epistemological, and ontological necessity and importance. Beauty in this book is what makes all things open to sensation and perception through their common embrace by imagination and myth. This means that beauty and aesthetic appreciation cannot be limited to only the pleasurable, and certainly beauty is far more than simply a function of individual taste.

The philosopher Arnold Berleant has written of what he calls "negative aesthetics." He considers beauty to be a force "that is exerted on the body and manifested in sensation," and that aesthetics "is as integral to the [human] organism as its biological features."[1] Given its bodily, biological reality and necessity, aesthetics must extend to the fullest range of human sensual and perceptual experience, including those that are distressing or harmful. "Aesthetic experience," says Berleant, "is not always benign."[2]

We so often imagine beauty as only pleasurable that we fail to recognize that aesthetic appreciation and response exist along a deep continuum. It is a mistake borne of a monotheistic cast of mind to polarize beauty against the ugly, trying to erect yet another useless dualism and dichotomy. Instead, says Berleant, "beauty can be discerned in many of

---

1. Arnold Berleant, "Negative Aesthetics and Everyday Life," *Aesthetic Pathways* 1, no. 2 (June 2011): 75–91. Available online at *https://hcommons.org/deposits/objects/ hc:21262/datastreams/CONTENT/content* (all page citations refer to the online version).
2. Ibid., 4.

the forms of ugliness since these are not opposites but only salient points of a nuanced, non-sequential, and complex range of aesthetic values that includes, for example, the bizarre, erotic, repugnant, and kitsch, along with the pleasant, the beautiful, and the sublime."[3] Moreover, even within this continuum, aesthetic appreciation and response can overlap and intermingle. "A dramatic situation, for example, may be at the same time bizarre, ludicrous, and pathetic."[4]

Artists recognize and make use of how images can impact us on many levels, both positive and negative and everywhere in between. Photographs and other visual depictions of war and catastrophe can both mesmerize and horrify us at the same time. The presentation of everyday items in the context of art (Andy Warhol's soup can) can draw attention to the aesthetic radiance of common objects. And, of course, some art is consciously intended to shock and disturb us. Beauty's power to show us things as they are includes its power to direct our attention to things we might not wish, or prefer, to see.

> Some artists deliberately press against the limits of perceptual and moral comfort. This may, in fact, serve as a social benefit by extending the range of endurable experience, as in scatological art, erotic art, pornographic art, and profanatory art. While deeply troubling to some, such art may perform a social function by accustoming people to face experiences that they consider unmentionable or anathema...[I]t may have value in enlarging our intellectual and physical as well as our emotional capacities. Even though some may find the art painful, it also may expand our capacity for experience and so enlarge our awareness and understanding. Art that is deeply disturbing to moral or religious feelings can, in fact, be artistically strong, as evidenced in work by Courbet and Dali.[5]

Just as art can occasion many forms of appreciation and response, our encounters with nature can also impress us in varying ways at once. I once listened to a lion pride hidden away in the bush as they devoured a prey. The murmurs and growls were interspersed with the sound of

---

3. Ibid., 3.
4. Ibid., 4.
5. Ibid., 6–7.

cracking bone. It was an experience both riveting and distressing that remains vivid in my memory years later. And in our everyday lives we can also experience how aesthetic appreciation and response can take various forms. We can be shocked and angered by an act of injustice, and simultaneously inspired and encouraged to rise up against it. Many a good deed has grown in response to the bad deeds of others.

We have seen that the repression of beauty has negative impacts on individuals, societies, and the larger environment because it leads to neglect and abuse. Berleant sees these negative impacts in varying intensities. The repression of beauty can result in an aesthetic anesthetizing that numbs us to the power of images. We become resistant to the images that we inhabit and so feel increasingly isolated and indifferent (Berleant calls this "aesthetic deprivation"). The longer this continues the more we risk losing our ability to aesthetically appreciate the world, resulting in "aesthetic damage." At its worse, this damage can result in actual "aesthetic harm."[6]

We can all think of experiences and situations that lie all along this spectrum—bland work cubicles with bad, buzzing lighting, the relentless barrage of advertising and 24/7 news accounts, salty processed foods that singe and deaden the tongue, elevator music, etc. Other instances are even worse—environmental pollution, overcrowding of buildings and humans, rapacious deforestation, strip mining, Arctic drilling, trophy hunting—aesthetic atrocities all. And this aesthetic distress extends to the *polis*—systemic racism, misogyny, poverty, lack of educational opportunity, social injustice, and toxic partisanship all offend us on many levels, including the aesthetic. All of these things are affronts to our aesthetic sensibilities, and, as we have seen, they can lead to a wide range of negative aesthetic responses that are revealed in symptoms that affect individuals, societies, and the environment.

The greatest danger comes when we no longer are able to sense these aesthetic affronts. We live at a time when we are most in need of our animal alertness, that direct recognition of danger and peril. And yet at the same time we are perhaps at a low point for these aesthetic responses. The sheer overload of our senses, the dulling of our responses to even the

---

6. Ibid., 9.

most offensive of acts and ideas, the retreat away from complexity and facts to the stupor of tribalism and belief—these all have left us anesthetized to the aesthetic atrocities all around us. We have stopped paying attention, and for an aesthetic animal that can have only one outcome. Purdy offers more wisdom here. Writing of how humans have so dramatically, and in many cases devastatingly, changed the landscape, he suggests that perhaps we could find ways of appreciating them in their altered form. Instead of ignoring them and writing them off in favor of other landscapes we consider pristine, we would instead focus our attention on them. "An aesthetics of damage," says Purdy, "a way of living with harm and not disowning the place that is harmed, might someday become its own version of beauty."[7] But first we must have the courage to reopen our animal hearts to the world as it is, turning down the volume to hear the eternal rustlings that are always there, always calling to us. We are long past the opportunity to "do no harm," and must rely on our aesthetic animal sensibilities to find new was to attend to our ecology of imagination.

Our aesthetic sensibility, our biological capacity to appreciate beauty in all of its various manifestations, lies at the heart of morality and ethics. We rely upon our aesthetic ability to be enraged by "ugly" ideas and repelled by "obnoxious" conduct to establish the parameters of the social order (a variety of cosmos). Indeed, that we apply overtly aesthetic terms like "ugly" and "obnoxious" to ideas and conduct that offend us points to the aesthetic underpinning of moral and ethical judgments. The drive for justice, freedom, equality, decency, kindness, and liberty are aesthetic pursuits, and they depend upon our aesthetic appreciation both to inspire our quest to fulfill them, and to encourage us to reject their oppressive counterparts. So, too, our ability to perceive the inhumanity, greed, and evil in some people is a function of aesthetic appreciation; beauty is showing us precisely who, what, and how they are. If we equate beauty with pleasure alone, then, we weaken the very aesthetic appreciation that we need to identify, and resist, the predators among us.

I cannot shake the feeling that there is something in our efforts to limit beauty to the pleasurable that also aids and abets our repression of

---

7. Purdy, *After Nature*, 245.

beauty. The stories you have read in this book about trying to divorce ourselves from nature, ignoring the obvious capabilities of the other animals, making beauty a utilitarian handmaiden to natural selection, confining soul to human introspection, doubting the inherent intelligibility of images, trying to quell the mystery of an image with the known of a symbol—these are not only repressions *of* beauty, they are defenses *against* beauty. Hillman adds more defenses: "wit and parody, appeal to the mind before the senses, sentimental literalism, sweetness, slickness without complexity, surface without depth."[8] Even within the realm of art, once presumed to be beauty's second home outside of nature, both artists and critics alike since the 1960s have waged war on beauty, leading to what Arthur Danto calls in his *The Abuse of Beauty,* "beauty dethroned."[9]

With so many defenses, what is it exactly that we are defending against? When we are defensive, it can be a legitimate response to a real threat, a raising of fists as the bully approaches. But it also can be an attempt at avoiding something that we don't want to engage or accept (the company I work for is unethical), a criticism that hits too close to home (you need to spend more time with the kids), or a perception of us by another that does not match our perception of ourselves (you're being a jerk). The defenses against beauty that are listed above pertain mainly to common themes of avoidance and a resistance to engaging beauty. But why would we want to avoid beauty, especially if it is so often pleasurable? It is difficult to imagine, even with the latent puritanism that retains such a foothold in the American mind, that we would erect so many defenses against something that is supposed to make us feel good.

I think that there is something about beauty that frightens us. That is why I am suspicious of going too far down the road with beauty and pleasure holding hands and smelling the flowers. I am concerned that limiting beauty to something *that is pleasing to us* is a tactical move of Barfield's "internalization," whereby we shift our focus away from

---

8. Hillman, "Practice of Beauty," 26.
9. Arthur C. Danto, *The Abuse of Beauty: Aesthetics and the Concept of Art* (Chicago: Open Court, 2003), 25.

attending to the greater world beyond the human to asking what that world means to us. It is a subtle but thorough-going and insidious move couched in the rhetoric of the self's quest for domination. By focusing too much on the pleasure that we can receive from beauty we risk getting distracted from the fuller depth of the images before us.

We stand before the *Venus de' Medici* (Uffici Gallery, Florence) and are overwhelmed by its beauty. We walk around it, viewing it from different angles, leaning in to see the details of pressed flesh rendered in marble, or then standing back to admire its power and presence. Rodin saw it this way:

> Is it not marvelous? Confess that you did not expect to discover so much detail. Just look at the numberless undulations of the hollow which unites the body and the thigh...Notice all the voluptuous curvings of the hip...And now, here, the adorable dimples along the loins...It is truly flesh...You would think it molded by caresses! You almost expect, when you touch the body, to find it warm.[10]

That is how an eye grafted on the heart sees. All of this can be immensely pleasurable. But the moment we shift our attention away from the *Venus* to focus instead on our pleasure we lose focus on the *Venus*. This shifting of attention is the avoidance that runs through the defenses against beauty that we listed above. The deeper question is what, or who, are we trying to avoid?

Consider: When we declare ourselves to be separate from nature, it is so we can set ourselves up as being above and having dominion over nature. When we ignore the obvious capabilities of the other animals, it is so we can declare ourselves exceptional and qualitatively and morally superior to them. When we make beauty a utilitarian handmaiden to natural selection, we do so because to say otherwise would contradict theories that we have already declared *must* be true and all-encompassing. When we confine soul to human introspection, we do so to render the world beyond our introspection mere dead matter (*res extensa*) over which we have control but to which we have no moral responsibility.

---

10. Rodin, in Goldwater and Treves, *Artists on Art,* 325.

When we doubt the inherent intelligibility of images, we do so because according to our "subjective" view it is only the human mind that can grant meaning. And when we try to quell the mystery of an image with the known of a symbol, we do so to subsume the image into the categorical pretensions of the rational mind that cannot tolerate the precision of ambiguity or the clarity given by multiple meanings held within the tension of an image. In each instance we are attempting to avoid the powers that be, and specifically we are attempting to avoid beauty's cosmological necessity. Instead of acknowledging that without beauty there would be no sensate and perceptual world whatsoever, we instead seek to emphasize our importance, indeed supremacy, in the general arrangement of things, as if it is we who make the world in our image.

The defenses Hillman names add other layers. A few answer to a common theme. Wit and parody, and slickness without complexity point to the bemused, clever, self-satisfied manner of the elite. According to this view, beauty is of our making, and so we can toy with it, mold it however we please, use our mental gymnastics and linguistic games to throw up such a cloud of obfuscating nonsense (I can think of, but will not use, a better word) that no one will be able to see through our charade to the nakedness of our mortal limitations or the shallowness hidden within our empty rhetoric. We have seen this cocksure attitude again and again in these pages, as with those who profess to believe in the rigors of science but instead simply proclaim their correctness (Watson and his followers) and those who feign open-mindedness but so easily fall into fundamentalism (Wallace and his followers).

The other defenses listed by Hillman we have seen, too. Surface without depth we hear in the claim that beauty is only skin deep, as if what is visible cannot also carry inwardness and mystery, the lie that Portmann has so ably refuted. The appeal to the mind before the senses reasserts the alleged, abstract superiority of veracity over mythical certitude in defiance of the actual lived spontaneity of animal action and behavior. Sentimental literalism and sweetness ply us with conceits and cliches, candies for the mind that romanticize beauty beyond all recognition; beauty a mere plaything, trivialized, stripped of power, dethroned.

If on the one hand we try to defend against beauty by shrinking it to mere pleasure alone, on the other hand we try to curtail its power by holding it in opposition to the concept of the sublime. The sublime is a creation of the eighteenth-century mind on holiday. We find it first in the accounts of three upper-class men—Anthony Ashley-Cooper, Third Earl of Shaftesbury, John Dennis, and Joseph Addison—on their travels through the Alps while on their Grand Tours. Each in his own way sought to differentiate their experience of the extraordinary grandeur and vastness of the Alps, *and the immense fear and terror they evoked,* from the more ordinary, pleasurable responses they associated with beauty. Dennis, for example, wrote that nature had executed the Alps in "Fury" and that unlike the pleasures of "Hills and Valleys, of flowry Meads, and murmuring Streams," the Alps "were mingled with horrours, and sometimes almost with despair."[11] Beauty was one thing, but the sublime was of a completely different order, outstripping all attempts at comprehension or understanding. *The sublime was terrifying,* like falling into an infinite abyss.

Edmund Burke gave the earliest definitive statement of the purported difference between the sublime and the beautiful in his *A Philosophical Enquiry into the Origin of our Ideas of the Sublime and Beautiful.* Although published in 1757, Burke had started working on the book before he was nineteen and held off publishing it for years.[12] In his book, Burke emphasized the importance of fear in the sublime, what he termed "not pleasure, but a sort of delightful horror, a sort of tranquility tinged with terror."[13] According to Burke, "Whatever is fitted in any sort to excite the ideas of pain and danger, that is to say, whatever is in any sort terrible, or is conversant about terrible objects, or operates in a manner analogous to terror, is a source of the *sublime.*"[14] And this fear is not like other fears. Rather the fear that accompanies the sublime is "the strongest emotion which the mind is capable of feeling."[15]

11. *The Critical Works of John Dennis,* edited by Edward Niles Hooker, 2 vols. (Baltimore: The John Hopkins Press, 1945), 2:381.

12. James Prior, *Life of the Right Honourable Edmund Burke,* 5th ed. (London: Henry G. Bohn, 1854), 47.

13. Edmund Burke, *A Philosophical Enquiry into the Origin of our Ideas of the Sublime and Beautiful* (London: Routledge and Kegan Paul, 1958), 136.

14. Ibid., 39.

15. Ibid.

For Burke this distinction was one of kind, not degree, leading him to conclude that beauty and the sublime are mutually exclusive. Beauty belongs strictly to "some quality in bodies, acting mechanically upon the human mind by the intervention of the senses." He goes on to list such qualities:

> On the whole, the qualities of beauty, as they are merely sensible qualities, are the following. First, to be comparatively small. Secondly, to be smooth. Thirdly, to have a variety in the direction of the parts; but fourthly, to have those parts not angular, but melted as it were into each other. Fifthly, to be of a delicate frame, without any remarkable appearance of strength. Sixthly, to have its colours clear and bright; but not very strong and glaring. Seventhly, or if it should have any glaring colours, to have it diversified with others.[16]

Contrast this with the sublime, which for Burke was preeminently an emotional experience of astonishment, awe, and terror:

> The passion caused by the great and sublime in *nature,* when those causes operate most powerfully, is Astonishment; and astonishment is that state of the soul, in which all its motions are suspended, with some degree of horror. In this case, the mind is so entirely filled with its object, that it cannot entertain any other, nor by consequence reason on that object which employs it. Hence arises the great power of the sublime, that far from being produced by them, it anticipates our reasoning, and hurries us by an irresistible force.[17]

He follows shortly thereafter with a quote from *Paradise Lost* of John Milton's description of Death, and concludes that "[i]n this description all is dark, uncertain, confused, terrible, and sublime to the last degree."[18]

Kant took up Burke's distinction and separation of beauty and sublime. He first addressed it in 1764 at age 40, and focused primarily on the differences of feeling in the two:

> The finer feeling that we will now consider is preeminently of two kinds: the feeling of the sublime and of the beautiful. Being touched by either is agreeable, but in very different ways. The sight of a

---

16. Ibid., 117.
17. Ibid., 57.
18. Ibid., 59.

mountain whose snow-covered peaks arise above the clouds, the description of a raging storm, or the depiction of the kingdom of hell by Milton arouses satisfaction, but with dread; by contrast, the prospect of meadows strewn with flowers, of valleys with winding brooks, covered with grazing herds, the description of Elysium, or Homer's depiction of the girdle of Venus also occasion an agreeable sentiment, but one that is joyful and smiling. For the former to make its impression on us in its proper strength, we must have a feeling of the sublime, and in order properly to enjoy the latter we must have a feeling for the beautiful. Lofty oaks and lonely shadows in sacred groves are sublime, flowerbeds, low hedges, and trees trimmed into figures are beautiful. The night is sublime, the day is beautiful. Casts of mind that possess a feeling for the sublime are gradually drawn into lofty sentiments, of friendship, of contempt for the world, of eternity, by the quiet calm of a summer evening, when the flickering light of the stars breaks through the umber shadows of the night and the lonely moon rises into view. The brilliant day inspires busy fervor and a feeling of gaiety. The sublime touches, the beautiful charms. The mien of the human being who finds himself in the full feeling of the sublime is serious, sometimes even rigid and astonished. By contrast, the lively sentiment of the beautiful announces itself through shining cheerfulness in the eyes, through traces of a smile, and often through audible mirth. The sublime is in turn of different sorts. The feeling of it is sometimes accompanied with some dread or even melancholy, in some cases merely with quiet admiration and in yet others with a beauty spread over a sublime prospect. I will call the first the terrifying sublime, the second the noble, and the third the magnificent. Deep solitude is sublime, but in a terrifying way.[19]

Kant returned to the subject twenty-six years later in his *Critique of Judgment,* where he continued to contrast beauty and the sublime. He limited beauty to "charms and with an imagination at play," while "the

---

19. Immanuel Kant, *Observations on the Feeling of the Beautiful and Sublime and Other Writings,* edited by Patrick Frierson and Paul Guyer (Cambridge: Cambridge University Press, 2011), 14-17.

sublime contains not so much a positive pleasure as rather admiration and respect, and so should be called a negative pleasure."[20] For Kant, through "formal order, proportion, and harmony of the beautiful the human subject experiences a pleasurable sense of alignment between the faculties of the mind and the mind's experience of reality, whereas before the turmoil of the sublime—which exceeds sense, measure, and order—the subject is powerfully made aware of its own limitations."[21]

Revising his earlier division of the sublime into three kinds, Kant later settles on two, mathematical and dynamic. In the first, the sheer magnitude of the sublime overwhelms what Kant considered the limited powers of the imagination which seeks help from reason, because it is only through reason that we can have an idea of infinity given in its totality (§26). Thus, "true sublimity must be sought only in the mind of the judging person, not in the natural object the judging of which prompts this mental attunement" (ibid.). In the dynamically sublime, reason once again proves its superiority over nature because through reason we are able to experience nature as frightening without being afraid. "[T]hough the irresistibility of nature's might makes us, considered as natural beings, recognize our physical impotence, it reveals in us at the same time an ability to judge ourselves independent of nature, and reveals in us a superiority over nature that is the basis of a self-preservation quite different in kind from the one that can be assailed and endangered by nature outside us. This keeps the humanity in our person from being degraded, even though a human being would have to succumb to that dominance" (§28). It is worth noting that in his discussion of beauty and sublime that Kant 1) subjugates imagination to reason, 2) declares humans independent from nature, and 3) declares humans superior to nature because of reason. All three ideas serve to repress, and defend against, beauty.[22]

---

20. Immanuel Kant, *Critique of Judgment,* translated by Werner S. Pluhar (Indianapolis and Cambridge: Hackett Publishing Company, 1987), par. 23.

21. Alexander Alberro, "Beauty Knows No Pain," *Art Journal* 63, no. 2 (Summer 2004): 38.

22. For a fascinating, and compelling, analysis of Kant's treatment of imagination in his *Critique of Judgment,* see Mark Johnson, *The Body in the Mind: The Bodily*

This exclusive distinction between beauty and sublime has remained more or less ingrained in Western thinking ever since Burke and Kant. However, within the area of art criticism, a number of writers have tried to defend beauty against its dethroning (Danto) by what they see as an unjustified elevation of the sublime, and have pointed directly to this attempt as seeking "to reduce the characteristics or features of the beautiful to a diminutive status."[23] Here again we see how reducing beauty to mere pleasure, and the associated denigration of imagination as inferior and subservient to reason, are attempts to limit beauty's autonomous power to instill awe, astonishment, and fear. From the elevated and lofty heights of the sublime there can be no such thing as terrible beauty because beauty must necessarily be associated with, and limited to, pleasure. As J. T. Boulton puts it in his introduction to Burke's *Philosophical Enquiry*, "by reserving to sublimity all that is impressive and awe-inspiring, [Burke] robs beauty of any power to be intensely moving, and leaves it a weak and sentimentalized conception. Beauty becomes, in fact, mere prettiness."[24]

There is a glaring overstep present in trying to oppose beauty and the sublime. The sublime became a theme in European letters after the republication of the ancient treatise *On the Sublime* (*Peri hupsous*), falsely attributed to the rhetorician Dionysius Cassius Longinus, which was first translated into English around 1652. The treatise is thought to date from the first century C.E. and presents the idea of the sublime within the context of literary criticism. According to the author, "the Sublime, wherever it occurs, consists in a certain loftiness and excellence of lan-

---

Basis of Meaning, Imagination, and Reason (Chicago: The University of Chicago Press, 1987). Johnson argues that "Kant is grappling with the recognition that imagination plays a far more central role in meaning and rationality than his own restrictive framework will allow" (161), and that although Kant "elaborates a notion of imaginative meaning and understanding *that makes possible* our more abstract and propositional structures" (169; emphasis added),... "ironically, his system forces him to separate [imagination] sharply from reason and understanding" (170).

23. Alberro, "Beauty Knows No Pain," 38, and references cited therein.

24. J. T. Boulton, in Edmund Burke, *A Philosophical Enquiry into the Origin of our Ideas of the Sublime and Beautiful* (London: Routledge and Kegan Paul, 1958), lxxv.

guage" (1.3–4). He enumerates five sources for the sublime, all of which depend on the gift of a "command of language":

> The first and the most important is (1) grandeur of thought... The second is (2) a vigorous and spirited treatment of the passions. These two conditions of sublimity depend mainly on natural endowments, whereas those which follow derive assistance from Art. The third is (3) a certain artifice in the employment of figures, which are of two kinds, figures of thought and figures of speech. The fourth is (4) dignified expression, which is sub-divided into (*a*) the proper choice of words, and (*b*) the use of metaphors and other ornaments of diction. The fifth cause of sublimity, which embraces all those preceding, is (5) majesty and elevation of structure.[25]

Although Longinus remarked upon overwhelming works of nature, he believed that words alone could be instruments of the sublime. The primary meaning of the word *hupsous* is "height," and Longinus repeatedly uses words that suggest vertical movement. And because what is "high" or "elevated" supersedes the normal and usual, for Longinus the sublime brought both the writer and the reader into a religious realm, where the writer was "inspired" and the reader "ecstatic."[26]

Given this association between height and the sublime, it is little wonder that the crags and precipices of the Alps so captured the imaginations of the young men embarked on their Grand Tours in the eighteenth century. Looking back on his *A Philosophical Enquiry,* Burke refused a request to expand on his ideas later in life, saying that he was "no longer fit to pursue speculative matters of that sort" because his older mind was occupied by "other and more active business."[27] Regardless of his state of mind in his earlier writings, the fact remains that Burke's step of declaring beauty and sublime as mutually exclusive is based on a pre-

---

25. Longinus, *On the Sublime,* translated by H.L. Havell (London: Macmillan, 1890), 8.1. Available online at *http://eremita.di.uminho.pt/gutenberg/1/7/9/5/17957/17957-h/17957-h.htm*

26. Casper C. de Jonge, "Dionysius and Longinus on the Sublime: Rhetoric and Religious Language," American Journal of Philology 133, no. 2 (Summer 2012): 276–77.

27. Prior, *Life of the Right Honourable Edmund Burke,* 47.

conceived *presumption* that beauty is limited to pleasure and is incapable of exerting the kind of power that Burke and others associated with the sublime. It is simply assumed that beauty cannot instill awe or feelings of terror, and so those powers are attributed to the concept of the sublime.

By trying first to limit beauty to the pleasures of meadows and streams, and then by denying beauty the power to awe and terrify by contrasting it with the sublime, we further the repression of, and defenses against, beauty and the inherent power of images. Freedberg reviews many accounts given to us by anthropologists of people's fear of being portrayed in images because "they might thereby fall into the possession and control of others."[28] Photography, especially, with its precise depiction of the individual, has been feared lest the photographer be able to devour the person, or gain possession of their soul, or cast spells upon them. And this fear was not only personal. People have also feared that the *anima mundi* can be threatened if its images are taken for bad purposes, "that a picture likewise blighted the landscape."[29] Even today, think how we throw up a blocking hand to the camera's intrusion. We can't help feeling that we exist in those images in a manner that extends beyond representation, that some part of us is taken away from us and put into the image. Think of how we feel violated if someone takes a photograph of us while we are asleep or without our permission. Freedberg writes compellingly of the long and widespread violence against images, the censorship, the defacing and destruction, and the iconoclasm and rejection of images as having inherent power that is such a big part of Western monotheism. All of these attacks on images give lie to claims that images are mere representations. Indeed, this array of defenses and attacks against images makes the point that images are inherently powerful, so much so that some people find images terrifying and intolerable.

It is the inherent power of images that beauty reveals to us so unambiguously. Despite our best efforts to pretend otherwise, we know that images are autonomous and independent, and that they neither depend upon us for their existence and significance nor can they be controlled by our will. The dreams come, a fox appears in the woods, an idea impresses

---

28. Freedberg, *The Power of Images*, 278–79.
29. Ibid.

itself upon us, an aroma takes us back through time to mom's warm, doughy kitchen, a starry night shows us how close infinity can be as we point with outstretched hand to touch and name the constellations (of which forty-two of the eighty-eight are named for animals, twenty-eight for objects, and only fourteen for humans). All of these are manifestations of images as psychic facts that cannot be translated to concepts, abstracted to symbols, or subsumed within the person. The power of images negates the fallacy of Barfield's "internalization" that would claim the powers we feel are mere projections.

The natural, divine order given by each image, its cosmos, belonged to the Greek goddess Themis. It was Themis who called the gods to counsel, and who gave natural divine law, as distinct from the laws made by mortals. Themis is the model for our Lady Justice and was depicted as holding a balance scale. But the blindfold we see on Lady Justice was a later addition and did not belong to Themis, rather Themis was a seer, and according to Aeschylus was the second prophetess at the Oracle of Delphi (the first being her mother, Gaia).[30] Themis represented the divine order which gods and humans alike were expected to follow. The etymology of her name means "that which is put in place," and so it was through Themis that humans learned the laws of justice and morality, rules of hospitality, good governance, how to conduct an assembly, and how to make offerings to the gods. To defy or ignore Themis was a transgression against the gods, an act of cosmic disorderliness, and such transgressions were responded to by Nemesis, another goddess who meted out "revenge for the violation of [Themis's] Order."[31]

This transgression has a name—*Hybris,* from which we get our "hubris." The repression of beauty, and the many defenses we have erected against beauty all point to this transgression. It is hubris that leads us to proclaim dominion over nature, to demean the other animals, to chain beauty to utility, and to deny the *anima mundi.* When we look at a mountain range in the distance and feel its sheer, insurmountable majesty, it is hubris

---

30. "Eumenides," in *Aeschylus,* translated by Herbert Weir Smyth, 2 vols. (London: William Heinemann; New York: G. P. Putnam's Sons, 1926), 2:273.

31. Karl Kerényi, *The Religion of the Greeks and Romans,* translated by Christopher Holme (New York: E. P. Dutton & Co., 1962), 121. Also see his discussion of *Themis,* 116–18, and *Hybris,* 118.

that leads us to think that this feeling must be a result of our projection, as if the mountains are not capable in themselves of being majestic. To think otherwise, we say, is primitive animism or stupid superstition. So, too, myths cannot be real, and poetry is but a pastime. Again and again, we try to lift ourselves up above nature and the other animals, declaring ourselves akin to god, and therein we transgress the cosmic order.

We fear beauty because beauty belongs to gods not to humans. Beauty will never bow down to our minds or succumb to our concepts and explanations. That is why we can never find a suitable definition of beauty, because beauty does not belong to the realm of mortal definition, indeed, even to pretend to define a god is yet another act of hubris. The gods don't need our definitions to be; they are always and everywhere inexorably present. Beauty remains despite our repression and defenses because Aphrodite is always there in all ways, and it cannot be otherwise. Our theories cannot subdue her, nor our insults drive her away. The gods never depart even if through our misconceptions we fail to recognize their presence.

In every instance of our defenses against beauty, we seek to dethrone beauty so that we may ascend to the throne. What beauty reveals to us, what we cannot bear to accept, what we have spent millennia trying to avoid, is that we are not really kings or queens, nor indeed are we akin to god. We defend against beauty because it reminds us of our mortal limitations and insignificance. When confronted with beauty we lose "our"-selves because we are released from the cult of subjectivity and are reunited with the ecology of imagination wherein we are just one image among other, a member of an egalitarian *polis* in which we are neither exceptional nor in charge. Beauty, like nature, does not need us, does not depend on us, and is not beholden to us.

Beauty's divine provenance necessarily confronts us with unfathomable mystery. And so the simple beauty of a fallen leaf will forever outstrip our efforts of understanding. There is no question that we know a great deal, but beauty always reminds us that there is much more that we do not know, things that we cannot know, and things that we do not know that the blackbird does know. Confronted with its inherent limitations, the rational mind is thwarted in its proclaimed dominion over all things and infuriated in its controlling desire for a Unified Theory of Everything, a concept so fantastic in its hubris that it can only be understood as that worst of transgressions—pretending, even worse believing, oneself to be a god.

If through our hubris we seek to rise above the other animals and indeed above everything else, too, then little wonder that the fear of falling is so intrinsic to our fear of beauty. We fall in love, fall into depression, fall off our high horse, fall asleep, fall ill, fall short, fall from grace, fall apart at the seams, fall silent, fall to pieces, fall to the wayside, take the fall, fall flat on our face, fall all over ourselves, fall in with bad company, fall foul of the law, fall prey to bad influences, and fall through the safety net. Things we want to keep track of fall through the cracks and important words fall on deaf ears. And then of course there is *the* Fall, that defining moment of original sin when we fell from blissful, innocent obedience to God to a state of guilty disobedience, a fall that according to Aquinas left us grievously and eternally wounded:

> Therefore in so far as the reason is deprived of its order to the true, there is the wound of ignorance; in so far as the will is deprived of its order of good, there is the wound of malice; in so far as the irascible is deprived of its order to the arduous, there is the wound of weakness; and in so far as the concupiscible is deprived of its order to the delectable, moderated by reason, there is the wound of concupiscence. [32]

Note that, according to the monotheistic cast of mind, reason is associated with the true, will with the good, and that the fall leads to disorder, ignorance, malice, weakness, and lustful desire.

Christian monotheism, high-minded spirituality, and hubristic rationality cannot help but see falling in negative terms, as if the only good place to be is on top (top dog, top brass, top tier, top shelf, top gun, top dollar, top of the world, top management, top of the heap). Traditionally, the mountain top is the place of spiritual inspiration, and "peak" experiences are always "elevating" and lead to moments of "highest" happiness

---

32. Thomas Aquinas, *Summa theologica,* translated by the Fathers of the English Dominican Province (New York: Benziger Brothers, 1947), I-II, q. 85, art. 3. (Available online at https://www.ccel.org/a/aquinas/summa/home.html)

and fulfillment. Peak-experience "seems to lift us to greater than normal heights so that we can see in a higher than usual way."[33] Given this strong preference for being on top, and with the uniform degradation of being anywhere else, it is little wonder that we resist anything that might knock us off our perch at the top of the *scala naturae*. The terrible beauty that Dennis called the sublime was shot through and through with this fear of falling; he wrote of the "Abyss" and the "frightful view of the Precipices."[34] Viewed from the peaks, the valleys and depressions that lay so far below are where, with one wrong slip, one ends up broken and lifeless. In our Western tradition, spirit belongs to the arid peaks and soul belongs to the moist valleys, which is why spiritual practices so often emphasize transcendence and avoid the depressions of the valley. One of the enduring mottos of Hillman's archetypal psychology comes from John Keats in a letter to his brother George where he wrote, "Call the world if you Please 'The vale of Soul-making.' Then you will find the use of the world."[35] Could our fear of falling also bespeak a spiritual fear of soul?[36]

The expressions of various kinds of "falling" listed above are all metaphorical, referring in various manners to a loss of control, status, health, or esteem, among others. Falling is antithetical to the heroic climb to the top, and instead is an act of humbling, soul's antidote to hubris. When confronted with beauty we cannot help but be humbled and fall silent, and the mythical importance of this muteness we have already discussed. Beauty takes us into the abyss of mystery that is given with each image, and it is this unfathomable mystery that the mind on the mountaintop

---

33. Abraham Maslow, *Religions, Values, and Peak-Experiences* (New York: Penguin Books, 1976), 61–62.

34. *The Critical Works of John Dennis,* 381.

35. John Keats in a letter to his brother George, April 28, 1819, in *The Letters of John Keats,* edited by Hyder E. Rollins, 2 vols. (Cambridge, Mass.: Harvard University Press, 1958), 2:102.

36. For an explication of the soul/spirit distinction and its implications, see James Hillman, "Peaks and Vales: The Soul/Spirit Distinction as Basis for the Differences Between Psychotherapy and Spiritual Discipline," in Benjamin Sells, ed., *Working with Images: The Theoretical Basis of Archetypal Psychology,* 2nd rev. ed. (Thompson, Conn.: Spring Publications, 2022). Hillman's essay was originally published in J. Needleman and D. Lewis, eds., *On the Way to Self-Knowledge* (New York: Knopf, 1976).

fears. The promise of the mountaintop is enlightenment, oneness with god, and transcendence. The beauty of images, which is another way of saying the power of images, keeps us in the valleys where images deepen and proliferate, refusing to be reduced to oneness or abstracted out of their place in the ecology of imagination. Images are comfortable with the "dark, uncertain, and confused," precisely the attributes that Burke said instilled the horror of the sublime.

All of this suggests that whenever we attempt to set ourselves apart and above nature and the other animals, we commit the transgression of hubris and so should expect the consequences of our transgression. Pride goeth before the fall, says the Proverb. The answer to our earlier question of what, or who, we are afraid of now becomes clear. The what that we fear is beauty and the indomitable power of images. The who that we fear is Aphrodite. Attempting to ascribe beauty a diminutive status by equating her with pleasure and denying her the power of the sublime draws danger from two quarters. First, as the tale told by Apuleius gives ample account, it is not wise to cast aspersions upon, or deflect the proper respect due to Aphrodite; she is most assertedly not all smiles and grace. Second, by disrespecting Aphrodite, and concomitantly trying to lift ourselves above the proper limitations of our mortal status, we transgress Themis and the divine order. We have pointed repeatedly to the catastrophic effects of repressing of beauty, but now we can identify the causes of these effects—our hubris and the resulting retaliation and revenge of Nemesis. I make this point with utmost seriousness. If the gods are in all things, then when we provoke the very gods that provide beauty and divine order, we risk unraveling the fundamental substrates of our mortal existence. Some have referred to a "tipping point" in the existential threat of anthropogenic climate change, a point where we take one step too far and there is no going back; slip from the precipice and the abyss awaits. That is the Fate of disrespecting and neglecting the gods.

It is important here to keep in mind the nature of polytheism and the proper mode of relating to the pantheon of gods given as images. Walter Burkert helps here:

> Polytheism means that the many gods are worshipped not only at the same place and at the same time, but by the same community and by the same individual; only the totality of the gods constitutes

the divine world. However much a god is intent on his honour, he never disputes the existence of any other god; they are all everlasting ones. There is no jealous god as in the Judeo-Christian faith. *What is fatal is if a god is overlooked.*[37] (Emphasis added.)

To overlook a god, says Burkert, "is to curtail the richness of the world."[38] To neglect Aphrodite, then, is to neglect the beauty that she provides and this in turn disrupts the divine order given with the general arrangement of images as cosmos. Nothing good can come of this.

The way back from the precipice, then, if we have not already toed past the tipping point, is to return to beauty and to respect and appreciate its manifestations in the full range of their powers, be they pleasurable or terrifying. Appreciation of beauty re-minds us, altering the habitual hubris of our mentation. Appreciation teaches us to not overlook the divine beauty that is everywhere given by the gods. By practicing appreciation, we recognize the gods in our practice, we realign ourselves with our proper place in the general arrangement of images, and in so doing we are restored to the richness of the world. If we can only learn to forgo our divine aspirations and remain contentedly among the living and the dead, then we might yet still avoid the mounting wave that approaches (Aphrodite arrived on a wave). But we must be clear. The gods do not care about us, and beauty will make no effort to redeem us. All that beauty can do is bring forth the power of images in all of their sensate, sensual, and sensible forms. The task of properly relating to images, of acknowledging, respecting, and appreciating them, is up to us.

---

37. Walter Burkert, *Greek Religion,* translated by John Raffan (Cambridge, Mass.: Harvard University Press, 1985), 216.
38. Ibid.

NINE

Homo Aestheticus

On an ordinary morning, I awake. Our bedroom is on the second floor so our windows, which are not covered by shades, look out onto trees and sky. My first act upon awakening is to observe both, thereby taking a first measure of the day. I stretch and yawn, rubbing the sleep from my eyes. I usually am awake before my wife, and I take joy in watching her still asleep. Then it's time to get up and get dressed, choosing what to wear today. Then to the bathroom, where I take a look in the mirror to straighten and adjust how I look. After that I go to the kitchen to make coffee, using the proportions of coffee to water that Jill and I prefer. While the coffee makes, roasting the air, I pet and feed our cat, receiving a meow and a purr in return, then take a look at the bird feeders out back, curious as to who the visitors are this morning. Once the coffee is made, I pour a cup, adding just the right amount of milk. No sugar for me. Then I settle on the couch with the cat and take that first sip of coffee—always so satisfyingly bitter. I spend some time with purrs and nuzzles, and then check the news to see what's going on in the world. I usually have about an hour of morning time before Jill gets up, so I make my breakfast, which varies from day to day according to what I have a taste for. Later, Jill comes down to begin her morning ritual. I get my morning hug, and then it is time for work.

That is an ordinary morning, and I ask that you observe it a series of aesthetic moments. Seeing, appraising, loving, choosing, arranging, making, preferring, smelling, petting, observing, tasting, preparing—each an aesthetic act, and each completely and utterly ordinary and mundane. And that is just the first hour; I could recount each and every following hour and the patterns would be similar as I inhabit my ecology of imagination and move through it based on the preferences and inclinations it affords me.

Allow me to go farther and suggest that Calleigh the cat is experiencing a similar series of aesthetic moments. She, too, welcomes me in her own manner according to her daily mood. She appears to enjoy her breakfast and our petting time together, just as each day she picks just the right spot for napping and grooming. There are times for play and times when she would rather be left alone. When she roams the house while Jill and I work she appears to find things of great interest, even if to our human senses they are the same things that were there the day before. She senses things that we don't, and her behavior and movements, so graceful, so sure, so certain, bring much beauty and joy to our shared household.

I have argued, if that is the right word, that aesthetic appreciation is bred in the bones, that aesthetic appreciation does not belong to the ephemeral or the elite but is as practical and down-to-earth as anything can possibly be. It is something that goes on all of the time, whether we are awake or asleep, and whether or not we are ever consciously aware of it going on. The problems that I have identified as repressions of or defenses against beauty are all associated with ideas that work against our nature as aesthetic creatures. The recommendations of Chapter Seven were directed toward restoring our conscious recognition (literally "re-thinking") of ourselves as images within a field of imagination, of vivifying our senses to be aware of the double sense of each image as it presents itself as sensate and sensible, and of establishing a habitual resistance to ideas and methods what would distract us from the beauty that is everywhere.

This is not a call to some kind of romantic-infused blissful reverie. One of the greatest disservices we have done to beauty is to romanticize it and to envision it only as something pretty and pleasurable. That is not the beauty of which I speak. The beauty of this book is given with each image just as it is, no matter how seemingly insignificant or mundane or how majestic or even terrifying. It is a paradox that equating beauty with pleasure or capping beauty's power with the concept of the sublime both serve to anesthetize us to the parade of beauty that appears before us in our everyday lives.

Thomas Moore writes compellingly of the beauty in our everyday lives in his *The Re-Enchantment of Everyday Life*. It is a wonderful book, a kind of handbook for reawakening the aesthetic senses that we have been pursuing in this book. Moore finds opportunities for enchantment every-where—in trees, food, homemaking, politics. His is a gentle but power-ful message, and when writing about our responsibility to the greater world of which we are a part, he arrives at a similar place as Hillman, who urged us to replace duty with a love born out of beauty. Instead of taking "responsibility" as duty or burden, Moore says that enchantment can provide a better motive:

> [W]hen we are charmed by a person or place, we will feel a strong connection, and from that intimacy we may want to be protective or responsible. Furthermore, motives of love lie deeper than those of obligation and are less anxious than those of narcissism—the need to be right and even righteous.
>
> If we felt at home on this earth and loved our home, we would do everything possible to keep it vibrant and healthy, and we would have a basis for human community.[1]

As the many examples that Moore gives make plain, beauty is not an abstraction. Beauty is always embodied, even when we imagine it in abstract or conceptual terms. Because it is embodied, beauty provides an immediate sense of place by focusing our bodily attentions on our ecol-ogy of imagination. Beauty helps to establish our sense of belonging, our sense of home, because it reveals the scale and reach of our imaginal eco-logical niche. We can imagine the vastness of infinite space, or the infini-tesimal smallness of quarks, but neither of those have much relation to the actualities of lived existence. "The stars I think about," said the artist Willem de Kooning, "if I could fly, I could reach in a few old-fashioned days. But the physicists' stars I use as buttons, buttoning up the curtains of emptiness. If I stretch my arms next to the rest of myself and wonder where my fingers are—that is all the space I need as a painter."[2] Beauty contains us by providing proper limitations to our daily lives within the context of our ecology of imagination.

---

1. Thomas Moore, *The Re-Enchantment of Everyday Life* (New York: Harper-Perennial, 1996), 44–45.
2. Willem de Kooning, in Dore Ashton, ed., *Twentieth-Century Artists on Art* (New York: Pantheon Book, 1985), 199.

Although beauty locates and grounds us within our imaginal ecology and the general arrangement of things, it also keeps us a bit off center (eccentric) through its affinity with the divine. As Portmann emphasized, the manifest form always suggests mystery, an inwardness that deepens our aesthetic experience by always lying beyond our grasp. A rock is just a rock, but that "just" should be taken to include the fullness of the rock's animate power, not a denial or minimizing of it. Just as every image is both precisely qualified and unfathomable, so, too, every mundane moment contains a potential epiphany. The distinction of sacred and profane is our distinction, and it is not a particularly useful one. The power of images instead demonstrates that the two go together. All things are full of gods.

By recognizing the power of beauty as always embodied (even the most transcendent claims of "out of body" experiences cannot be made without resort to the body), I want to emphasize a lesson that we learn most clearly from our fellow animals. Beauty cannot be separated from *bios,* from our animal lives and the diversity of our biotic and abiotic surroundings. The occasions of beauty, even if we perceive them as ephemeral or respond to them through rhapsody or ecstasy (the supposed emotions of the sublime), are not themselves ephemeral. Just as beauty is not abstract, so, too, beauty is not transcendent. We encounter beauty as we live within beauty, as aesthetic creatures existing within a vibrant context of other aesthetic creatures, animals we call images and images we call animals. And here we add, too, the many other psychic facts that beauty reveals. Although we might not think of them as alive in the way that animals are alive, the plants, rocks, buildings, oceans, soil—all of the other images that come together to constitute our ecology of imagination—are presented to us as animate, each individual cosmos ensouled in its own manner. *Bios* is revealed through beauty, presented as images to the imagination, and contextualized and made sensible through myth.

This intimate connection between *bios* and beauty lies at the heart of Sewell's project in *The Orphic Voice.* Where I use words such as beauty, image, and imagination, Sewell, the poet, uses poetry or language-as-poetry. Her claim is perhaps more explicit than mine, because she urges "the challenging vision of a biology extended into study of the human

mind, with language and poetry as part of its essential methodology."[3]
Her focus on language naturally leads her to include *logos* with *bios*,
where we have been attending more to the inherent sensibility of *bios*
as presented through images in manners not limited to spoken language.
From my perspective, and I emphasize that this is not a statement of
conflict with Sewell's beautiful and powerful work, image and myth
precede and animate language of whatever sort. Having said that, Sewell
is certainly correct that language-as-poetry is

> the most perfect development of word-language to which is allotted
> the task of empowering as medium and instrument all the middle
> ranges of our thinking, including thinking about living things and
> ourselves. Poetry is one of our most practical inventions, but it is not
> completed and never will be.[4]

The opportunity she suggests is one of critical importance because it is
through the "inclusive mythology" offered by language-as-poetry that
biology might get closest to a methodology that could "match the principle of inclusion inherent in all of [biology's] living and organic and
synthetic subject matter."[5] Here Sewell echoes our earlier assertion that
appreciation has to learn how to proceed from that which it seeks to
appreciate. "For all ways of thinking at their best establish a relationship
between the formal properties of the system of thought being employed
and certain properties in the subject matter."[6]

Because beauty and *bios* go together, beauty can reveal the most mundane of things as exquisite and unique, something that the comparative
nature of language-as-science cannot do. This is why beauty is so often
associated with the arts, where language-as-poetry (and here we must
not be literal and think that "language" applies only to words) comes as
close as mortally possible to presenting an image in its uniqueness. So,
too, the image as presented poetically is at once precise and mysterious,
capable of generating many perspectives but incapable of being held in
any singular perspective. More, because poetry and art at their best help

---

3. Sewell, *The Orphic Voice*, 287.
4. Ibid., 47.
5. Ibid., 44.
6. Ibid.

to extend our perceptual powers, they show us aspects of the world we would otherwise not see. As Herbert Marcuse observed, "The truth of art lies in this: that the world really is as it appears in the work of art."[7] Art is how we show the world to one another. "The artist does not draw what he sees," wrote Edgar Degas, "but what he must make others see."[8]

Sewell's attempt to bring together language-as-science and language-as-poetry in common cause, and thereby to overcome the erroneous belief that as languages they are different in kind rather than degree (I would say they differ in style) mirrors our attempt to see different methodologies and theoretical frameworks as first and foremost imaginative acts. Science, too, is a way by which we show the world to one another. Just as there are many styles associated with all manner of human endeavors, so, too, the many styles of thinking and theorizing belong first to imagination. That some styles of thinking and theorizing attempt to distinguish themselves by denying and rejecting their birthright in imagination is perhaps to be expected, especially with casts of mind that are prone to be precocious in their exclusive mythologies. But perhaps we can still hope for an eventual homecoming and reconciliation that reunites them with their more inclusive kin. The return, after all, is part of the prodigal's story.

If beauty and *bios* go together, then the various biotic and abiotic forms that contribute to the ecology of imagination can all be said to be aesthetic. I maintain that this aesthetic dimension is not incidental or complementary, but rather essential and constitutive. In terms of humans, this suggests that our aesthetic capabilities are given with our biotic constitution, not only *Homo sapiens* but *Homo aestheticus*. Although we have for so long declared "wisdom" as our defining characteristic and have tried to use it to declare our superiority over the rest of earthly creation, I maintain that it is our powers of appreciation that distinguish us, not as superior, but as thoroughly embedded in and dependent upon our ecology of imagination. Where through *sapiens* we would rise above and be separated, through *aestheticus* we remain grounded and at home.

---

7. Herbert Marcuse, *The Aesthetic Dimension: Toward a Critique of Marxist Aesthetics* (Boston: Beacon Press, 1978), xii.

8. Goldwater and Treves, *Artists on Art*, 308.

There is another sense of wisdom that contributes to and gives further expression to our appreciative sensibilities. This is the wisdom of Sophia that originally referred to the skills of a craftsperson, carpenter, sculptor, and seafarer. "Sophia originates in and refers to the aesthetic hands of Daedalus and of Hephaistos, who was of course conjoined with Aphrodite *and so is inherent to her nature.*"[9] (Emphasis added.) The wisdom that is found in the hands is the wisdom that we have said teaches the mind, and so it is the interplay between Sophia and Aphrodite that imbues us with our greatest gifts, the gifts that allow us to appreciate the cosmos and to partake in its crafting. Understood through this divine lens, *sapiens* and *aestheticus,* wisdom and appreciation, remain together in the embodied imagination that is their source.

We will have more to say about the aesthetics of crafting, but first we need to look more closely at the power of appreciation and the implications of *Homo aestheticus.* If the primary human gift to the ecology of imagination is the breadth and depth of our appreciation, then appreciation can give us new ways of imagining the repression of beauty and what might come with the lifting of such repression.

First, appreciation is grounded in respect and love. Both Portmann and Lorenz emphasized that love and respect were necessary for observation, and Rilke posited that the greatest task we can offer to another is to stand guard over their solitude. Please note that these efforts of appreciation are not directed inwardly toward our understanding, but rather are methods of appreciation whereby we gain access to the imaginative depth of our fellow biotic and abiotic inhabitants—they are efforts to engage *with them.* We cannot hope to engage an image in its precise context, mood, and scene without this foundational respect and love for the image's integrity. We might also here remember Themis, and her teachings about how to relate properly with the gods and the general arrangement of things (cosmos) through respect and humility.

Appreciation thereby eviscerates any potential separation between human and cosmos. As one image among other images, bound together within a common ecology, all images exist first and foremost within an aesthetic array of particulars, each sensate, sensual, and sensible in its

---

9. Hillman, *The Thought of the Heart,* 34, and citations therein.

own manner, each affording other images potentialities according to their natures, and each engaging its ecology through appreciation. This relationship via imagination can be distinguished from functional inter-actions. The Gaia Hypothesis, for example, imagines all things as being subsumed within one organic whole. Despite its mythic sounding name, the Gaia Hypothesis belongs more to the myth of hypothesizing all-encompassing theories than it does to the myth of Gaia. It sees things in terms of parts belonging to a whole, and its responses tend to be moralistic in terms of duty and obligation.

Appreciation based in respect and love takes a different approach to relationships. Laura Sewall writes that our tendency is to perceive objects while being insensitive to the relationships between them. As an alternative, she gives an example from Barry Lopez describing an Inuit way of perceiving. Where an object-centered view might say "a male wolf does this," an Inuit might say, "a male wolf, on a mid-summer's day in which the clouds were particularly billowy and white, when the sun was nearly overhead, and when a caribou grazed within a half mile, does this."[10] See how here the relationships are necessary attributes of the wolf and its ecology of imagination. The wolf is not extricated from its context as a separate "thing," but makes sense only within its context. Further, the wolf remains within reach within a context of relatable scale and is not conflated with ideas of all-encompassing wholeness. We discussed this earlier when we looked at how images cohere and are given all at once. This style of relationship is neither functional nor causal, it is aesthetic, the way the brush strokes of a painting or the notes of a song are all mutually dependent upon one another. Another way of saying this is that part of Aphrodite's gift in making the cosmos visible includes a manner of relating with one another and our ecology of imagination that is based in beauty and love.

> When fueled by beauty and sensuality, our relationship with the visible world may move our hearts. As the visible world becomes meaning-ful and vital, we feel it in our bodies. The sensory world thus becomes

---

10. Laura Sewall, "The Skill of Ecological Perception," in Theodore Roszak, Mary E. Gomes, and Allen D. Kanner, eds., *Ecopsychology: Restoring the Earth/Healing the Mind* (New York: Sierra Club Books, 1995), 208.

directly embodied in us; *the relationship is visceral, and subjective experience becomes sensuality.* We fall in love.[11] (Emphasis added.)

The emphasis added is crucial. Appreciation is visceral; it moves our hearts and is carried in the blood. When we appreciate images through an intimate relationship with them, we have no need for bloodless, disembodied subjectivity and regain our sensual place in an embodied, animalized cosmos.

The biologist E. O. Wilson calls the human's deep attachment to other living organisms "biophilia." This love for life, says Wilson, points to an "innate tendency to focus on life and lifelike processes."[12] Elsewhere he describes biophilia as the "innate emotional affiliation of human beings to other living organisms."[13] Wilson is quite right that our fascination and desire to connect with other living organisms is "innate" in that it is given with our nature as *Homo aestheticus.* But I would suggest that this innate love is not limited to living organisms. Home might be where the heart is, but the heart is also where home is. Our sense of place, of being embraced, held, and supported is given to us by the other images of our ecology of imagination both biotic and abiotic. It is not a matter of being alive or not. What matters is that our ecology of imagination is animate, ensouled. That is the source of our emotional *affiliation* with the world, a bond that feels like family because we *are* family, members of an imaginal household that secures our place at the table through love and mutual respect.

Appreciation, then, makes no clear-cut distinction between biotic and abiotic. Although acknowledging that these concepts intend to refer to different kinds of entities as living or non-living, appreciation is more interested in the animate nature of images in all of their various manifestations. In cultures everywhere, rocks and hills and valleys and prairies are both ensouled and ensouling. Appreciation inhabits the *anima mundi,* reading the signs, looking for portents and omens. In

11. Ibid., 209.

12. Edward O. Wilson, *Biophilia* (Cambridge, Mass. and London: Harvard University Press, 1984), 1.

13. Edward O. Wilson, "Biophilia and the Conservation Ethic," in Stephen R. Kellert and Edward O. Wilson, eds., *The Biophilia Hypothesis* (Washington, D.C.: Island Press, 1993), 31.

such a world, what matters is what is there, whether visible or invisible. All the different kinds of sense that we have discussed are brought into play to engage an ensouled cosmos. Rocks speak their own language, their meanings held in their stratifications and fissures, sand tells time as it runs through our fingers, stars constellate in animal forms, clouds show us faces and predict the weather, which also presents a vast range of temperaments. Meanwhile, the ocean whispers to us in a conch shell. This same animated force exists in other "abiotic" forms that we might typically, but wrongly, want to exclude from our definitions of nature as being manufactured or human-made. Skyscrapers can be as majestic as mountains, or they can fail to inspire when defeated by cheap materials and poor design. Human-made parks can transport us with their beauty such that people will even come from places we might consider "real nature" to experience them. Meanwhile, other human-made parks can come across as cold and artificial. You can always tell the latter because the kids decide to play elsewhere, like a cat preferring the cardboard box over the toy that came in it.

This recognition of *anima mundi* answers to White and Purdy's call for a deep need for an animistic and polytheistic connection between human and cosmos. This is a kind of religion without need of belief or proselytizing. When we approach the world through appreciation, we avoid the capital-N gloss that obscures nature's intrinsic diversity and proliferation. Images as cosmos, and the careful attention to the eachness of images within the context of their ecology of imagination bring an animation and aliveness that is directly perceived and deeply felt. "[T]he imaginative world," wrote Wallace Stevens, "is the only real world, after all."[14]

We sometimes forget that for the vast expanse of our evolution as hominids (around four million years) we were utterly natural beings. What we think of as modern humans, *Homo sapiens sapiens,* (and I cannot help but notice that we choose to double-down on *sapiens* when talking

---

14. Wallace Stevens in a letter to L.W. Payne, Jr., March 31, 1928, in *Letters of Wallace Stevens,* selected and edited by Holly Stevens (Berkeley and Los Angeles: University of California Press, 1966), 252.

about ourselves), have only been around for about forty thousand years, and we did not become domesticated to living in towns and villages until about 7500 BCE. And although writing was invented about 4000 BCE, reading and writing did not become culturally significant until the invention of the printing press six hundred years ago.[15]

So, for over three-fourths of the time *Homo sapiens sapiens* have existed, we did so as nomadic hunter-gatherers in small groups of 25 or so. The transmission of shared cultural experiences was oral. During this time the human relationship with nature, if indigenous hunter-gatherer societies within the historic era can be taken as examples, was animistic. Nature was perceived and engaged with as if it was full of spirits, gods, demons, and invisible forces. Other animals, especially, were taken as divine presences. This mythopoetic perspective was evolved from even earlier predecessors, so it seems reasonable to suggest that modern humans retain some semblance of this perspective today. Indeed, given the time needed for evolutionary change, it is extremely unlikely that the last ten thousand years of "Western" civilization has somehow eclipsed the preferences and predilections of our immense prehistory. We were *Homo aestheticus* long before we became *Homo sapiens,* and I maintain that we remain so today.

There are strong and serious strands in modern evolutionary thought that argue our aesthetic sensibilities first evolved during our nomadic,

---

15. I am indebted for this evolutionary sketch to Ellen Dissanayake, *Homo Aestheticus: Where Art Comes from and Why* (New York: The Free Press, 1992), 203. Out of respect for her fine and innovative work, I would like to make clear that the idea of *Homo aestheticus* came to me before I encountered her book. And, while writing this book, I also came across an extraordinary interview with James Hillman where he also uses the term: "James Hillman on Changing the Object of our Desire," *https://www.youtube.com/watch?v=rFaOXO6hLOU&t=1931s*. Hillman likely coined the term in 1989, where he described *Homo aestheticus* as "the human as a sense-enjoying, image-making creature. We are sensate creatures, animals in an ecological field that affords imagistic intelligibility." Hillman, "Back to Beyond," 117. Lastly, Wolfgang Welsch also uses the term in his *Undoing Aesthetics,* translated by Andrew Inkpin (London: Sage Publishing, 1997). We each have our own meanings, but I think what we share is the idea that the human capacity for appreciation is intrinsic to *being* human; appreciation is not incidental but constitutive to human life.

savannah-dwelling, hunter-gather days.[16] That may or may not be the case, but it is certainly true that indigenous cultures around the world have perceived, and still perceive, the biotic and abiotic world as animate. I am suggesting that this manner of perception is constitutive of *Homo aestheticus*. When we appreciate the power of images, we necessarily perceive the world as ensouled because that is how the world presents itself to our imagination. We perceive images as powerful because they are powerful, and it is their imaginative power that affords us the opportunity for appreciation. To deny the psychic facticity of the world is folly and leads to unfortunate consequences:

> Few would deny that the ideals of Western civilization are transgressed more often than they are exemplified, and that the civilization that continues to profess them is in increasingly disturbed and perilous straits. What has gone wrong? It is as if while we were becoming more and more enlightened and "civilized"—distancing ourselves from the exigencies of nature and the superstitions of the tribe—we were also progressively forsaking ancient, elemental, human satisfactions and ways of being...No wonder that life with all its comforts and perpetual novelty seems still somehow phony, bland, and superficial.[17]

Where we run aground is by once again confusing the realms of *verum* and *certum*. We think that to take these ancient ways of being seriously we must take them *literally* as being "true" according to *verum*'s standards. But as we saw earlier, appreciation is not constrained by *verum*'s mythical stance. Appreciation belongs to the realm of beauty, imagination, and myth, and it engages the world as an animalized cosmos alive with portents and signs. Appreciation does not need to make truth claims or declare how things "really are."

Each person will appreciate images differently because each image provides its own perspectives and sensibilities. It is perfectly fine if a particular tree moves me but has no effect on you. Neither the tree nor my

---

16. See, e.g., Denis Dutton, *The Art Instinct: Beauty, Pleasure, and Human Evolution* (Oxford: Oxford University Press, 2009).

17. Dissanayake, *Homo Aestheticus*, 4.

appreciation of the tree needs validation beyond our mutual relationship. This is the nature of intimacy, and it is difficult to imagine a feeling more appropriately called spiritual or religious than intimacy. To intimate something is to communicate about it delicately and indirectly, to be suggestive; to be intimate with something means to bring it close, to breathe it in. It is through intimacy that we become most acutely aware of the borders between us and the other members of our ecology of imagination, and intimacy also teaches us how those borders can suddenly feel porous, intertwined, blurred by love and yet somehow simultaneously strengthened and solidified. Intimacy is what guarding solitude feels like.

As we have seen repeatedly, appreciation is inherently pluralistic. There is never one final, absolute appreciation of anything. Our statements about things, despite their declarative style, are always partial and limited, always open to further perspectives and articulations. Intimacy plays a part here, too, as we return again and again to the closeness that intense interest and desire demands. And every time we return there is more to discover, more to appreciate.

The same respect and love that binds us to our ecology of imagination also relativizes us in our relationship to the other animals. We no longer feel the need to proclaim our superiority or denigrate their abilities. Ethology depends upon imagination, and as we lovingly observe the details of animal forms and behaviors, we cannot help but feel an enduring connection between us and them. We feel in our bodies that the differences between us and them are indeed only a matter of degree, not kind. We can marvel at their extraordinary sensibilities, delight in the joys they so obviously display, and stand in awe of their "their inarticulate wisdom, their unhesitating achievement, and above all their static reality" (Frankfort).

Despite our rational prowess, or indeed perhaps because of that prowess, we seem one step removed from the directness of the worldly embrace that we observe in other animals. It is so hard for us to set aside doubt and fear and uncertainty and simply to do what the world affords us. Their trust in the world intimates a courage that is of a degree greater than ours, at least if by "ours" we mean adult humans. The baby crawling on the floor has that trust, that courage, but somewhere along the line we misplace it. Appreciation is the way to regaining that trust because appreciation restores our animal faith in mythic certainty and the courage that is bred in our bones. Appreciation, as we have said, is visceral, muscular; we feel it in the heat of the blood and the roar of the heart. We are never more alive than when in the thrall of beauty.

There is something empowering about more fully acknowledging our limitations as animals. Humility brings with it a deepened appreciation for the capabilities that we do have. We cannot match the extraordinary range of how other animals perceive the world—the precision of a bat's echolocation, the range of a bird's ultraviolet vision, or the dog's discerning sense of smell. And yet we humans are capable of perceiving beauty across a limitless range of potentials. Even if we might "rationally" know better, we cannot help but to pick up and pocket a smooth river pebble, or stand with uplifted face in a summer rain, or lean close to see *Venus*'s adorable dimples "molded by caresses." We humans find beauty everywhere, in plants, landscapes, snakeskins, and butterflies. We listen to the myriad ways that different leaves talk to us in the wind, or the haunting call of an owl at dusk. We sing and dance and play and tell stories, all for no reason other than the doing, delighting in the beauty of the world even as we know that we perceive only a slice of it. This broad and deep capacity to appreciate the beauty of each image as its own cosmos is what constitutes us as *Homo aestheticus*.

Appreciation's inherent pluralism and its attachment to the eachness of images are also antidotes to fundamentalism. Because appreciation attends to the imaginative polytheism of an ensouled cosmos, it avoids the dichotomies and oppositions that flow from a monotheistic cast of mind. Appreciation easily holds various viewpoints simultaneously and is not subject to the laws of logic because appreciation does not belong to the realm of *verum*. So, we can easily appreciate the proliferation and beauty of animal forms as pertaining to sexual selection while also standing with Portmann that unaddressed phenomena suggest that some animal forms exist simply to exist ("to stand out"). For appreciation, meanings do not have to be exclusive or exclusionary because appreciation embodies what Sewell refers to as an inclusive mythology. A perspective based in beauty, imagination, and myth appreciates scientific theories in terms of the myths they enact and does not fall prey to claims of absolute truth or declarations of how things "really" are.

The gift of appreciation is the primary contribution of *Homo aestheticus* to the greater world, and that appreciation affords the greater world opportunities that it would not otherwise have. Chief among these is love. When you appreciate the beauty in something, you cannot help but be attracted by it. You want to be closer to it so as to discern every detail. The love that arises from such encounters deepens our respect and interest. At the same time, we want to take care of that which we love, to protect and honor it. Appreciation, then, embraces the greater world with a love that adds to its freedom. Because *Homo aestheticus stands* guard over the solitude of that which it loves, those things can more fully express their beauty and, as Portmann would put it, their self-presentation. We need only think about how we feel when we are loved to understand this empowerment. We become more fully realized when we are loved, more truly who and what we are. And with this deepening we become more beautiful. Think of the radiance of the bride and groom on their wedding day, how beautiful they are.

Beauty, then, is not in the eye of the beholder but can be encouraged and deepened by the eye of the beholder. Beauty exists unto itself, but it also thrives when it is appreciated. There are stories about sculptors saying that a statue already exists within the stone and that the art of sculpting is to release the form hidden within. Indigenous peoples often believed that fire lay latent in wood, waiting to be ignited. These imaginings are similar to how love interacts with soul. In the Apuleius tale, it is Cupid's love that allows Psyche to reach her fullest form as an immortal, and in her fulfillment she became even more beautiful, divinely so. Appreciation thus holds together the divine trinity of beauty, love, and soul. All are dependent upon one another, require one another, and are incomplete without one another.

We have alluded throughout this book to some of the consequences of the repression of beauty. In both human and environmental terms, the repression of beauty results in disorders of love and soul. In the human realm, some examples are the desperate quest for personal identity, the extreme and toxic polarization of partisan politics, the cruel terror of bigotry, and the grotesque disparity between the haves and have nots. The environmental consequences are painful even to consider, from anthropogenic climate change, to the loss of biodiversity, to the rapacious abuse of natural resources. All of these can only occur when love and soul are disordered. When beauty is repressed, the general arrangement given by cosmos falters and the natural order tips. What was of a piece becomes fractured, scattered, splintered, and broken. The too common human malaise of feeling disoriented, anxious, depressed, and isolated stems directly from the abuse of beauty and the concomitant disorder of love and soul. So, too, the neglect and exploitation of the environment, the sheer ugliness of it, denotes the absence of beauty's ordering powers. It is no accident that in the vast literature about aesthetics and beauty that reference is so often made to harmony, composition, proportion, and symmetry. While these are often posited as formal components of beauty, a better way of imagining these terms is that they point to the cosmological ordering power that resides in beauty.

The cosmological function of beauty as bestowing order can also be imagined in terms of mathematics. There is much beauty in the clarity and precision of mathematical forms. Sewell suggests that the "formalism and rigorous necessity of mathematics make it more...akin to those formalizing tendencies of matter and body."[18] In other words, mathematical forms correspond and are correlated with the "natural" ordering that is inherent in matter.

> If a system of necessary form is something we share with matter, logic or mathematical process may be thought of as an inherent characteristic of matter itself in its own progress toward form. If mathematical activity is a development and prolongation by the human mind of those activities by which matter, animate and inanimate, operates on itself, this might explain why the results of mathematical thinking can be referred back to matter with such signal success. The extent of the correlation between mathematics and physical reality...might be not an astonishing correspondence of apparent opposites but the *family agreement* of two terms of a similar progression. Mathematics may be the evidence not of man's emancipation from the material world but of his absolute solidarity with it.[19] (Emphasis added.)

Here again, Sewell shows us how all thought, even that considered abstract and purely conceptual, remains embodied. The beauty of math-

---

18. Sewell, *The Orphic Voice,* 36.
19. Ibid.

ematics mirrors the sensate beauty of the embodied image and the sensual ordering given by cosmos that is made inherently sensible by myth. Mathematics reveals the family relationship that exists within the imaginal household of an ecology of imagination.

To summarize, the primary gift of *Homo Aestheticus* is appreciation. Through appreciation, humans create opportunities within their ecology of imagination that expand and deepen the aesthetic potential for other members of the imaginal household. By increasing beauty, appreciation also increases love and soul, and with this increase comes a fuller sense of cosmos and the general arrangement of images given by beauty and myth. Mathematics might be one way this order is imagined, but the style of order that is inherent in cosmos is aesthetic order, the order given by the manifest forms and behaviors of embodied images within the context of their imaginal ecology. The gods were hardly a peaceful, well-mannered bunch, but they nonetheless presented themselves in terms of Themis' divine order. As mere mortals, we must always remember that their ways are not always apparent to us, and so we must resist attempts to "lay down the law" about how things are supposed to be. Reducing "order" to uniformity or rote obedience misses the point of aesthetic order that results simply in each image presenting itself as itself.

Although appreciation is our primary gift to the general arrangement of things, we have also been blessed with the powers of creation—not only *aestheticus* but *artifex*. The root meaning of *artifex* is the skill of a craftsperson and can apply to all manner of making and creating. It can certainly be extended to the arts in all their various forms, but its root meaning is where it remains most closely attached to appreciation in the manner that we have been speaking. All kinds of human creativity, even those we tend to think of as intellectual or abstract, are embodied acts. The skill of craft lies in the body, and in many instances is located in the hands. The prominence of the hands also implicates the importance of maintenance ("to hold by the hand"). If we imagine the loving care that a craftsperson devotes to his or her tools and the emotional attachment that they have to their tools, we start to get a feel for the deeper connections between making and maintaining. (As a boy, Picasso carried a paint brush around in his pocket.) Both are deeply participatory experiences, and both require a simultaneity of appreciation and action. We mentioned earlier how a mechanic must appreciate and respond to the materials at hand, knowing when to press and when to stop according to an intuitive physicality learned by repeated encounters and experiments. As bodily actions, making and maintaining are also erotic actions. By this I mean that while some kinds of making and maintenance can be done in a cold and detached manner, others are carried out with passion and love. We can approach maintenance as a moral obligation or a chore and turn it into a duty or a burden. But when we love the things we maintain, the attention we give to them comes not only willingly but with great pleasure. We take care of them because we appreciate them and want to spend time with them. By tending to them lovingly we help them to be more fully what they are and in return we receive the pleasures of service and appreciation.

It is our aesthetic animal sensibilities that sustain and drive us to create, adorn, ornament, make, and maintain. The skills found in the hands of a painter or mechanic, the body of a dancer or a sailor, the ear of a musician or therapist, or the taste of a chef or curator are all part of our animal natures and all depend on our aesthetic animal powers of appreciation. Just as being loved allows us to become more fully who and what we are, so, too, by appreciating and loving the world we find ways to make it more beautiful. Part of our natures as *Homo aestheticus* is not only to be part of the world but also to alter the world through our talents, skills, and creations. We simply cannot help but be cosmetic creatures, constantly finding ways to more beautifully delineate, color, and blush the face of things.

With these ideas in mind let's reconsider how we started this chapter. My morning routine includes appreciation, making, and maintenance, and often they are happening all at once. Feeding the cat, making coffee, and making breakfast, for example, provide opportunities for all three. I take great pleasure in cooking and have spent a lot of time learning how to cook. I especially delight in the techniques of cooking, the hands-on part. Fresh ingredients are often beautiful in a variety of ways. The tools of the trade—good knives and cookware—bring joy every time they are touched and handled. The balance of my favorite knife or the minimalist, utilitarian lines and weight of a plain saucepan are sources of constant pleasure. The steeling of a blade before use or the preheating of a pan are part of the rituals of cooking. Knowing when the butter is ready for the eggs, how to beat the eggs and season them, how to stir them, and when to take them off the heat so they finish to the desired texture and consistency are all part of an aesthetic whole that combines appreciation, making, and maintenance.

Another example from later in the day. Again, it is food. Grocery shopping for me is a direct and powerful encounter with *anima mundi* embedded in the most mundane of daily routines. When I pick ingredients for our meals, I always have this notion that there are particular things that I am meant to pick. I am unwilling to just grab any old potato. In the pile there are potatoes that are the right potatoes, the ones that want to go home with me. And so I look, touch, and feel until I settle on the ones that call out to be selected. By the time I get to the checkout line I don't have a basket of fungible items; I have the makings of a homemade meal based on mutual desire, hand-picked with attention and care because the ingredients deserve it and so does the meal to come. It is only fitting that we say thanks when we sit down to table. Where we go astray is failing to see that it the food that blesses us.

These might seem like trite examples, and they are somewhat intended as such. What I am suggesting is that every aspect of daily life provides opportunities for both *aestheticus* and *artifex,* for appreciation and skillful attention and crafting. Folding clothes, tending the garden, washing the car, writing a book, singing a song—the potential to appreciate and increase beauty is everywhere. But please keep in mind that the reason for striving to do all of these things well, the reason for appreciating and attending to them, is because *they* deserve it. Although it is certainly true that doing something well brings us pleasure and satisfaction, we should take that pleasure as something given to us as a gift. If all things are full of gods, then approaching and treating all things with care and respect is a matter of aesthetic propriety, a constant remembering and honoring of the divine that exists within all things.

Rilke insisted that beauty is everywhere. If so, then we can find opportunities for appreciation everywhere. So, too, we can contribute to the increase of beauty through our skillful makings and respectful maintenance. Whether it is through the caring and careful doing of everyday acts, or through the more sophisticated (in the sense of Sophia) talents and skills of the craftsperson, artisan, and artist, we can add beauty to an already beautiful world. Humans everywhere cannot help but decorate, ornament, embellish, and enhance. It is as if we want to share the beauty that we find and appreciate with others, and, to the extent that our proclivities, talents, and skills allow, to give expression to the beauty that is given to us as individuals—a painter paints, a writer writes, a carpenter builds. Indeed, as *Homo aestheticus* this is what we are in the world for, it is our role in the household to appreciate, make, and maintain, a role that arises from love, not obligation, and that is carried out not as duty but as devotion.

TEN

Return to Beauty

Ellen Dissanayake, in her book *Homo Aestheticus,* argues that the human penchant for craft and art, what she calls "making special," is an intrinsic behavior of hominids that has evolved over the past four million years. In keeping with the prevailing evolutionary perspective, she posits that, because humans everywhere engage in artistic pursuits, "these must serve some purpose, even if it is not immediately evident."[1] She spends the rest of the book trying to tease out what such purposes might be.

While Dissanayake focuses her attention on the making of art, I have tried to focus our attention on the human gift of aesthetic appreciation, especially of beauty as it appears in nature and everyday life. Just as Dissanayake asserts that making special is intrinsic to humans, I have asserted that aesthetic appreciation is intrinsic to humans and that beauty, imagination, and myth are part and parcel of an aesthetic basis for human life. Unlike Dissanayake, however, I feel no need to find a utilitarian purpose for our aesthetic gifts. This does not mean that there might not be such a purpose, but I prefer to leave open the possibility that beauty can exist simply to exist and that the proliferation and diversity of manifest forms throughout nature might suggest a parallel or even precedential force at play, and that force is beauty. I maintain that before survival or reproduction there is first and always beauty, that things first appear as images within an ecology of imagination, that things are made visible and perceptible through Aphrodite's smile, and that *this aesthetic presentation precedes and perhaps sustains evolutionary processes.*

We have seen that one of the ways we have attempted to repress beauty is by trying to ignore or deny the embodied imagination. It is remarkable,

---

1. Dissanayake, *Homo Aestheticus,* 44.

and troubling, that the idea that non-human animals, and to a degree even human animals, were mere automata held sway for so long. We face a similar fundamentalism today in a crushing ideology that tries to turn all manifest forms and behaviors to utilitarian ends. But let's resist here, and demand an answer as to why animals, including humans, are *not* all automata? Surely that would be the most parsimonious outcome— all animals mere brutes acting on instinct, each thoroughly predictable in its own way, each enduring solely for the sake of endurance, each mating without desire, reproducing only as an endless means in itself. Simple, tidy, boring. What need for beauty, play, or love in a world of robotic simplicity?

And yet that is not how things are. Instead, there is the incredible diversity of the world that presents itself to us in seemingly endless variety. Evolution itself contributes to this proliferation of forms by constantly putting forth new manifestations of life as if driven by some deep need for aesthetic expression. Our own powers of appreciation are similarly diverse in their preferences and inclinations, each of us being called by some things and not others, each of us finding our unique place in the ecology of imagination through love and the burning desire not for anything and anyone, but for particular things and companions that capture our heart and soul. And then there are the sparks of imagination that seem to imbue all humanity with an irrepressible desire to create, whether it be crafting tools, building a village, or making art. Beauty abounds, shining in the sheer presence of the myriad images that we inhabit, that we are.

There is a seeming paradox, however, in what I have been saying. On the one hand, I have said that the repression of beauty is one of the most catastrophic and enduring of human errors, a potentially irredeemable act of hubris. On the other hand, I have maintained that beauty remains everywhere, and that as humans we are constituted by our aesthetic gifts. How can both claims be true?

The resolution of this seeming paradox is revealed in our symptoms, both personal and environmental (and we have already pointed out that they are inseparable). The repression of beauty ultimately results from bad ideas and the elevation of belief over our direct, tacit engagement with the many images that constitute our ecology of imagination. We have seen throughout this book the devastating impact of monotheism and its progeny – fundamentalism, dualism, zealotry, and the positing of antagonistic opposites and dichotomies. Claims of human superiority and exceptionalism seem to be necessarily correlated with such views, along with the concomitant claim that the rest of the world belongs to us and is under our dominion. The psychological symptoms that affect both humans and the greater world arise from bad and ugly ideas, ideas that divorce us from our proper place in the general arrangement of things, that displace us from the cosmos, that lock us out from the warm embrace of our household. It is not we who need therapy, it is our ideas.

Despite ideas that repress or defend against beauty, our embodied imagination is constantly and fully engaged with and by beauty. *It is the dissonance between our malformed ideas that repress beauty and our lived reality as beings fully immersed in beauty that is the source of our discontents.* As we have seen, some areas of biology and psychology have begun to push back on these ideas. Rejecting the separation between humans and nature, restoring the inherent multiplicity to nature in all of its particularity, renewed respect and appreciation for our fellow animals, resisting single-minded evolutionary theories that insist beauty must be either utilitarian or inconsequential, the resurgence of animistic and polytheistic imagination, recognizing that biology requires beauty, imagination, and myth (Sewell would say poetry) as part of its methodology, and embracing an aesthetic basis of mind are all steps in the right direction. But there is vastly more to be done.

I began this book by saying that "We exist to appreciate beauty, to create beauty, and to be beautiful. That is all the world asks of us. Nothing more is required." We have now had an opportunity to see the far-ranging ramifications of this simple premise. The premise is easy to say, but it is extraordinarily difficult to implement. Breaking habits is hard and breaking bad habits especially so. We all live in a world permeated with traditions that isolate us from our proper places within our respective ecologies of imagination. These traditions constitute our reality, but they are in fact illusions. We are aesthetic animals who have forsaken beauty. We must return to beauty, but the road back is long.

Like all major transformations, the return to beauty requires a breakdown. We must free ourselves from the ideas that bind us if we are to dissipate our anesthetized stupor and fully grasp the life-sustaining power of appreciation. Gone the monotheistic cast of mind and its paternalistic promises of superiority and control. Gone fundamentalism and its false and fragile promises of truth and security. Gone the hubris that we stand alongside the gods and apart from the animals. But, as with every breakdown, there is an interim period where we feel unsupported because the old ideas upon which we used to rely are gone. And the more certain and sure we were of those old ideas, the more difficult this interim period becomes.

The repression of beauty is so thoroughgoing that the return to beauty can occasion an existential fear within the monotheistic cast of mind. It is so fundamentally wed to the idea that we are separate from and superior to the other things of the world that the very thought that it could be mistaken brings about virulent, even violent, resistance. When a life is constructed upon belief, and that belief is challenged, it feels like life itself is at stake. The exclusive mythology of this style of monotheism is very difficult to let go because it feels so safe and satisfying. It has answers, or at least the promise of answers. It claims to know how things are, what is true, what is real. It has standards that, if not agreed upon, are at least uniformly imposed. It is King because it has declared itself King, and as subjects we are expected to be obedient if we are to receive the promises of protection and stability.

When this exclusive mythology is internalized and adopted by the individual, we become an isolated self that is separate and unknowable to other individuals. This "exclusive" mythology has two connotations, one as excluding other perspectives, and two as being "exclusive" as in special, elevated, and qualitatively distinct and better. And so, an exclusive mythology makes us feel like we have answers, that we know what is true and real, and that we are necessarily better than those who might think differently. Exclusive mythology cannot help but posit a world of us versus them. Moreover, under an exclusive mythology, individual life is understood as constricted by rules, regulations, and moral imperatives. Independence, which we proclaim an inalienable right, is imagined to mean standing alone and apart, each person an island.

Viewed from within its bubble, the alternatives to this exclusive mythology are automatically cast in terms of inevitable opposites. If there are no sure answer then there must be confusion, if there is no absolute truth then there must be relativism, if there is no reality then there must be illusion, if there are no uniform standards then there must be chaos, if there is no protection then there must be danger, and if there is no agreed upon order then there must anarchy. Faced with such (false) alternatives, and unable to see other alternatives because of the blindness we have made for ourselves, we dig in and harden our defenses. Perspectives that challenge our exclusive mythology are necessarily seen as enemies that challenge our "traditional" values and our "accepted" ways of life, where both "tradition" and "accepted" are just further tools used by our exclusive mythology to protect our borders and keep our walls intact. Locked behind the gates, it becomes us against them, insiders and outsiders, tribe against tribe.

The breakdown of this exclusive mythology occurs when we finally recognize that the King is mortal, not divine, that his proscriptions cannot hold, and that his promises cannot be fulfilled. Then the center collapses and we fall into the abyss. At first, and sometimes for a very long time, all of our fears feel realized. All of things that we believed and held as true and real have fallen away, we feel dazed and confused, and uncertain of how to move or where to go. Without the set standards provided by the King we feel chaos and disruption. Without the King's protection we feel vulnerable and weak. And then, slowly, the fear turns into anger against the King, not because of what he promised but because he wasn't able to keep his promises. With nothing to hold on to, bitterness and cynicism become our crutches.

There comes a point during any breakdown when the future is uncertain. Sometimes people stay on crutches for a long time. But in the case of this particular King, there is a welcoming alternative. Appreciation's inclusive mythology offers a different kind of stability through the inherent sensibility of myth. Because images are presented in a precise context, mood, and scene, they naturally cohere and hold together, not because of some outside hand that contains them but because they *are* contained, each image a cosmos of internal relations and cohesions, at once sensate, sensual, and sensible. Mythic certitude embraces each of us and provides us our particular, embodied place, revealing the world as trustworthy, supportive, and accommodating. And as we begin to regain our footing, we find that the ground is solid. No longer having a need for a center, we can come to delight in the eccentricity that is our individual characters. Instead of fretting about how to move or where to go we find ourselves already underway. As our senses rebound, we begin to look around and explore our surroundings. We find that there are others like us here, a community of kindred spirits inhabiting a household where all are required and welcomed. Although we have learned through our break-down that there are things worth fearing, we nonetheless begin to feel secure in our new home. And as we become more trusting we begin to see more and more beauty. It is everywhere, it seems, just as Rilke said.

Soon, the other members of this newly constituted household begin to reach out to us, seeking our talents and skills. We become needed, appre-ciated, and our wings begin to grow. We no longer need the King to tell us who or what we are and have no need for a tribe or a pledge of allegiance. We simply are as we are, and as we grow more beautiful from being nur-tured by the love of others, we become stronger and more content. As others guard our solitude, we become more and more ourselves and more and more willing and capable to guard the solitude of others, love beget-ting love. Courage resides in the heart, and so as the heart is strength-ened by love we become more courageous, more comfortable within the mystery and unknown that is most of things. Fear remains, as it should because there are things worthy of fear, but with our newfound courage we are more willing and able to look critically at the things that we once took as gospel. We realize that the things we thought we couldn't live without are now gone and yet here we remain. The inclusive mythology of appreciation helps us to see and appreciate the world anew, including the exclusive mythology that we once so thoroughly believed. This last point is important – an inclusive mythology includes an appreciation for the exclusive mythology and its considerable talents and attributes. Because appreciation does not need belief, there is no need to fall into the traps of dilemmas and oppositions, and so there is no need to ostracize or reject what an exclusive mythology has to offer. When we return to beauty there is a place for everyone, the only difference is that we refuse to elevate anyone to King.

An inclusive mythology is a different animal from an exclusive mythology. The latter makes us feel constrained within borders and necessarily at odds with "others." The former acknowledges the limitations or our particular ecology of imagination, but also appreciates that it exists within a broader environment of other ecologies with whom we are not necessarily at odds. Habitats flow one into the other, support one another, and require one another. Instead of "outsiders," an inclusive mythology sees the potential of neighbors and friends. As individuals we no longer feel the need to have absolute answers, to posit verifiable truths, or to declare things as they really are. There is a natural flux to life, like floating on the sea; things change, and we learn to ebb and flow with the tides, to ride the currents, and surf the waves. That others have perspectives different from ours is accepted as commonplace and not necessarily threatening. Instead of other viewpoints having to be wrong they can be entertained as possible new avenues for our own perspectives. Instead of hard and fast rules and regulations, and the shaming pressures of moral imperatives, appreciation teaches us to respond to each thing in a manner appropriate to its nature. Independence no longer sets us apart but reminds us that our freedom comes from being "in" dependence, held, supported, and encouraged by the greater world.

In addition to individuals, society, too, can be restored to its ecology of imagination through appreciation and the return to beauty. Aristotle posited that humans are by nature political animals, and that we necessarily come together into groups because we have an impulse to enter into partnerships with others. The social order is yet another example of cosmos, and the polis benefits when it is motivated by and structured according to beauty. Imagine if policy debates and election contests were based on aesthetic concerns. Social injustice, inequality, and toxic partisanship would be rejected as ugly and disorderly. Instead, we would recognize that beauty is a civic necessity and strive for policies and politics that encourage fairness (one sense of which means pleasing or charming) and respectful civic engagement among equals. We would develop cities and towns that favored aesthetic concerns with inviting public spaces and pleasing architecture that called people to gather and interact. And we would recognize that poverty, lack of educational opportunities, and the crime that too often results from them are affronts not only to society's well-being but also to our aesthetic sensibilities. If we appreciated our fellow citizens and did our best to guard their solitude, we would guarantee their economic and educational needs so that they might more fully realize their gifts and characters and thereby increase their beauty and that of the *polis*.

Guided by beauty, economics would lose its predatory and selfish connotations. Instead, we would recognize that economics and ecology share common roots with *oikos,* our "eco," at their heart. Economics combines *oikos* and *nomos,* home and management, and so an economics ordered by beauty and seen within the context of an ecology of imagination refers to household management. A properly managed household takes care of all of its inhabitants, visible and otherwise. It is frugal and careful with its resources. Once reconnected to the household of ecology, economics would be naturally sensitive to protecting habitats and the broader environment. It would be bad economic policy to place profit over preservation and protection because to do otherwise would be hubristic and disrespectful. Instead, economics would save one of its favorite terms— appreciation—by restoring its aesthetic meanings. Increased value would mean not only monetary increase but also an increase in that which matters to us, what we care for, esteem, and treasure. So, too, the many other words already embedded in our economic thinking—bond, yield, safe, credit, duty, interest, share, debt—would regain their natural connections to love, attention, caring, and gratitude.

When we consciously embrace our role as *Homo aestheticus,* it cannot help but dramatically affect the greater world. We become acutely aware of the devastating consequences of our prior hubris. Because we appreciate the world, we come to love the world. And when we love the world, we want to protect it, respect it, take care of it. Not so we can get something in return, but because the world is an ensouled place that deserves love, respect, and care. It sounds exaggerated to say, but if humans actually appreciated the world there would be no anthropogenic climate change, scarcity of water, pollution, or rapacious deforestation because it would be unthinkable to do such things. We would no longer want cheap, disposable items because we would no longer think of ourselves primarily as "consumers." Appreciation teaches us the value of manufactured goods in the old meaning of "hand-made," and so we would desire objects of beauty and quality, objects that last and to which we can become attached through time.

If this view of relating to the world in terms of appreciation, love, and respect sounds unduly romantic or pollyannish, that is because we refuse to give up our crutches. What I am saying could not possibly be more practical and doable. It refers not to a utopia (literally "no place") but to a thorough grounding in an ecology of imagination where we fulfill our household roles with grace and pleasure. It is our current ways of relating to the world as foreign and hostile that are fantastic, incredible, and catastrophically hubristic.

When we return to beauty, we see that we are included in the nature of things. Nature is not somewhere else but right here, within reach of outstretched arms. The bird's nest, the beaver's lodge, and my home are different in degree, not kind. My footprints belong in the sand as much as the sandpiper's, the sky outside my window is the same sky that caps the mountain range, the water from my tap is linked to the falling rain and melting snow, and the salt in my body connects me to the vast sea that lies bluing beyond the pines. I am in nature because nature is in me, the planets within, just as the old stories used to say. By returning to beauty, we regain appreciation for the nature in all things, thereby restoring the natural wonder available to us through the acts of our own creation—architecture, urban design, traffic patterns, roads, bridges—all aesthetic constructs as natural as the trees and rocks that grace the landscape.

The return to beauty also places us alongside our fellow animals. We once again recognize their divine spirituality, their ineffable grace, and their intrinsic nobility. We might name them, but we do not own them, and they have no need for anthropomorphism to bestow their memories, dreams, and reflections. They teach us how to be who and what we are by showing us through their presence and behavior who and what they are. There is no subterfuge with animals, they are as they appear to be and therein lies their extraordinary beauty. By learning to appreciate them, the other animals refine our observations, teaching us to adapt our methods and understanding to them, showing us how to relate on terms other than our own. In so doing, the other animals deepen our connection with our own ecology of imagination. The blackbird is involved in what I know, but I, too, am involved in what the blackbird knows because we are kindred beings, sharing a world where there are many ways to fly.

By learning to appreciate and respect the other animals we also learn how to better appreciate and respect one another. To meet a new person with the idea that they might potentially become a friend does not make us weak or foolhardy. If the person shows us otherwise, then appreciation teaches us to adjust our views and respond accordingly. As animals we are quite aware that there are predators and dangers; indeed, the more adept we become at appreciating images in terms of their self-presentation the more adept we become at recognizing things for what they are and what they portend. Aesthetic appreciation and animal faith go together, and animals know the difference between friend and foe. When we strive to appreciate things, we are at our intuitive and instinctual best because our embodied imagination regains its animal focus and sophistication. As De Waal has written, "it's hard to fool an ape."[2]

That each person will appreciate beauty in their own way also means that each person will afford their ecology of imagination unique aesthetic opportunities. Each of us has the potential to increase beauty both through the responses we engender from others and through our own aesthetic maintenance and makings. In the first case, appreciation can occur without further actions on our part because our aesthetic affordances are what constitute us. In the second case, we increase the opportunities for aesthetic appreciation directly through our creative abilities to craft, enhance, embellish, ornament, and decorate. The making of beauty increases appreciation because the making itself depends on appreciation. Every craftsperson or artist must look, listen, touch, smell, and contemplate their work. Making something beautiful entails being able to appreciate its unfolding beauty during the process of creation. A painter doesn't know a painting is finished until she steps back and sees that it is finished. A chef tastes the stew and learns that it needs more salt. A teacher phrases and rephrases a lesson until the student's eyes glimmer with understanding. All along the way, appreciation lives in the body as it interacts with the materials at hand. We might even imagine that

---

2. Frans de Waal, *Our Inner Ape: A Leading Primatologist Explains Why We Are Who We Are* (New York: Riverhead Books, 2005), 59.

the appreciation we have of another's making is possible because of the appreciation they put into it. A gift of soul-making.

The autonomy of images and their independent power and integrity lie at the heart of appreciation. All through this book I have been saying this in different ways because it is the aspect of appreciation that is most difficult for us. Because of the long repression of beauty, and our belief that somehow, we, the beholders, are what matter most, we find it difficult to just sit quietly and watch. It is so hard for us to observe without preconception or interpretation and to have the patience to allow images to present themselves in their own way. In part this is because we feel that we should be *doing* something, as if the image isn't enough in itself without our input. To admit otherwise takes courage because we must give up the pretensions of control and understanding. Images have no need of our explanations. Only a heart bolstered by love can engage the mystery of images in their limitless depth. Images can be so clear and evident, and at the same time they are forever hinting at more. Love and intimacy teach us this, how we can feel so close to the beloved at the same time that they remain mysterious and enigmatic. Perhaps that is why love is at once so frightening and irresistible; frightening because we are powerless before it, irresistible for the same reason.

The return to beauty brings us home. Not a prim garden of meadows and flowers, but a vibrant, visceral, pulsating world of beating hearts, muscles flexing under coat and skin, countless watching eyes, and blackbirds involved in what we know. Back home, we once again feel the certainty of our animal faith as we move through our ecology of imagination with a familiarity bred in the bone. We move more slowly than before, though, not in a hurry like we once were. We take more time with things, giving them the attention that they are due, listening instead of explaining.

That appreciation slows down life is one of its greatest gifts to us. We have for so long been taught, instructed really, that it is good to be busy, and that idle hands belongs to the devil, that it is a blessed relief to feel otherwise. Appreciation arrests our movement, the way a fox suddenly seen in the woods stops us in our tracks. Savoring takes time, just as creating something beautiful not only takes time but also refashions our experience of time. Time, after all, is not a commodity, not something that is really spent, consumed, wasted, or taken; time is not money. Instead, appreciation teaches us that time is inextricably bound with beauty's atemporal, divine presence. Time might fly when we are having fun, but it can also stand still when we are in the thrall of beauty; the way a kiss can linger, or that love can last forever.

It is good to come home, especially when it could have been otherwise. Given our transgressions and the neglect of our household, the gods could have changed the locks. But it appears that we are still welcome. At home we are recognized and acknowledged, and quickly fall back into familiar patterns and traditions. However special we might have felt before coming home, whether through accomplishments or accolades, when we walk back through that door, we are just us. The other members of the household know who we are, and in their knowing they remind us of who we are. Back at home, we all have our places and our roles, our respective gifts and limitations. Back at home, we are loved (because if we are not loved then we are not truly at home), and with this love we are restored to the beauty of who and what we are.

Back at home, the trees in my front yard greet me in the morning, the sky portends the day, and my sleeping wife's face traces a smile on my lips. I shake off the sleep and prepare for the day ahead. Calleigh the cat says good morning in her own way, content because she, too, is at home. As the coffee brews, the dreams of the night slowly fade into the light of day, no longer seen but still present like an afterthought. They pop up from time to time, sometimes a help, sometimes a distraction, and sometimes just to pass through while tending to their own doings. They belong here, too. We share a home together.

This morning is cloudy, and the forecast calls for rain. I look forward to it; rainy days are good days. They tend to be more contained and peaceful, and the hours take longer than usual to turn. Sometimes I wish the sunny days could learn from their rainy kin how to linger; sunny days always seem to leave too soon. It's warm today and the winds are up a bit ahead of the approaching front. The windows are open, and I can already smell the rain. As I pour my coffee, the first drops fall.

Cloudy, rainy days like this seem to inspire contemplation, and so they are good days to spend time with the words and ideas that have for so long been my animal companions. Kept inside by the rain, I look forward to hearing and watching Jill move about the house, pursuing her own imaginings as I stand guard over her solitude. Outside, the birds are busy and as I sip my coffee, I watch them come and go. The birds don't seem to mind the rain, somehow.

And neither do I.

CODA

A Blessing

by James Wright

Just off the highway to Rochester, Minnesota
Twilight bounds softly forth on the grass
And the eyes of those two Indian ponies
Darken with kindness.
They have come gladly out of the willows
To welcome my friend and me.
We step over the barbed wire into the pasture
Where they have been grazing all day, alone.
They ripple tensely, they can hardly contain their happiness
That we have come.
They bow shyly as wet swans. They love each other.
There is no loneliness like theirs.
At home once more,
They begin munching the young tufts of spring in the darkness.
I would like to hold the slenderer one in my arms,
For she has walked over to me
And nuzzled my left hand.
She is black and white,
Her mane falls wild on her forehead,
And the light breeze moves me to caress her long ear
That is delicate as the skin over a girl's wrist.
Suddenly I realize
That if I stepped out of my body I would break
Into blossom.

From James Wright, *Above the River: The Complete Poems and Selected Prose.*
© 1971 by James Wright. Published by Wesleyan University Press

ACKNOWLEDGMENTS

This book is the culmination of many years. I have been blessed by exceptional teachers and colleagues, foremost among them Thomas Moore and the late James Hillman. More than any others, they saw something in me worth encouraging, and changed my life in ways that I can never repay. Benjamin Ladner first ignited my interest in Elizabeth Sewell and the worthy pursuit of loving and serving Sophia. Jay Livernois has never let me take the easy road, and through his example has sharpened my talents and tastes. Doug Pollock provided valuable insights by reading an early version of the book, making it better through his friendship and wisdom. Steve Pruett-Jones and Melinda Pruett-Jones provided critical advice on evolutionary biology, helping to educate and focus my thinking. I am honored that Margot McLean contributed her beautiful art for the cover of this book and am deeply grateful for Klaus Ottmann's careful and sophisticated editing that helped to more fully realize this book. Lastly, and most importantly, this book would have never been written without Jill Mateo, who was an active participant in its writing from the beginning, guiding me through the intricacies of animal behavior and evolutionary biology, reading early drafts, and offering revisions. She opened my eyes to the blindness of my own making, she guards my solitude, and she has made me more than I could have ever been without her.

Alberro, Alexander. "Beauty Knows No Pain." *Art Journal* 63, no. 2 (Summer 2004), 36–43

Allen, Colin, and Marc Bekoff. *Species of Mind: The Philosophy and Biology of Cognitive Ethology* (Cambridge, Mass.: The MIT Press, 1997)

—. and Michael Trestman. "Animal Consciousness," in *Stanford Encyclopedia of Philosophy* (Winter 2017 Edition), available online at *https://plato.stanford.edu/archives/win2017/entries/consciousness-animal/*

Aquinas, Thomas. *Summa Theologica,* translated by the Fathers of the English Dominican Province (New York: Benziger Brothers, 1947). Available online at *https://www.ccel.org/a/aquinas/summa/home.html*

Ashton, Dore, ed. *Twentieth-Century Artists on Art* (New York: Pantheon Book, 1985)

Apuleius. *Metamorphoses (The Golden Ass),* vol. 1: Books 1–9, edited and translated by J. Arthur Hanson, Loeb Classical Library 44 (Cambridge, Mass.: Harvard University Press, 1996)

Augustine. *City of God,* vol. 4: Books 12–15, translated by Philip Levine, Loeb Classical Library 414 (Cambridge: Harvard University Press, 1966)

—. *The Catholic and Manichean Ways of Life,* translated by Donald A. Gallagher and Idella J. Gallagher (Washington, D.C.: The Catholic University of America Press, 2017)

Baker, James Austin. "Biblical Views of Nature," in *Liberating Life: Contemporary Approaches to Ecological Theology,* edited by Charles Birch, William Eakin, and Jay B. McDaniel (Maryknoll, N.Y.: Orbis Books, 1990), 9-26. Available online at *https://www.religion-online.org/article/biblical-views-of-nature/*

Barfield, Owen. *Poetic Diction: A Study Meaning* (London: Faber and Faber, 1928)

—. *History in English Words* (Great Barrington, Mass.: Lindisfarne Press, 1988)

—. *Saving the Appearances: A Study in Idolatry* (Middletown, Conn.: Wesleyan University Press, 1988)

Bekoff, Marc. "Cognitive Ethology and the Explanation of Non-human Animal Behavior," in *Comparative Approaches to Cognitive Science,* edited by Herbert L. Roitblat and Jean-Arcady Meyer (Cambridge, Mass.: The MIT Press, 1995), 119. Available online at *http://cogprints. org/157/1/199709002.html*

—, and Dale Jamieson, eds. *Readings in Animal Cognition* (Cambridge, Mass.: The MIT Press, 1999)

—, and Paul W. Sherman, "Reflections on Animal Selves," *Trends in Ecology & Evolution* 19, no. 4 (April 2004): 176–80

Berleant, Arnold. "Negative Aesthetics and Everyday Life," *Aesthetic Pathways* 1, no. 2 (June 2011): 75-91. Available online at *https:// hcommons.org/deposits/objects/hc:21262/datastreams/CONTENT/content*

Berry, Patricia. "An Approach to the Dream," *Spring: An Annual of Archetypal Psychology and Jungian Thought* (1974): 58–79. Reprinted in Patricia Berry, *Echo's Subtle Body: Contributions to an Archetypal Psychology* (Thompson, Conn.: Spring Publications, 2017)

Boakes, Robert. *From Darwin to Behaviourism* (Cambridge: Cambridge University Press, 1984)

Borgia, Gerald, and Gregory F. Ball, "[Review of] *The Evolution of Beauty: How Darwin's Forgotten Theory of Mate Choice Shapes the Animal World and Us* by Richard O. Prum," *Animal Behavior* 137 (2018), 187–88. Available online at *https://science.umd.edu/biology/borgialab/ Animal%20behavior%20review%20of%20Beauty.pdf*

Bowler, Peter J. *Evolution: The History of an Idea* (Berkeley: University of California Press, 1989)

Burke, Edmund. *A Philosophical Enquiry into the Origin of Our Ideas of the Sublime and Beautiful* (London: Routledge and Kegan Paul, 1958)

Burkert, Walter. *Greek Religion,* translated by John Raffan (Cambridge, Mass.: Harvard University Press, 1985)

Burton, Robert. *The Anatomy of Melancholy* (London: Thomas Tegg, 1840)

Carter, Marion Hamilton. "Darwin's Idea of Mental Development," *The American Journal of Psychology* 9, no. 4 (July 1898): 534–59

Cartmill, Matt. "Animal Consciousness: Some Philosophical, Methodological, and Evolutionary Problems," *American Zoologist* 40, no. 6 (December 2000): 835–46

Caston, Victor. "Epiphenomenalisms, Ancient and Modern," *The Philosophical Review* 106, no. 3 (July 1997): 309–63

Cavalieri, Paola, and Peter Singer, eds. *The Great Ape Project: Equality Beyond Humanity* (New York: St. Martin's Griffin, 1994)

Conches, F. Feuillet de. *Méditations métaphysiques et correspondance de N. Malebranche* (Paris: H. Delloye, 1841)

Corner, James. "Representation and Landscape: Drawing and Making in the Landscape Medium," *Word & Image: A Journal of Verbal/ Visual Enquiry* 8, no. 3 (1992): 247–75

Cornford, Francis M. *Principium Sapientiae: The Origins of Greek Philosophical Thought* (Cambridge: Cambridge University Press, 1952)

Coyne, Jerry. "An Evolutionary Biologist Misrepresents Sexual Selection in *The New York Times,*" available online at *https:// whyevolutionistrue.com/2017/05/08/an-evolutionary-biologist-misrepresents-sexual-selection/*

Cronon, William, ed. *Uncommon Ground: Rethinking the Human Place in Nature* (New York: W.W. Norton, 1995)

Danto, Arthur C. *The Abuse of Beauty: Aesthetics and the Concept of Art* (Chicago: Open Court, 2003)

Darwin, Charles. *On the Origin of Species by Means of Natural Selection, or the Preservation of Favoured Races in the Struggle for Life* (London: John Murray, 1861)

——. *The Descent of Man and Selection in Relation to Sex,* 2nd ed. (London: John Murray, 1874)

——. Letter to Asa Gray, April 3, 1860. Darwin Correspondence Project, "Letter no. 2743," available online at *https://www.darwinproject.ac.uk/letter/DCP-LETT-2743.xml*

De Jonge, Casper C. "Dionysius and Longinus on the Sublime: Rhetoric and Religious Language," *American Journal of Philology* 133, no. 2 (Summer 2012): 271–300

De Waal, Frans B. M. *Are We Smart Enough to Know How Smart Animals Are?* (New York: W.W. Norton, 2016)

——. "Fish, Mirrors, and a Gradualist Perspective on Self-Awareness," *PLOS Biology* 17, no. 2 (1994): 1–8

——. *Our Inner Ape: A Leading Primatologist Explains Why We Are Who We Are* (New York: Riverhead Books, 2005)

Dennis, John. *The Critical Works of John Dennis,* edited by Edward Niles Hooker, 2 vols. (Baltimore: The John Hopkins Press, 1945)

Dewsbury, Donald A. *Comparative Psychology in the Twentieth Century* (Stroudsburg, Penn.: Hutchinson Ross Publishing Company, 1984)

Dissanayake, Ellen. *Homo Aestheticus: Where Art Comes from and Why* (New York: The Free Press, 1992)

Dugatkin, Lee Alan. *Principles of Animal Behavior,* 2nd ed. (New York: W.W. Norton, 2009)

Dutton, Denis. *The Art Instinct: Beauty, Pleasure, and Human Evolution* (Oxford: Oxford University Press, 2009)

Finkelberg, Aryeh. "On the History of the Greek κοσμοσ," *Harvard Studies in Classical Philology* 98 (1998): 103–36

Fisher, John Andrew. "The Myth of Anthropomorphism," in Bekoff and Jamieson, *Readings in Animal Cognition,* 3–16

Frankfort, Henri. *Ancient Egyptian Religion: An Interpretation* (New York: Harper Torchbooks, 1961)

Freedberg, David. *The Power of Images: Studies in the History and Theory of Response* (Chicago and London: The University of Chicago Press, 1989)

Freud, Sigmund. *Civilization and its Discontents,* translated by James Strachey (New York: W.W. Norton, 1961)

——. *The Future of an Illusion,* translated by James Strachey (New York: W.W. Norton, 1961)

Gallup Jr., Gordon. "Can Animals Empathize? Yes," *Scientific American* 9, no. 4 (Winter 1998): 66–71

Goldwater, Robert and Marco Treves, eds., *Artists on Art from the XIV to the XX Century* (New York: Pantheon Books, 1945)

Gibson, James J. *The Ecological Approach to Visual Perception* (Hillsdale, N.J.: Lawrence Erlbaum Associates, 1986)

Griffin, Donald R. *The Question of Animal Awareness: Evolutionary Continuity of Mental Experience* (New York: The Rockefeller University Press, 1976)

——. *Animal Minds* (Chicago and London: The University of Chicago Press, 1992)

Harrison, Peter. "Descartes on Animals," *The Philosophical Quarterly* 42, no. 167 (April 1992): 219–27

Harvey, Paul H. and Jack W. Bradbury. "Sexual Selection," in *Behavioural Ecology: An Evolutionary Approach,* edited by J.R. Krebs and N.B. Davies, 3rd. ed. (Oxford: Blackwell Scientific Publications, 1991), 203–33

Heisenberg, Werner. *Physics & Philosophy: The Revolution in Modern Science* (New York: Harper & Row, 1962)

Hillman, James. *Re-Visioning Psychology* (New York: Harper and Row, 1975)

——. "Peaks and Vales: The Soul/Spirit Distinction as Basis for the Differences Between Psychotherapy and Spiritual Discipline," in *Working with Images: The Theoretical Basis of Archetypal Psychology,* edited by Bejamin Sells, 2nd ed. (Thompson, Conn.: Spring Publications, 2022)

——. "An Inquiry into Image," *Spring: An Annual of Archetypal Psychology and Jungian Thought* (1977): 62–88

—. "Further Notes on Images," *Spring: An Annual of Archetypal Psychology and Jungian Thought* (1978): 152–62

—. "Image-Sense," *Spring: An Annual of Archetypal Psychology and Jungian Thought* (1979): 130–43

—. "Cosmology for Soul," *Sphinx: A Journal for Archetypal Psychology and the Arts* 2 (1989): 17–33

—. "Back to Beyond: On Cosmology," first published in *Archetypal Process: Self and Divine in Whitehead, Jung, and Hillman*, edited by David Ray Griffin (Evanston: Northwestern University Press, 1989) and reprinted in *Uniform Edition of the Writings of James Hillman*, vol. 8: *Philosophical Intimations*, edited by Edward S. Casey (Putnam, Conn.: Spring Publications, 2016)

—. "On Mythical Certitude," *Sphinx: A Journal for Archetypal Psychology and the Arts* 3 (1990): 224–43

—. "The Practice of Beauty," *Sphinx: A Journal for Archetypal Psychology and the Arts* 4 (1992): 13–28

—. *The Soul's Code: In Search of Character and Calling* (New York: Random House, 1996)

—. *Inter Views: Conversations with Laura Pozzo on Psychotherapy, Biography, Love, Soul, Dreams, Work, Imagination, and the State of the Culture* (Woodstock, Conn.: Spring Publications, 1991)

—. *The Force of Character and The Lasting Life* (New York: Random House, 1999)

—. *The Thought of the Heart and the Soul of the World* (Thompson, Conn.: Spring Publications, 2021)

Huxley, Thomas H. *Method and Results: Essays* (London and New York: Macmillan, 1904)

Iamblichus, *Life of Pythagoras*, translated by Thomas Taylor (London: J. M. Watkins, 1818)

Ingold, Tim. "Tool-Use, Sociality and Intelligence," in *Tools, Language and Cognition in Human Evolution*, edited by Kathleen Gibson and Tim Ingold (Cambridge: Cambridge University Press, 1993), 429–46

James, William. "Are We Automata?" *Mind* 4, no. 13 (January 1879): 1–22

Johnson, Mark. *The Body in the Mind: The Bodily Basis of Meaning, Imagination, and Reason* (Chicago: The University of Chicago Press, 1987)

Jones, Adam G., and Nicholas L. Ratterman, "Mate Choice and Sexual Selection: What Have We Learned Since Darwin?" *Proceedings of the National Academy of Sciences* 106, Supplement 1 (June 16, 2009): 10001–8. Available online at *https://doi.org/10.1073/pnas.0901129106*

Jung, C. G. *The Collected Works of C. G. Jung,* vol. 8: *Structure & Dynamics of the Psyche,* edited and translated by Gerhard Adler and R. F. C. Hull (Princeton:, N.J.: Princeton University Press, 1969)

—. *Collected Works of C. G. Jung,* vol. 13: *Alchemical Studies,* edited and translated by Gerhard Adler and R. F. C. Hull (Princeton, N.J.: Prince-ton University Press, 1970)

Kant, Immanuel. *Critique of Judgment,* translated by Werner S. Pluhar (Indianapolis and Cambridge: Hackett Publishing Company, 1987)

—. *Critique of Pure Reason,* translated by F. Max Müller (London: Macmillan, 1881)

—. *Observations on the Feeling of the Beautiful and Sublime and Other Writings,* edited by Patrick Frierson and Paul Guyer (Cambridge: Cambridge University Press, 2011)

Kaufman, Kenn. *A Field Guide to Advanced Birding: Birding Challenges and How to Approach Them* (Boston: Houghton Mifflin Company, 1990)

Keats, John. *The Letters of John Keats,* edited by Hyder E. Rollins, 2 vols. (Cambridge, Mass.: Harvard University Press, 1958)

Kerényi, Karl. *The Religion of the Greeks and Romans,* translated by Christopher Holme (New York: E. P. Dutton & Co., 1962)

Kokko, Hanna. "Fisherian and 'Good Genes' Benefits of Mate Choice: How (Not) to Distinguish between Them," *Ecology Letters* 4, no. 4 (July 2001): 322–26

Kortland, Adriaan. "Chimpanzees in the Wild," *Scientific American* 206, no. 5 (May 1962): 128–140

Koyré, Alexandre. *From the Closed World to the Infinite Universe* (Baltimore: The John Hopkins University Press, 1979)

Kugler, Paul. "Image and Sound: An Archetypal Approach to Language," in *Spring: An Annual of Archetypal Psychology and Jungian Thought* (1978): 136–51

Larson, Edward J. *Evolution: The Remarkable History of a Scientific Theory* (New York: Random House, 2006)

Longinus. *On the Sublime,* translated by H. L. Havell (London: Macmillan, 1890). Available online at *http://eremita.di.uminho.pt/ gutenberg/1/7/9/5/17957/17957-h/17957-h.htm*

Lovejoy, Arthur O. *Essays in the History of Ideas* (New York: G.P. Putnam's Sons, 1960)

Marcuse, Herbert. *The Aesthetic Dimension: Toward a Critique of Marxist Aesthetics* (Boston: Beacon Press, 1978)

Marx, Leo. "The Idea of Nature in America." *Daedalus* 137, no. 2 (Spring 2008): 8–21

Morgan, Conwy Lloyd. *An Introduction to Comparative Psychology* (London: Walter Scott, Ltd., 1894)

Maslow, Abraham. *Religions, Values, and Peak-Experiences* (New York: Penguin Books, 1976)

Moore, Thomas. "Musical Therapy." *Spring: An Annual of Archetypal Psychology and Jungian Thought* (1978): 128–35

—. *The Re-Enchantment of Everyday Life* (New York: Harper-Perennial, 1996)

Nagel, Thomas. "What Is It Like to Be a Bat?," *The Philosophical Review* 83, no. 4 (October 1974): 435–50

Onians, Richard Broxton. *The Origins of European Thought: About the Body, the Mind, the Soul, the World, Time, and Fate* (Cambridge: Cambridge University Press, 1988)

Patricelli, Gail L., Eileen A. Hebets, and Tamra C. Mendelson. "[Review of] *The Evolution of Beauty: How Darwin's Forgotten Theory of Mate*

Choice Shapes the Animal World and Us by Richard O. Prum," *Evolution* 73, no. 1 (2019): 115–24

Percy, Walker. *Diagnosing the Modern Malaise* (New Orleans: Faust Publishing, 1985)

Portmann, Adolf. *Animal Forms and Patterns: A Study of the Appearance of Animals,* translated by Hella Czech (London: Faber and Faber, 1948)

—. *Essays in Philosophical Zoology: The Living Form and the Seeing Eye,* translated by Richard B. Carter (Lewiston, N.Y.: The Edward Mellen Press, 1990)

—. *New Paths in Biology,* translated by Arnold J. Pomerans (New York: Harper & Row, 1964)

Prior, James. *Life of the Right Honourable Edmund Burke,* 5th ed. (London: Henry G. Bohn, 1854)

Prum, Richard, O. *The Evolution of Beauty: How Darwin's Forgotten Theory of Mate Selection Shapes the Animal World—and Us* (New York: Doubleday, 2017)

Purdy, Jedediah. *After Nature: A Politics for the Anthropocene* (Cambridge, Mass.: Harvard University Press, 2015)

Rich, Adrienne. *What is Found There: Notebooks on Poetry and Politics* (New York: W.W. Norton, 1993)

Rilke, Rainer Maria. *Letters to a Young Poet,* translated by Reginald Nell (London: Sidgwick and Jackson)

Ritvo, Harriet. "Animal Consciousness: Some Historical Perspective," *American Zoologist* 40, no. 6 (December 2000): 847–52

Rollin, Bernard E. *The Unheeded Cry: Animal Consciousness, Animal Pain, and Science* (New York: Oxford University Press, 1989)

Romanes, George. *Animal Intelligence* (London: Kegan Paul, Trench & Co., 1982)

—. *Mental Evolution in Man: Origin of Human Faculty* (London: Kegan Paul, Trench & Co., 1988)

Rosen, Jonathan. *The Life of the Skies: Birding at the End of Nature* (New York: Farrar, Straus, and Giroux, 2008)

Roszak, Theodore, Mary E. Gomes, and Allen D. Kanner, eds. *Ecopsychology: Restoring the Earth/Healing the Mind* (New York: Sierra Club Books, 1995)

Safina, Carl. *Beyond Words: What Animals Think and Feel* (New York: Henry Holt and Company, 2015)

Santayana, George. *Scepticism and Animal Faith: Introduction to a System of Philosophy* (New York: Charles Scribner's Sons, 1923)

—. *The Sense of Beauty: Being the Outline of Aesthetic Theory* (New York: Charles Scribner's Sons, 1896)

Schwarz, Astrid, and Kurt Jax, eds. *Ecology Revisited: Reflecting on Concepts, Advancing Science* (Dordrecht: Springer, 2011)

Sewall, Laura. "The Skill of Ecological Perception," in Roszak, et al., *Ecopsychology*, 200–15

Sewell, Elizabeth. "Bacon, Vico, Coleridge and the Poetic Method," in *Giambattista Vico: An International Symposium*, edited by Giorgio Tagliacozzo and Hayden V. White (Baltimore: The John Hopkins Press, 1969), 125–36

—. *The Orphic Voice: Poetry and Natural History* (New York: The New York Review of Books, 2022)

Stark, Rodney. *For the Glory of God: How Monotheism Led to Reformations, Science, Witch-Hunts and the End of Slavery* (Princeton, N.J.: Princeton University Press, 2003)

Stevens, Wallace. *Letters of Wallace Stevens,* selected and edited by Holly Stevens (Berkeley and Los Angeles: University of California Press, 1966)

Teleki, Geza. "They Are Us," in Cavalieri and Singer, *The Great Ape Project*, 296–302

Uexküll, Jakob von. *A Foray into the Worlds of Animals and Humans,* translated by Joseph D. O'Neil (Minneapolis and London: University of Minnesota Press, 2010)

Vining, Joanne, Melinda S. Merrick, and Emily A. Price, "The Distinction between Humans and Nature: Human Perceptions of Connectedness to Nature and Elements of the Natural and Unnatural," *Human Ecology Review* 15, no. 1 (Summer 2008): 1–11

Walker, Stephen. *Animal Thought* (London: Routledge & Kegan Paul, 1983)

Wallace, Alfred Russel. *Darwinism: An Exposition of the Theory of Natural Selection With Some of Its Applications* (London: Macmillan, 1889)

—. *Natural Selection and Tropical Nature: Essays on Descriptive and Theoretical Biology,* 2nd ed. (London: Macmillan, 1895)

Warden, C.J. "The Development of Modern Comparative Psychology," *The Quarterly Review of Biology* 3, no. 4 (December 1928): 486–522

Watson, John. "Psychology as the Behaviorist Views It," *Psychological Review* 20, no. 2 (March 1913): 158–77

—. *Behaviorism* (New York: W.W. Norton, 1925)

Weidensaul, Scott. *Of a Feather: A Brief History of American Birding* (New York: Harcourt, 2007)

Welsch, Wolfgang. "Animal Aesthetics," *Contemporary Aesthetics* 2, no. 2 (2004). Available online at *https://digitalcommons.risd.edu/cgi/viewcontent.cgi?article=1026&context=liberalarts_contempaesthetics*

—. *Undoing Aesthetics,* translated by Andrew Inkpin (London: Sage Publishing, 1997)

Wheelwright, Philip. *Heraclitus* (Princeton, N.J.: Princeton University Press, 1959)

White, Jr., Lynn., "The Historical Roots of our Ecologic Crisis," *Science* 155, no. 3767 (March 10, 1967): 1203–207

Williams, Raymond. *Keywords: A Vocabulary of Culture and Society* (New York: Oxford University Press, 1985)

Wilson, Edward O. *Biophilia* (Cambridge, Mass. and London: Harvard University Press, 1984)

—. "Biophilia and the Conservation Ethic," in *The Biophilia Hypothesis*, edited by Stephen R. Kellert and Edward O. Wilson (Washington, D.C.: Island Press, 1993)

Wilson, Frank. *The Hand: How Its Use Shapes the Brain, Language, and Human Culture* (New York: Vintage Books, 1999)

Wohlleben, Peter. *The Hidden Life of Trees: What They Feel, How They Communicate* (Vancouver: Greystone Books, 2015)

Zahavi, Amotz. "Mate Selection—A Selection for a Handicap," *Journal of Theoretical Biology* 53 (1975): 205–14

www.ingramcontent.com/pod-product-compliance
Lightning Source LLC
Chambersburg PA
CBHW020531270326
41927CB00006B/529